SCEPTICAL ALWAYS

A VIEW AT THREE QUARTER TIME

SCEPTICAL ALWAYS

A VIEW AT THREE QUARTER TIME

IAN PLIMER

connorcourt

PUBLISHING

Published by Connor Court Publishing Pty Ltd, 2025

CONNOR COURT PUBLISHING PTY LTD
PO Box 7257
Redland Bay QLD 4165
sales@connorcourt.com
www.connorcourtpublishing.com.au

ISBN: 9781923568167

Cover design by Ian James

Printed in Australia

We breathe in air with 0.04 per cent carbon dioxide and exhale air with more than 4 per cent carbon dioxide. If one is passionately committed to Net Zero, the solution is simple: drop dead.

\- Ian Plimer

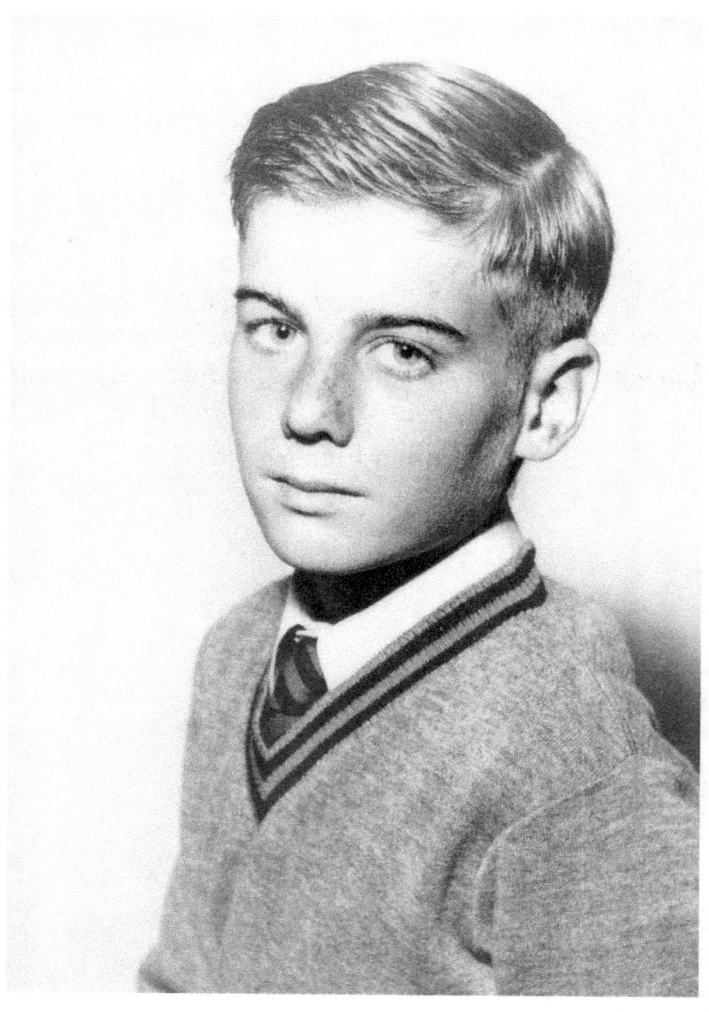

Normanhurst Boys' High School, school photograph as a
12-year-old

About the Author

PROFESSOR IAN PLIMER is Australia's best-known geologist. He is Emeritus Professor of Earth Sciences at the University of Melbourne, where he was Professor and Head of Earth Sciences (1991-2005) after serving at the University of Newcastle (1985-1991) as Professor and Head of Geology. He was Professor of Mining Geology at The University of Adelaide (2006-2012) and in 1991 was also German Research Foundation research professor of ore deposits at the Ludwig Maximilians Universität, München (Germany). He was on the staff of the University of New England, the University of New South Wales and Macquarie University. He has published more than 140 scientific papers on geology and was one of the trinity of editors for the five-volume *Encyclopedia of Geology*. He has published numerous chapters in books and is a regular contributor to *The Spectator Australia* and various Sky TV programs.

This is his fifteenth book written for the general public, the best known of which are *Telling lies for God* (Random House, 1994), *Milos-Geologic History* (Koan, 1999), *A Short History of Planet Earth* (ABC Books, 2000), *Heaven and Earth* (Connor Court, 2009), *How to get expelled from school* (Connor Court, 2011), *Not for greens* (Connor Court, 2014), *Green Murder* (Connor Court, 2020) and *The Little Green Book* (Three Volumes, Connor Court, 2023).

He won the Leopold von Buch Plakette (German Geological Society), the Clarke Medal (Royal Society of NSW), the Sir Willis Connolly Medal (Australasian Institute of Mining and Metallurgy). He is a Fellow of the Australian Academy of Technological Sciences and Engineering and an Honorary Fellow of the Geological Society of London. In 1995, he was Australian Humanist of the Year and later was awarded the

Tea Gardens, NSW, 1956, Ian Plimer with younger brother.

Ian Plimer, Pymble, NSW, 1965

Centenary Medal. He was Managing Editor of *Mineralium Deposita*, president of the SGA, president of IAGOD, president of the Australian Geoscience Council and sat on the Earth Sciences Committee of the Australian Research Council for many years. He won the Eureka Prize for the promotion of science, the Eureka Prize for *A Short History of Planet Earth* and the Michael Daley Prize (now a Eureka Prize) for science broadcasting for a story included in this anthology (*The environmental impact of creation*). He was an advisor to governments and corporations and was a regular ABC broadcaster.

Professor Plimer spent much of his life in the rough and tumble of the zinc-lead-silver mining town of Broken Hill where an interdisciplinary scientific knowledge intertwined with a healthy dose of scepticism and pragmatism are necessary. His time in the outback has introduced him to those who can immediately smell a scam. He is Patron of Lifeline Broken Hill and the Broken Hill Geocentre. He worked for North Broken Hill Ltd and was a director of CBH Resources Ltd, Ivanhoe Australia Ltd, Ivanhoe Electric Inc, Sun Resources NL and Kefi Minerals plc. In his post-university career he was proudly a director of a number of ASX-listed public companies (Silver City Minerals Ltd, Niuminco Group Ltd, Lakes Oil NL) and is now a director of various unlisted private Hancock Prospecting iron, energy, research and copper exploration companies.

A new Broken Hill mineral, plimerite $ZnFe_4(PO_4)_3(OH)_5$, was named in recognition of his contribution to Broken Hill geology. Ironically, plimerite is green and soft. It fractures unevenly, is brittle and insoluble in alcohol. A ground-hunting rainforest spider *Austrotengella plimeri* from the Tweed Range (NSW) has been named in his honour because of his "provocative contributions to issues of climate change". The author would like to think that *Austrotengella plimeri* is poisonous.

Ian Plimer with late mother, father and younger brother, Port Stephens, 1956

Preface

As a geologist, I have been to some pretty interesting parts of the world off the beaten track where one meets unusual characters, frauds, fools, fanatics, tragedy and danger. I am nothing special, any geologist can write rip-roaring yarns about the fickle finger of fate because of the working life we have enjoyed and we all have colleagues who have died in helicopter, plane and car crashes, who have died from some dreadful disease caught while in some God-forsaken place, died underground or have been shot at. Much of my geological fieldwork has been done in outback Australia and in the Islamic world and work in these areas forms the basis of many of the stories which can be read in no particular order. Current geological work takes place in Saudi Arabia, Ecuador and outback Australia. Geology is very humbling. When the Almighty made that fourth dimension we call time, He made an excess of it for geologists.

Observation underpins geology and most of my observations were recorded in field books and then written as short stories that were edited later before publication. Only a small selection of stories is presented here. Other stories were letters to friends about people, places and thoughts and some stories have been previously published in *the skeptic*, *Quadrant*, *The Independent Weekly*, *The Spectator Australia*, *The Australian*, the Institute of Public Affairs, newspapers, blogs, WWW sites, annual conferences of the Australian Skeptics, public lectures and broadcasts on various ABC National shows (e.g. Occam's Razor).

The first story I wrote as a reminder of a family incident was *Fred* (1971) and stories thereafter are collated in chronological order. There are not too many stories in the late 1990s, a time when I was engaged in litigation with fraudulent creationists and the flurry of recent stories were written when I had time on my hands in various cancer clinics. The theme of the stories is about people, off the beaten track places and fundamentalist nonsense that pervades society as knowledge, some stories have a twinge of front bar poetic licence and many are autobiographical. Of course I intertwine my science in these stories.

One of the recurring themes I have written about over the decades in my capacity as a geologist educator has been anti-science. When I published on creationism, I was the darling of the left as they erroneously thought I was attacking Christianity and, now that I write on the myth of human-induced climate change, I am apparently expressing far right-wing views and am the left's public enemy No 1. However, my criticism of the creationists concerned their abuse of the scientific method and their use of bad science to gain power over people. My criticism of the green Marxist environmental movement has been their abuse of the scientific method and their use of bad science to gain power over people.

Some have interpreted my writings on creationism as an attack on Christianity. Not so. My best-selling book *Telling lies for God* (1994) contained a Foreword by a prominent Anglican Archbishop who joined me in attacking creationism and many of my arguments were formulated during long fluidised discussions with a close friend, a physicist and now a high church bells-and-smells Anglican Archdeacon, The Venerable Dr Edwin Byford. My attacks on creationism were actually a defence of Christianity from the wasteland of fundamentalism. Some religions and denominations have not been able to cope with advances in science.

Fundamentalists have not changed whereas many Christian denominations have changed as the understanding of the physical world has changed yet the spiritual world is unchanged. During that time I met many Christian fundamentalists, I even had one as a co-litigant and, well before Islamic fundamentalism reared its ugly head again in the West, I was curious to know what make fundamentalists tick.

If Christianity has something unique to offer then it is contemplation, something we have all experienced at a funeral. Christianity gives hope, Christianity allows for forgiveness and recognises that everyone has feet of clay. The eye of contemplation follows all strands of knowledge and religion, at its core it has a unique strength: faith. Science cannot measure a religious experience, faith, contemplation and hope and hence there cannot be an integration of science and religion. Religion deals with the world within whereas science deals with the world without.

Oubth-ut-Allah derives from geological work in Iran in 1978 just before the revolution of 1979 that led to Ayatollah Khomeni returning to Iran. Geological work in Africa can be harrowing and *Postcard from Africa* (1980) was written as a letter when much of Africa was at half time during ghastly civil wars. *Skid marks in the desert* (1983) was a very close call when I survived a jet aeroplane crash. This opened my eyes to safety and criminal negligence and very nearly robbed me of a few decades of life. As a result, I enjoy life, friends and fluids and find critics painfully amusing. I try to adhere to the edict: "*The person who wins the game of life has had the most laughs*".

Getting conned is part of travel to foreign lands (*Street wise*, 1987) and it's always nice to have it done with charm and no malice. Just as we go through cycles of having crazes such as yo-yos, there are cycles of vacuous pseudoscientific codswallop such as crystal power (*Crystal healing*, 1987) and all sorts of clapped-out fads claiming that there are energies unknown to science. These are cons of the credulous and ignorant.

Work in the red dirt country of the Australian outback led to the stories *A bender with Blackie* (1989), a true story about an outback trip with a close personal friend the then Mayor of Broken Hill (later to become the Labor Member for Murray Darling), *Outalpa Springs* (1993) a vignette about one of the many lonely graves lost in the remote outback and *Green view from the red dirt* (2015), a story about and written at the Arkaroola Wilderness Sanctuary, one of the most beautiful areas of the outback and a place that every Australian should visit at least once in their life.

When I first went to Turkey in the late 1980s, it was a secular country that had enjoyed six decades of growth resulting from the vision of Karmel Ataturk, who I consider was the greatest political leader in the 20ᵗʰ Century. He took education away from the mullahs, created a secular society with religious tolerance, looked westwards, industrialised the country, built infrastructure, made Turkish the official language and reduced the influence of the fundamentalist Sunni Arabs. Turkey has now regressed into an Islamic dictatorship and Sunni fundamentalism is rearing its ugly head again. Turkey was booming for three decades although some people, especially those in remote mountainous areas, still had a hard life. I wrote about young Turks I met in 1991 (*Aleşehir, Kücükyenice, The flautist, Şapdağ girl, Gümüsler*) and tried to show the poverty, tragedy and anti-women attitudes that still existed towards the end of the 20ᵗʰ Century.

In 1994, I visited south-eastern Turkey during a lull in the war between the Kurdistan Workers' Party (PKK) and the Turkish Army to make a *Four Corners* TV program and do *Stern* interview about the alleged beaching spot of Noah's Ark. One evening we were hosted in the mountains, maybe Iran, Iraq or Armenia, by Abdullah Õcalan of the militant PKK who spoke of the plight of the Kurds to *Stern*. Õcalan is still in prison so I write nothing. Various stories about Noah's Ark which allegedly beached in south-eastern Turkey and unbalanced evil exploitative creationist fundamentalism were written in 1994 *(Goosestepping for God)*.

The environmental impact of creation (1993) was a light-hearted attempt to unite the Biblical creationism with modern environmentalism. It went to air on Occam's Razor for which I won the ABC's Michael Daley Prize. *Resources for 10 billion humans* went to air on ABC Radio National (1988). These were broadcast at a time when the ABC was not fully politicised into an out-of-control green Marxist network unrepresentative of those who fund it and specialising in moralising mendacious moaning. Such programs would now not be broadcast because they are not supportive of the ABC carping groupthink.

Creationists have a fundamentalist literal interpretation of the Bible and a Noachian "Great Flood" some 4,000 years ago underpins their dogma. One of the reasons I was so vocal about creationism was that the leaders claimed that it was underpinned by science and should be taught on an equal time basis with evolution in all school science courses. Creationism, like global warmism, ignores elementary geology and hence is not science. As a Chair in Geology now for more than three decades, it was and still is my place to profess my discipline in public about fundamentalist Christianity attempting to change Earth geological history and global warming activism dressed up as science terrifying children. There is no place for the teaching of religious and scientific nonsense to uncritical ill-educated school children and creating trauma, depression, guilt and fears in children.

Creationism is essentially anti-religion and kills people emotionally and intellectually whereas climate activism kills countries economically, creates great suffering for the poor and is the end result of the anti-intellectual dumbing down of the education system over five decades. It appears that I have lost this battle because, although creationism is not taught in the school science syllabus, all sorts of other nonsense such as human-induced climate change and environmentalism are preached with religious fervour in schools to children who do not have the basics of reading, writing, expression and elementary chemistry, physics, biology and geology and hence are unable to critically evaluate what is taught as "science".

My concerns about the dumbing down of the education system were expressed in the parody *Why Australia lost the Three Day War with Upper Volta* (1989) which went to air as an Occam's Razor program in 1989. As one who has an interest in making a better society through education and science and as one who has devoted much of his life to education, I was greatly influenced by the 1852 book by John Henry Newman (*The idea of a university*) that envisaged a university community in which students were taught *"to think and to reason and to compare and to discriminate and to analyse."* This is what I tried to do in my university teaching and nearly thirty years later, my parody using Upper Volta, which in 1984 had changed its name to Burkina Faso, has shown to be disturbingly true. Ask any former university student of mine. I was one of the few during a time of falling standards who tried to teach young people to question, think and be critical. I don't think I failed.

I have always been intolerant of intolerance and fundamentalism. I see little difference between the fundamentalism and abuse of science by creationists and the fundamentalism and abuse of science by the global warmists (*The theology of climate change*, 2009; *Global warming; meet creationism*, 2020). Climate change is the new religion that has filled a theological vacuum as Christianity retreats due to relentless attack from post-modernism in the West and genocide in the Islamic world.

In some of my earlier books nearly thirty years ago I wrote about climate change and the lack of evidence for human-induced climate change, but as the warmist dogma got more heated and gained traction in the public, I wrote more on this junk science (*Malice in wonderland*, 2006; *The long history of climate*, 2007; *One volcano can ruin your whole ideology*, 2009, *Sea level rise*, 2009) concurrent with writing the international best seller *Heaven and Earth* (Connor Court, 2009). After publication of *Heaven and Earth* (2009), *How to get expelled from school* (2011) and *Not for greens* (2014) were also published by Connor Court concurrently with writing *Stop climate change* (2011), *Human-induced climate change: Why I am sceptical* (2012), *Renewable energy targets* (2013) and *Australia's influence on global climate* (2014).

Some of my writings must have hit home because the Gillard Labor-Green government established a web site to try to answer the 101 questions that I encouraged school children to ask their teachers about climate change in *How to get expelled from school* (Connor Court 2012). The answers were hilarious, contorted, self-serving and commonly wrong and reminded me of how the creationists would set up panels, booklets and conferences to show that my criticisms of them were unfounded.

I am bad for the businesses of creationism and climate activism that uses fraud to create a job for life hence, rather than addressing the arguments I raise, they can only use *ad hominem* attacks. Your taxes paid some $500,000 for this Federal government website which was an attempted kneecapping and, with a change in government, the site was immediately withdrawn. This shows that the claim that climate activism is science is wrong. It is political activism by anti-capitalist greens and Marxists. A man's worth is measured by the quality of his enemies. It appears that I am worthless because my enemies are not of quality yet I appear to have upset a large number of people over the years. This, of course, causes me endless sleeplessness as I deeply care about *bien-pesant* opinions. I get many emails from the critics and I have learned to realise that just by opening the email I had already spent too much time on it. Every time I write a piece on climate change based on published data in *The Spectator Australia*, there are howls of complaints from a few of the normal suspects and support from an army of correspondents who tear the critics apart. I hope this book brings joy to many readers and creates apoplexy with others who think they live in a demon-haunted world.

As the effects of climate change policies started to hit the community hip pocket, I continued to point out that the climate change ideology was unscientific, had huge economic costs and whatever we humans did, we could not change nature. *Stop climate change* (2011) was written as a result of activists illegally entering Kirribilli House and unfurling a ”Stop climate change“ sign on the roof. Although this may have gained a few seconds of infamy on television, it just showed the ignorance and vacuousness of the environmental movement.

Human-induced climate change: Why I am sceptical (2012) was a response to the unbalanced criticism I had from my books where the critics, who had not read the books, seemed to think that scepticism was not the mainstay of science and attacked the man rather than addressing the argument. None of this has made one iota of difference to the rabid warmists who have embraced their ideology without rationality, logic and the breadth of integrated interdisciplinary knowledge hence there is no way that they will change their position using logic, rationality and knowledge, especially if they have their snouts in the trough.

As a result of weak-kneed governments unquestioningly accepting the green ideology, we now have a country with an excess of coal, gas and uranium, a huge energy export market, skyrocketing domestic energy costs and not enough domestic energy to run an industrialised society. Of course, if one is logical and believes that human emissions of carbon dioxide actually drive global warming, then the only reliable source of energy that does least damage to the environment is nuclear fission.

One is constantly disappointed with governments of all colours and their civil servants. Much of this disappointment arises from the fact that the new breed of politicians has never had real jobs and treat politics as a career for life rather than a calling in the service of their fellow man after a successful life in another domain. They follow public opinion rather than leading and their lack of leadership as ministers has allowed green left bureaucrats to take over their departments. Such politicians do nothing for the country as a result of not risking their political capital. For example, rather than stop harm to Australia with the global warming fraud, their eyes just glaze over when the matter is raised. The civil service holds the public and politicians in contempt and only they know best. And, because of this, they live in the lap of luxury in the ersatz city of Canberra. The politicians hold the public in contempt until such time as they want your vote to allow the rorts to continue.

The concentration of civil servants in Canberra has led to political decisions unrelated to reality. These same people take no risks in life yet have benefits that far outweigh the benefits of those in the productive private industry sector of the economy who actually pay them. Furthermore, red, black and green tape is crippling the productive economy of Australia and hence decentralisation may inject a bit of reality into civil service decisions and policy. At the time of publication, red, black and green tape was costing Australia $176 billion *per annum*. My solution in *How to make Australia efficient* (2012) was published as an article in *Quadrant* and each of the places cited I know in my capacity as a geologist hence I am able to extol the virtues of all of these towns.

It has been a great privilege to work in the outback and come across sobering scenes (*Outalpa Springs*, 1993), some great characters (*A bender with Blackie*, 1989) and survivors who know how to live life (*Švejk sedition*, 2021). In today's world we have our nutters who are not harmless (*Crystal healing*, 1987) and those woke folk who are unstitching our Western democracy without replacing it with something better (*Cancel Mozart*, 2023).

One volcano can ruin your whole ideology (2008), *Climate crimes* (2015), *Green view from the red dirt* (2015), *Human emissions of hot air* (2017), *One lonely molecule* (2017), *Cash levels rising* (2020), *Talking Tonga* (2022), *Snot* (2022), *Eat beef, save the planet* (2022), *Rain, rain, go* away (2022), *The joys of drinking* (2022), *The Earth is already at Net Zero* (2023), *Bring back blackbirding* (2023), *Let's be Cretans, not cretins* (2024), *History in remote hills* (2024), *Cop this!* (2024) and *The carbon crisis* (2025) were aimed at informing most and annoying some readers. They were penned for and published by *The Spectator Australia* some thirty years after I had first written about the myth of human-induced global warming. For years I have been arguing that the hip pocket will change what is a green Marxist politicised science policy unrelated to science and not rational scientific argument, evidence and history.

This is now starting to happen as the community recognises that there has been no measurable climate change for thirty years despite dire predictions and, as a result of failed green policies to reduce carbon dioxide emissions, the cost of energy has soared, jobs are being lost and climate activists have done a pretty good job at despoiling the environment with their wind and solar industrial complexes. Various stories about minerals, resources and my concerns as a patriot for the future of our nation entitled *Minerals critical crisis* (2025), *Fertilise or fail* (2025), *Egyptians and leftie loonies* (2025) and *Incurable disease* (2025) were published in *The Spectator Australia* which also had the temerity to reject some articles submitted about green steel, hydrogen and other lunatic green schemes.

A final thank you to Tony Zollo for his incisive criticisms and corrections and my ever patient publisher Dr Anthony Cappello for his work in preparing my manuscript for publication.

The precious Noah's Ark being guarded by a Turkish Soldier. The Durupinar formation, located in the Doğubayazıt district of Ağrı, Turkey,

Contents

Fred

"Hello, I'm your grandfather."

My mind raced. This old codger looking down onto my bed could only be my maternal grandfather. I was gobsmacked. Sometimes a poker face is just not possible. Some 15 years earlier, my paternal grandfather had departed this mortal coil to eat infinite quantities of haggis and listen to the angels play bagpipes. He was an opinionated nasty old bugger, he could not relate to women or children. He used to live in the sleep-out on the back veranda hidden by a canvas blind. His endless nicotine and mustard gas coughing frightened me as a little boy, as did his lack of communication, long nasal and ear hair and enormous hooter.

It was better when he went to the War Veterans' Homes, first at Narrabeen and then at Yass. It was an exciting excursion to visit him at Yass which involved walking to the station, travelling to Central in a suburban train and then the long trip to Yass in a steam express train. At Yass Junction, another steam train met the express train and the ride into Yass was along the centre of the main street in a steam train. Whenever I see a picture of a steam train, I can still smell it. It is marvellous how the brain remembers smells better than any other sensation. Later when we had a few more shekels and my father's MS prevented him from walking, my mother used to drive us to Yass in a dreadful third-hand clapped out Vauxhall Velox.

I enjoyed visiting the Yass War Veterans' Home. My grandfather and mother did not get on, my father used to spend the time sitting with his father chatting and I used to wander around talk to all the other war veterans in their rooms, the library and in the gardens. Some of them were limbless, others badly affected by chlorine and mustard gas in the

First World War, some were scarred and blinded and all enjoyed having a visitor, even if he was an unrelated curious little boy. Some of them would ask me to read to them. None of them spoke to me about the horrors of war, they were probably too traumatised. I got the feeling then that many of these men were lonely and never had family visitors.

My grandfather's passion was football. This I shared with him. His home team, which he had followed all his life, was Heart of Midlothian. They won the Scottish Cup in 1956. Granddad would never stop talking about this event which, of course, changed the course of Western civilisation. He seemed to like war. He served as an ambulance officer in the Boer War, the Boxer Rebellion and both World War I and World War II. He cheated on his age in both the Boer War and World War II.

What happened in his youth in South Africa and China? Who knows? He never spoke about it. It must have been ghastly at the Somme picking up the pieces of dismembered soldiers. On leave in London in 1916, he met a fragile lonely young aristocratic lady during the depths of World War I, begat my father in January 1917 and married the mother-to-be a month before my father's birth. Mother and child were sent by ship from Southampton to Sydney. Whether this was because she was married to a Scotsman, married to someone of lower class or conceived a child out of wedlock we'll never know. Maybe he wanted his wife and son to have a better life in Australia. He never lost his strong brogue and never returned to Edinburgh.

As a child, I was told that my maternal grandfather had died before I was born. He had fathered three daughters and my blind grandmother brought them up during the Great Depression and World War II. This was a herculean struggle from which my mother never recovered, she was bitter that she never had an education and was bitter that in her time women never had the same rights as men. She became a Pankhurst-type feminist. For a child, the death of someone old seemed a reasonable explanation for the lack of a maternal grandfather. There was the honour of widowhood. It was a reasonable explanation. Reasonable until the time an old codger was standing beside my hospital bed.

My paternal grandmother had died when I was a year or two old and there were photographs of her in the normal places. On the piano and on the lounge room mantle piece above the fire place. She was occasionally referred to with reverence. A fine-looking aristocratic woman to whom my father, an only child, was greatly attached. The photograph on the piano I remember well. She looked kindly at me while I was attempting to master Czerny's children's piano exercises. She exuded confidence, softness, sadness, distance and sacrifice. She died young. I learned to practice scales while reading a book and I felt that she was chastising me for not fully applying myself to the task at hand.

My mind was racing while imprisoned in a hospital bed. It then dawned on me that I had never seen a photograph of my maternal grandfather. He was never mentioned in any conversation. He just did not exist in my childhood. Yet this man standing over my hospital bed had a strong family resemblance. He was the right age. Old, proudly upright and bald as a badger.

"Thanks for coming to visit me. How did you find me?"

"Bessie told me. My name is Frederick. You can call me Fred if you wish. I hear it is nothing major."

Bessie, Elizabeth, was his daughter. My mother.

"No. I should be out in a day or two. I don't know whether it was the red wine or a chicken which tasted a little off. Never been a chicken lover and I love good red wine but it does not love me."

He had the city discomfort, a squint, uprightness and slenderness of a bushie so I tested the water.

"In your day, I would have died of peritonitis. Not today, it is a simple operation."

I wanted to try to use the name Fred. A new grandfather with a name.

It suited him. He looked like a Fred. He also looked tired, strained and pained.

"I hear you spend a lot of time out bush. I spent many years at Mount Isa and in the Irvinebank area. Do you know where Irvinebank is?"

"Oh yes. The Atherton-Irvinebank road is one of the worst in Australia. Many have come to grief there, especially in the wet." I was speaking his language.

"How do you know that?"

"I'm doing some work underground at the Wolfram Camp mine, just north of Dimbulah off the Mt Mulligan road on the other side of the Walsh. I'm sure you know it Fred. The old four compartment shaft, the Leisner, is still in operation. Goes down to the 400 ft level with a sump on the 500 ft level. It's still a good producer of wolfram, bismuth and moly. I've got to know many mines in the Herberton, Irvinebank, Petford and Emuford areas. I often travel up that way in the dry. Got caught on the wrong side of the Walsh a few wets ago so I've learned my lesson. That part of the world has a great and rich mining history and a large number of really interesting mineral deposits, especially Chillagoe, the town that led to the demise of Red Ted Theodore. In the old days, there were some fantastic tin mines in the Irvinebank area. The old Vulcan Mine was the richest tin mine in Australia. A real freak of nature. Why were you in Irvinebank?"

I thought that this rather verbose chat about an area he knew might make Fred more comfortable. A conversation about a little-known area in far north Queensland was a starting point for a new relationship. I did not want a conversation of questions and answers. Far too strained and had the potential of being too nosey.

"I was a quantity surveyor for some of the public road works until they retired me last year. I used to calculate and cost the amount of materials needed for public works. A job for an experienced person. Not a young person's job and I can't see why they had to retire me."

Fred started to relax and went on to tell me that he was quite upset that he had been forcibly retired at the tender age of seventy-four. He thought that he had successfully cheated on his age for decades and that he would be able to work until he died. However, he must have let something slip. Without work, he could not escape. Forcible retirement had given him the opportunity to come south and to try to make his final peace with his three daughters. An opportunity to meet his grandchildren for the first time. Hardly children as they were now all adults and he had a few great grandchildren.

"I've bought a few little articles in for you to read while you are confined. I hear you live a very busy life and now that you have been slowed down, you'll probably be able to catch up on reading."

"Thanks. I'll start on them today."

"Nothing special. For some years I've been contributing to various magazines and I thought that as a scientist you might be interested in some of my ideas."

I was given a pile and inch or so thick containing a few hundred pages of articles. These were carbon copies on foolscap airmail paper. They were clearly Fred's only copy of his life's work.

"These look like your own copies. I'll read them and get them back to you presently."

"Don't concern yourself with that. They are for you."

During my first hour with my new grandfather, he gave me his life's work. He was desperate to communicate with his family, to tie up all loose ends and to have some communication with his grandchildren. A man in his mid-seventies does not have that long to live and there was a whole lifetime to catch up. He seemed to put a lot of faith in me. He had planned to give his life's work to a grandson that he'd never met at their very first meeting.

I must have displayed great shock when he announced that he was my grandfather. He must have realised that I'd been told that he was dead and that he was never part of anyone's life. He seemed bitter that he'd been killed off. Killed off from a grandson with whom he could communicate. A grandson who actually knew where Irvinebank was. A grandson who spent enough time in the bush to be non-judgemental. He must have realised that I was somewhat different from the other city-bred desk-driving shiny bums. So little time left and so much catching up to do.

It was a short visit. After he left I spent the rest of the day in thought and reading his life's work. Unlike my paternal grandfather, he was strongly anti-war. A humanist. He was very Australian and spoke like an educated man. Self-educated. He did not like the bosses, capitalists, Poms or Yanks. He could not tolerate mental or physical indolence. He hated the Nazis. He hated the Communists. He wrote on atheism, a new world order, nature, Esperanto and politics. All heavy serious stuff that was in vogue in the 1920s and 30s. All the stuff that the left wingers of the 1930s were passionate about. Years of thinking and writing under canvas by the light of a tilley lamp in the bush. Fred's life carefully crafted by an ancient portable Remington. A Remington typewriter with a very worn lower case 'e' that had dropped half a line. His Remington was his only asset, his only joy and his salvation from the past. He couldn't afford to use too much paper so all his life was single-spaced on rice paper with all corrections still *in situ*. How on Earth did he keep so much paper perfectly preserved over so many wet seasons?

Unfortunately, there was very little biographical writing. Just a few snippets to give me a measure of the man. Was he a man of high principles or was he a little unsteady in his convictions? He lived in times when there was great hostility in Australia between the Catholics and Protestants. In job advertisements, employers were able to state "*Catholics need not apply*". As a committed anti-papist, he had organised groups of similar like-minded gentlemen to go to the fish markets very early on Fridays to buy up all the fish and leave nothing for the Catholics. It was a totally pointless way of making a stand especially as he was a regular at the fish markets for years. Once it had worked the first or second time, many more fish would have been brought to market and his pocket could obviously not stretch that far. Had he thought it through or was he being mischievous? Was he a man of passion to the point of being obsessive? A troublemaker. A non-drinker. A non-smoker. A non-gambler. A non-voter. A non-person. He did not exist, even to his immediate family. What made him tick?

One more hospital visit and then I was able to visit him in a small flat adjacent to his sister's house. Fred was the only son. He had a brother who died as an infant. God knows what his childhood was like with his nine sisters. As a child, I had met the last surviving five of his unmarried sisters, all of whom were talented in their various ways. Music, literature, art, teaching, and languages: all had a calling at which they excelled in times when there was massive discrimination against women in the workforce.

Childhood excursions to visit the ever-diminishing number of great aunts at "*Elizabeth Farm*" near Parramatta had a routine. First a train trip with a change at Central. Then a walk from Granville station, meetings and greetings on the veranda with a powdery kiss mixed with stale scent and the smell of age followed by a brief recital on the grand. I was to play *Für Elise*, Mozart, Chopin, Czerny or any other classical piece for my gathered great aunts. I was a poor pianist but, even then as a child, I had a great love of classical music that has been with me all my life. It was beautiful to play on a grand compared with the old upright at home. Reward was a cup of tea with scones and then I was dismissed to play under the macadamia tree while adults' talk took place. All I needed was two half bricks and the trip to the great aunts was heaven. This was one of the greatest joys of my frugal childhood. These nuts were like forbidden fruit. Sweet, meaty and a long after-taste. The Protestant ethic was fulfilled. I had to work to eat.

Although the company of adults was not inviting, I was never allowed inside while the adults' talk took place. It was of no concern. I was a child, free to gather and eat as many macadamias as possible. I had no interest in the conversation of the adults. I explored the garden and cellar although I never fully explored all the rooms of "*Elizabeth Farm*". In hindsight, it was clear that some of the talk was about Fred. He might not have had direct contact with his wife and children, but he would have had contact with his sisters. Never did we go to *"Elizabeth Farm"* with my maternal grandmother. There may have been friction between her and my great aunts because Fred had left her. The farm had been the family home of three generations for some seventy years and, although he may have been a touch feral, Fred's nine sisters were not. Fred had been killed off just in case the neighbours knew that there had been a divorce or separation in the family. Killed off to enable the upbringing of pure children, untainted by a family scandal. As a child I knew that I was from a superior family background because there was no divorce, no family scandal, no children out of wedlock, no alcoholism and no Catholics.

In fact, it was the opposite. I was often reminded that my maternal grandmother's father was an eminent scientist. He was a Fellow of the Royal Society (FRS). When I showed interest in minerals as a child, I was given a mineral specimen that, I was told, my FRS great grandfather studied and made his name. Later in life when I was an avid reader of the scientific literature, I learned that this was not quite true. My interest in minerals and geology grew and, as a teenager, I was given a wonderfully preserved trilobite fossil. It too, I was told, came from the collection of my famous great grandfather.

With time on my hands in my hospital bed, additional geological knowledge since childhood and a thumbnail sketch of my new grandfather, it became obvious. The trilobite fossil was from Beetle Creek, near Mount Isa in northwestern Queensland. My FRS great grandfather could not have collected the fossil because the collecting site was not known in his lifetime, the Mount Isa deposit had not been discovered by Campbell Miles and my great grandfather was constrained to NSW as the government analyst. As a teenage child, I was not aware that I had a maternal grandfather but Fred must have known that I existed. He also probably knew from his sisters that as a child I had a great interest in geology and the outdoors. He must have gone bush specifically to collect a present for his unknown grandson who had an interest in geology.

As a child, I was fascinated with the perfect pattern of this extinct beast that gave me a window into ancient environments more than 500 million years ago. The delicate pygidium, the partially preserved cephalon, the upstanding thorax and the strong pleural furrows. I knew the trilobite like the back of my hand. My trilobite was my companion on my path through childhood. I learned by heart the genus and species names of my trilobite's extinct relatives much the same as children today know the dinosaur fossils and their families. Although I have had numerous rock and mineral collections, which I have since given away, I still have my trilobite. It proudly sits next to my desk. My link with childhood. The token of my unknown grandfather's affection and intellectual encouragement.

It was only after the resurrection of Fred that a family tree appeared. I was now told that Fred had deserted his wife and three young daughters. Fred has broken off the engagement to my grandmother before marriage. He was uncertain and not convinced that the union was that of lifelong soul mates. He needed physical and mind space. He needed time. After pain, pressure and persuasion, Fred finally married my grandmother. I know nothing of the early years of marriage except that he was continually reminded that his earlier cancellation of the engagement was a shameful, ignominious and dishonourable breach of promise. He was obviously not a gentleman and not to be trusted. I suspect he had been endlessly nagged about his alleged poor character. There was only a certain amount of this that Fred could take. He took flight.

I was told that he disappeared during times of greatest need and that he did not even support his family. My knowledge of Fred's sisters, Fred's background and Fred's sense of ethics and morals suggested that this was not the case. His deserted wife never worked, never took in washing or ironing and, although she struggled in times when social security did not exist, she survived. At those times, everyone was poor and struggled. Furthermore, his abandoned daughters were able to find him very quickly after his ex-wife died and he returned from the bush. There must have been contact and maintenance must have provided over all those years for his wife and children. For me, it became indisputable that Fred provided for his wife and daughters during those decades of marital separation. The non-smoking, non-drinking, non-gambling Fred also died poor with no assets after a frugal life in the bush.

As part of eternal punishment, Fred's contact with his grandchildren was banned. My *Redlichia* fossil was the proof that he cared and that he tried to make contact with his flesh and blood that was interested in rocks. During his forty-year absence, he probably occasionally lost himself in the fragrance of another lady. Did he fall in love? Do I have an auntie or uncle somewhere or Queensland or New Zealand where there was a Frederick Swann who may have had a number of interesting relationships? It matters not.

I was pleased to know that I was normal, that the family had a few skeletons in the cupboard and that I was part of an ordinary dysfunctional family. I had a grandfather for three years of my adult life. We had much contact, interesting conversations and became close. After I moved back outback, I learned of his death well after his funeral. I could easily have been contacted and I would have attended the funeral but even in death he was the patriarchal pariah. It was deemed that, even with death, affection was denied. I guess I was not told as punishment for fraternising with the family black sheep.

Over time, I have come to value heretics, freethinkers, dissenters, black sheep, pariahs, sceptics, whistle-blowers, unusual people and others of principle. I have also found that over time, I have nothing in common with those that go through the motions of life, work, experiences and affections. I enjoy people of passion.

Fred would give one of his memorable faint smiles if he knew that I had turned out to be a troublemaker.

I wonder if it's hereditary?

(1971)

Oubth-ut-Allah

It was all a big mistake. I should never have been there but, once there, I was stuck in mountainous north-eastern Iran in winter. Because the rocks of the Kopet Dağ Mountains, east of Mashhad, had been heated at high pressures, they resembled the rocks of Broken Hill. Thereafter, all resemblance ceased. At that time, I was a Broken Hill resident and very active publishing in the international scientific literature on Broken Hill geological matters. The Imperial Persian Ministry of Science in 1977 requested my services for an investigation of the Kopet Dağ Mountains because their Bafq zinc-lead-silver deposit was coming to the end of its life and Iran wanted a replacement zinc-lead-silver deposit. The brief was simple. Another Broken Hill would be just fine, thank you very much. Once in the Kopet Dağ Mountains, I immediately realised that there was no chance of another Broken Hill that had formed in a remarkable period of Earth history 1,685 million years ago and the Kopet Dağ rocks were far younger as shown by brachiopod fossils.

Although the Kopet Dağ area was the wrong geological environment for a Broken Hill-type zinc-lead-silver deposit, the area had never been mapped and the rocks retained the history of continental collision processes in that part of the world that took place hundreds of millions of years ago. It was clearly worthwhile to stay and complete the task but not with my Broken Hill geological mind set.

In the Shah's time, Mashhad was an interesting city. It was my base. It was at the end of the line, an outpost for the military and a hot bed of a mullah-driven revolt. Like many Islamic cities, it had stunning mosques, foetid markets, chaotic traffic through which a thread of order ran, vibrant bazaars, beggars, gravity-defying buildings and a small wealthy group of business people. In early 1978, the smell of revolution permeated the air. Everywhere was pro-Shah bunting, photographs and propaganda but it was a different picture in the mosques, universities and at private meetings.

It did surprise me that my lectures at Ferdowsi University at Mashhad required two M-16 bearing soldiers at the back of each lecture theatre. I wondered if they understood geology? I wondered if they understood English? Would I disappear forever if I said "*bum*"? For security reasons, I was forbidden to meet university staff or students. I was prohibited from taking students out into the field to teach them mapping techniques. It was forbidden to take photographs and I was prohibited from leaving Mashhad for mapping in the mountains without my Savak driver. The security police, Savak, had well and truly earned their reputation for brutality and a brush with Savak meant imprisonment, clearing out of congested prisons and a premature embrace with Allah. Yet at private parties and dinners, there were copious quantities of the local alcoholic firewater and not very generous discussions about the Shah. The revolution took place in 1979 and, as with so many populist and people's revolutions, the new regime was far worse than that which it replaced.

I had a task to achieve, I had my colonial topographic maps as aerial photographs were forbidden and smuggled satellite photographs. I had a miniature Japanese camera which could be carried in my bulky winter clothing. Each day, my Savak driver would purchase the day's provisions of bread, yoghurt and nuts from the market and collect me from my host's fortified villa to drive me up the mountains. It never seemed to worry my Savak driver that, despite the fact that I'd never been to the area in my life before, I knew exactly where I wanted to go, knew all the roads and village tracks and already knew much about the geology of the area. His job was to shadow my every movement and to stop me fraternising with nomads, villagers or any other human being. He certainly was not there to protect me. My maps and photographs had been cut to the page size of my field book, these he never saw and the electronic cacophony of my camera was silenced by the howling snow-laden northerly winds.

My first few days in the field were a general reconnaissance of the area to be mapped. This involved walking great distances at altitude, climbing very steep snow-laden slopes and carrying far too many rock samples. All this was necessary to get the feel of the area before systematic mapping could commence. I was in my early 30s and at the peak of physical fitness. The reconnaissance work exhausted my Savak driver who had led an indolent chain-smoking life and, if he ever had a time of peak fitness, then it was in the geological past. It was then that he made a decision on behalf of the Shah and I was deemed to be no threat to the Shah's Iran. Thereafter, he spent the whole day sleeping and smoking in the vehicle awaiting my return from mapping in far off mountains. Some would call this the perfect job. He never understood how I could navigate in this far off unknown land without maps. He never seemed to care about anything.

Fieldwork was constrained by snowdrifts on the northern slopes of hills and the lack of outcrop in areas covered by debris left behind during the retreat of glaciers about 12,000 years ago. Rocks cropped out on the ridges and in the ravines and mapping was by ridge and valley traverse. In many isolated steep ravines, caches of used cartridges and machine gun belts were piled high in what could only have been clandestine training grounds. It was not surprising that at altitude in the depths of winter, I only rarely saw a villager or nomad however armed villagers, mujahedeen and bandits were clearly very active. Was this a normal alpine training ground for those involved in cross border smuggling or was it the boys in the mountains preparing for the inevitable Iranian revolution?

The people in these mountain areas clearly had every reason for revolution as they were miserably poor, had no land ownership, no infrastructure, little food and no employment. It appeared that subsistence agricultural production in summer was supplemented by the sporadic mining of small quantities of gypsum developed on limey sandstones. One summer crop failure and disaster awaited in winter. The mountain people I met were always kind and friendly and, without my Savak driver, I felt safe. Preparations for a revolution concerned me a little however, I was pleased that my Savak driver and his revolver were not with me when such large bore weaponry was floating around in the mountains.

I left the most remote mapping part of the mountains until the last. I needed to get mountain fitness and mapping is such a steep remote area would be far more efficient if I had a good geological understanding of the adjacent areas. Mapping of the last isolated mountain areas was fascinating. The ancient valley floors were steeply sloping, indicating that the area had undergone recent uplift and tilting associated with the collision of the Indian sub-continent with Asia. This process is still going on and has created the Himalayas and the Tibetan Plateau. It was clear that the Kopet Dağ Mountains were still rising because of the steep topography and frequent earthquakes. The sloping uplifted older valley floors were covered with glacial debris and were deeply incised in a sequence of inter-connecting north-south and east-west ravines. Meltwaters had exploited cracks in the bedrocks, had cut out ravines and the bedrocks were now only exposed on the floors of the ravines that were up to 80 metres deep.

Once in these ravines, it was almost impossible to climb out and it was necessary to follow them some kilometres into the mountains before the ravines became a mountain watercourse. Further downstream, these ravines broadened to become a deep flat-bottomed valley that hosted the occasional village serviced by a qanat, the underground water canal that taps melt waters from high in the mountains. Qanat is a useful word for Scrabble players because if one has a Q without a U then there is still hope.

The qanats of Persia are a marvellous system of underground canals dug thousands of years ago. The canals are lined with boulders, have a service way and have ventilation shafts or wells each kilometre or so. They are still well maintained despite the fact that some run for scores of kilometres underground from the source in the mountains to the valley floor. Because qanats are dug in impermeable clays and are structurally supported, they rarely collapse and the water does not become muddy.

In fact, the clays naturally extract salts and natural pollutants from the water. Qanat water is fast-flowing and supports no algal blooms, thanks to the clays and the lack of light. The bulk of the water is used by villagers for the spring and summer alpine melt water irrigation of grain and fruit crops. Qanats are engineering projects that have been environmentally friendly for thousands of years, unlike many costly modern environmental projects that commonly fail and are of no benefit to humans.

The villages use the water for drinking, cooking and the washing of clothes. Wells into the qanat have a wooden bucket on a levered pole to enable the collection of water from depth and the large boulders around the tops of the wells are covered with freshly washed brightly coloured clothes. The village wastewater flows along surface watercourses that, because of impervious clay-rich sediments, do not connect with a cobble-lined qanat up to 60 metres below the surface. Qanats are inhabited by blind white fish and the unpolluted water is crystal clear and teeth chilling.

The domed alpine village huts are made from mud mixed with donkey dung, houses have walled yards, pens for livestock and almond, pistachio and fig trees. The villages have no electricity, no reticulated water, no sewage system, no schools, no shops, and no medical clinic and are inaccessible by motor vehicle. If villagers are ill or seriously injured, then there are two alternatives: die or get better. Until the next time. The winding narrow rocky cavernous mud tracks through the villages make them impassable to any vehicle. These villages are yet to experience the 20th or 21st Centuries. Each village has a central square ornamented by a large fruit tree surrounded by benches for village elders and it is only in larger accessible villages where there is a mosque. However, small or remote villages have a social structure led by the village headman elected to this position by the male village elders. It is the headman's responsibility to ensure that the old ways are followed.

Villages are connected by donkey tracks, many of which follow the qanats down slope. Without qanats, the mountainous areas of northeastern Iran would be unpopulated. The view of some in wealthy Western society that the people in such areas are peasant nobility connected to Nature is laughably naïve. Mountain folk live or die on the seasons, it is a constant struggle with the elements and survival is a day-to-day problem. These people are not concerned about the environment, they just want to eat. Given half a chance, they leave their tribal lands for a better life in the cities. And they do.

Maps of the ravine areas were unreliable as no villages or tracks were marked. Such areas would have arisen after the making of the maps. Geological mapping of the ravines was always interesting as one was never certain about what was around the next corner. Was it a village? An impassable waterfall or cliff? An interesting outcrop or even an old mine? Old ruins? Furthermore, mapping in the ravines was frequently in the sun and out of the biting northerlies.

Quite often when I was working alone in these isolated areas, I felt that I was not alone. Sometimes, one met a miner, shepherd or villager going about their daily business. Very often, one was shadowed by villagers, most of whom had never seen a geologist at work. It must have appeared very strange. A foreigner in peculiar clothes on village lands, occasionally hitting a rock with a strangely-shaped hammer, writing on the rock, writing on a plastic bag, putting a rock into a plastic bag, putting the bag into a knapsack, writing in a book and constantly photographing this strange hammer laid to rest on outcrops. Why did this foreigner stop at one outcrop for quite a time yet ignore other rock outcrops? How strange. There must have been deep and meaningful discussions in the villages each evening about what I was doing.

In the ravine country of the Kopet Dağ Mountains, I often felt that I was been watched. A long time in the bush had given me good observation skills and a sixth sense. I neither saw nor heard anyone. Once when I turned the corner in a steep ravine, I was met by a dozen armed horsemen lining the cliffs thirty metres above me. Wild, bearded, fiery, robed men with belts of high calibre ammunition and automatic weapons pointed at me. No escape. No way to go. A Butch Cassidy and Sundance Kid moment. Even if I were armed, I was still easy target practice as there was no cover. What would be the point anyway? It looked like a quick death by the brothers Kalashnikov in the wilds of mountainous Iran.

With the barrel of his gun, the head horseman indicated to me to climb up a track from the ravine to his horsemen. This I did, they surrounded me and started to excitedly converse in Farsi. While my knapsack was being searched and my body searched for weapons, the guns were still trained on me. I decided that if I moved slowly and deliberately, then I would be non-threatening. I was asked if I was American but showing them my passport was pointless because no one could read our alphabet or had knowledge of English or French. They probably couldn't read. By using the labels on my clothing and by drawing in my field book, I was able to convince them that I was not American. They might not have known about Australia, kangaroos or where the country was but they knew that I was not American. The maps and satellite images were of no interest whatsoever which was a relief as the satellite images were clearly of American origin. It was a relief to know that my armed Savak driver was asleep in the car miles away. His presence would have guaranteed annihilation.

By using the barrel of a gun, the head horseman directed me to share a horse with the smallest horseman. Our band of horsemen took me high into the mountains and we eventually stopped at an outcrop of highly weathered ophiolitic rocks. Such rocks are a slice of the ocean floor thrust up onto continents after continental collision. I had seen ophiolite sequences in many parts of the world and was not surprised to see the outcrop stained by a patina of the bright green copper carbonate mineral called malachite. Malachite was probably found by Neolithic folk who passed bright green specimens around the fireplace. Someone may have thrown the specimen into the fire and the reaction of malachite and heat would have boiled off carbon dioxide and water. The remaining copper oxide would have been reduced by charcoal to copper metal. When the fire had died, shiny prills of copper metal on rock would have been seen and the Neolithic people would have scratched, beaten with a rock and bent the metallic copper. This is probably the way copper was discovered. As with so many discoveries, they were accidental and driven by curiosity. Since antiquity, malachite has been one of the main ores of copper and, when in its massive form, can be used for jewellery.

It then dawned on me why the horsemen had taken me away. They must have been watching my harmless geological mapping for days and, after discussions in the village, had decided that I might be able to help them as their own personal geological consultant. They were crushingly poor and it was obvious that I could provide them with advice on whether such a malachite outcrop was worth mining to provide food for the village. I demounted and was watched with great interest while I measured the dimensions of the ophiolite outcrop with my tape and compass and dug a small pit through the weathered malachite-bearing rock to the fresh unweathered rock. The guns were now in saddle holsters as the horsemen realised that I had finally understood what was required of me. In their eyes, I was clearly not very bright but could be of use to them. They were right. I could survive in my world but not in theirs.

Ancient sea floor rocks commonly contain copper minerals at the sites of old sea mounds and mid ocean ridges. The primary copper mineral is the golden yellow copper iron sulphide, chalcopyrite. Upon exposure to air, chalcopyrite tarnishes to a display of peacock colours and eventually combines with oxygen and carbon dioxide in air and water to form secondary copper minerals such as the green malachite or the blue azurite. A rarer copper mineral, the chestnut-coloured copper iron sulphide bornite, tarnishes even more quickly. Bornite was named after the Austrian mineralogist Ignaz von Born (1742-1791), a close friend of Mozart. It is commonly called peacock ore. Producing copper from chalcopyrite by smelting requires heat whereas smelting of bornite gives out heat hence it is sought after by smelters. Did the Kopet Dağ malachite derive from bornite? Alas, no.

It formed from chalcopyrite, a mineral that is currently forming in the Mid Atlantic Ridge and East Pacific Rise where the ocean floor is being pulled apart as the ophiolite sequence forms. The copper deposits of Cyprus, exploited since antiquity, formed 120 million years ago on the ocean floor before being thrust up as a Mediterranean island and a belt of ophiolites across southern Turkey. With the thrusting of ophiolites onto the land, the ancient sea floor rocks are dismembered, huge amounts of water flow through them and much of the ophiolite is converted to serpentine. These catastrophic processes smear out chalcopyrite into fractures and veins and are often responsible for converting a massive chalcopyrite deposit into numerous uneconomic veins.

The presence of malachite in the Kopet Dağ Mountains could possibly indicate the presence of a massive chalcopyrite deposit at depth. There may even be platinum minerals, chromite or even the serpentine mineral chrysotile, sometimes incorrectly called asbestos. Inspection of the ophiolite showed that it was sheared, converted to serpentine and had numerous veins, some of which contained sporadic grains of chalcopyrite. In my field book, using Persian numbering, I drew a three-dimensional diagram of the malachite stainings and showed the head horseman that there were only about five saddlebags of malachite that could be easily won from this locality. As there was neither water nor acid nearby, the malachite could not be converted on site to copper. Malachite stains along shears in rocks can be deceptive because there is only thin paint of malachite along the shear and the whole body of rock is not composed of malachite.

We mounted and rode to the next locality, also an ophiolite, where I repeated the exercise. At this locality was the black hard heavy mineral chromite, an iron chromium oxygen mineral typical of ophiolites. It was no surprise to find chromite. This mineral is the sole source of chromium for the steel industry. Chromite from ophiolites is rich in chromium and normally occurs as numerous small dismembered pods, thin layers and isolated grains. The bulk of the world's chromite occurs in the eastern Transvaal of South Africa. It contains less chromium than ophiolitic chromite but occurs as thick massive seams that are mined by mechanical means and then beneficiated. Chromite is a low-priced commodity that is sold on the international market the same way as other traded commodities and is subject to the same international pressures of supply and demand, exchange rate and commodity price.

The low capital cost mining of small isolated pockets of a low unit value commodity in such a remote area clearly made chromite mining not viable, despite the extreme poverty (hence low costs) of the people in the area. It was just not possible to explain such concepts to the horsemen so I dismissed the chromite locality on the basis of its small size. Another two localities where there was surface malachite staining were visited and then the horsemen took me down from the mountains into a ravine-protected village served by a qanat.

The head horseman also doubled as the village headman. Horses were hobbled in the yard of a village house, the guns and ammunition were wrapped in oily rags to be hidden somewhere and sweet black tea, yoghurt and bread was served. The village horsemen were charming hosts and there was much discussion with the other villagers about the events of the day which, although disappointing, were a great talking point. I regretted not being able to use my geological skills to be able to help these wonderful people out of what looked like permanent gripping poverty. The only possible commodity that the Kopet Dağ ophiolite could have provided the village was platinum. Even small quantities would have put many meals on tables.

I borrowed one of the village baking trays, collected sand from the watercourse and water from the qanat and showed the village people how to pan for heavy minerals. I used a bullet to show how a heavy object can be concentrated by panning and tried to describe that a heavy silvery white mineral (either osmiridium or isoferroplatinum) panned from watercourses high in the mountains draining the ophiolite is very valuable. I hope I managed to communicate the message.

Towards sunset, a village youth was instructed to guide me back to the car. We took a long circuitous route such that the setting sun behind us allowed me to see the car and prevented the Savak driver from seeing me or my young guide. My guide shook my hand and disappeared into the sun.

I was saddened that I could not give my friendly armed horsemen some better geological news.

(1978)

Drinking on the job with Ken Maiden, fellow geologist,
Namibia, 1994.

Postcard from Africa

The French, Portuguese, Spanish, Belgian, German and English colonial powers left Africa quickly and did not prepare the local people for decision making, power and government. The Italians failed to get a foothold and got thumped in Ethiopia and the Dutch had an influence in the Cape. The French and English left an education system and the English and Germans left a legal system. Most black African countries are now totally and absolutely corrupt. They are run by army leaders, local warlords and clan leaders, all of whom have their snouts in the trough. While the average person starves, the leaders live in palaces, have private jets and rob their own countries of all the wealth. Money is spent on well-equipped private armies who wipe out the political opposition, wipe out rival clans and conduct systematic genocide by starving the population. God help you if you are a woman and the army drops in for a chat.

These countries generally put out their hands and ask the United Nations for aid to feed the population, especially after weather events, crop failure and civil war. Church and humanitarian aid groups try to help on the ground and often pay with their lives. Aid is often stolen and funds derived from stolen aid is then deposited in European banks. Almost nothing is put back into schools, hospitals, roads, bridges, potable water and reliable reticulated electricity. These facilities are generally paid for by aid organisations and, as the money passes through numerous sticky hands, then the facility built is not maintained and falls apart in a few years. Driving on some African roads requires time, a well-maintained robust vehicle, swerving skills and a wallet full of money for bribes in order to go from A to B.

Survival is grim in Angola, a former Portuguese colony. It is in the tropics, has fantastic fertile soils, good rainfall, permanent water and is rich in minerals and oil. The Portuguese left overnight and no one had been trained to run government, the civil service, the police, the army, the revenue-earning mines and productive farms. In fact, as was done in East Timor, the Portuguese destroyed all geological maps and scientific reports on the mineral resources. Some of this information was in libraries in other parts of the world and later was given to Angola (and East Timor). Angola quickly collapsed into civil war between the major clans. The government clan financed their side of the civil war by selling oil and the rival clan financed the war by selling diamonds illegally mined from their patch of ground.

Unnamed pilots from an unnamed country told me how it was done. Old World War II freighter planes (DC3) still exist and fly in Africa. The DC3 carried about 3 tonnes of freight and, if the air temperature is cool, they can add another half tonne. The take off is from illegal airstrips in neighbouring countries and the plane is loaded with weapons, ammunition and some food. All freight is in corn bags labelled as humanitarian aid. The planes fly at night at tree top height with no lights so they cannot easily be shot down or detected on radar and, when in Angola, they climb and then put on the landing lights some 200 metres before touchdown on short unsealed airstrips cut out of the jungle. The freight is unloaded quickly by a mob of men and the lighter plane can just clear the trees upon take off. The only freight coming back to the neighbouring countries is not heavy and is in the pockets of the crew. Diamonds. If a pilot does three or four such trips, then he can make enough money to buy his own plane. I met one of these chaps, a pilot in his twenties who owned his own Boeing 727 jet. Some planes crash or go missing and, of course, the crew don't survive. Other crews are killed on the ground after delivery of the weapons. No one reports such plane crashes and no one officially knows anything. This is little different from the drug smugglers of South America. There is no concern about one's fellow man, very high rewards if successful and numerous opportunities for a quick dollar. And a quick death.

Even if there was no gun running, the weapon of mass destruction is everywhere. The machete or bush knife is essential for survival in a subsistence economy. Most males have their trusty machete for clearing tracks and fields. Young boys all have their own machete. It is a right of passage, is cheap to operate, no money needs to be spent for a gun or ammunition and it can easily be sharpened on any stone. The machete has killed more in Africa than guns.

Although the 25-year long civil war in Angola has theoretically ended, Angola still has 20 million land mines spread all over the country. There are already 600,000 amputees in Angola, no agriculture can be undertaken because the legless can't work and the fields have land mines. Most of the land mines are made mainly of plastic and hence can't be easily located by metal detectors, no one can afford the $1,000 needed to find and explode an $8 land mine and hence a fertile rich agricultural country cannot produce food. If the country was organised and those in power were concerned about the quality of life of their fellow countrymen, these countries would boom.

The adjacent countries are different but the end result is the same. Although Zambia has had no long civil war, it is little different regarding starvation, poverty and disease. Various parts of the country are run by clan warlords. There are no laws. There is no system to keep the community running. If you want to do anything, you must bargain with fourteen-year old boys holding an AK47 (Kalashnikov). Even if some sort of deal is struck, there is no guarantee that the arrangement will work for a week, a day or even an hour. Life has absolutely no value at all. There are bodies lying in the streets that have clearly been there for some time. They provide protein for packs of dogs. Infected decomposing bodies pollute the waterways and people who use this water have lifelong problems with gut viruses and parasites. A country that was once rich has been reduced to total chaos. Farmers use sticks because they have no tools, there is no employment, no health care, no social security and no viable profitable industries. The whole infrastructure and financial base of the country has been wasted in twenty short years. The country is so far in debt to the international community, that no one will lend them money to get them out of their predicament. And if they are lent money and the debts were forgiven, there is no structure to stop them doing exactly the same again. Why would you lend them money? It would only be stolen by some politician gangster and not used for its designated purpose. How can you lend money to a country that has no government or banking system? Who will pay the money back? In some countries when you throw a coin up in the air, it does not come down. Zambia is one such place.

Zambia was originally a colony that produced 30% of the world's copper and was known as the breadbasket of Africa. Chile is now the world's biggest copper producer from deposits that have far less metal in them than those in Zambia. The land is so rich and the tropical rainfall in so regular that three crops a year can be grown. The country built magnificent cities, airports, roads, schools, universities and hospitals and had a generous social security system. Zambia had industry driven by cheap hydroelectricity and exported food and minerals to other countries. It was once wealthy. Now the population dies from starvation, murder, malaria and AIDS.

After Zambia became proudly independent, it drifted into Marxism. They became very anti-white and anything that had been done by the former white colonial population was not continued because it was politically incorrect. All of the mines and farms became the property of the government who had no experience in management, no technical experience or knowledge and no ability with budgets and planning. There was the political view that the country was now independent, it could do whatever it wanted to do and that everyone was to have a job. Nothing was maintained or repaired, no new employment-generating industries were started, everything started to fall apart at the seams until everything actually did fall apart. By then, it was too late. What were the richest copper mines in the world and the richest agricultural country in Africa very quickly collapsed because of poor inexperienced management, overstaffing by untrained incompetents in order to give everyone a job, bad decisions because of inexperience and lack of knowledge and there was no re-capitalisation.

Unlike an oil well where capital is up front, mines continue to require working capital as hard-working equipment needs to be replaced and processing plants need to be modified as ore changes in characteristics with depth. Mining and agriculture were exploited and there was no continuing investment to keep the ship afloat as all of the monies generated were taken by government. These once profitable industries now started to make a loss and, to make matters even more difficult, commodities are sold on a global market where global prices and exchange rates cannot be dictated by the miner or farmer. Once exchange rates are tampered with to make these primary industries profitable, then it becomes prohibitively expensive to buy machinery made outside the country such as Caterpillar dozers, trucks and tractors. Once that happens, the country is in a death spiral. This is what happened in Zambia. It has happened in many other places and still happens all over the world.

Rather than fix the problem, the country continually devalued its currency. This meant that everyone still had buckets full of money (which was politically popular), but Zambia then was not only unable to afford foreign mining and agricultural equipment but could not afford the foreign specialists who would have solved their problems. To make matters worse, foreign specialists were sent packing and journalists were jailed just in case they exposed the shambles. The country put no money into roads, housing, health, hospitals and schools and had no machinery to build such infrastructure. The costs of everything escalated and inflation was crippling. It became impossible to drive across a country that once had four lane freeways. Towns that originally had infrastructure for 100,000 people now held a million or more people with no additional infrastructure. In a country that has one of the highest rainfalls in the world, there was no tap water because pumps had broken down and electricity to drive the pumps could not be generated because of a lack of generator spares and maintenance. Because of the lack of potable water, the lack of sewage systems, the lack of medical facilities and over-population, cholera came back with vengeance. It had all but disappeared in the good times and now was rampant. Hundreds of thousands of people died from diseases that are easily curable and were wiped out in other countries a long time ago. In more recent times, Zimbabwe became a very good example. It was a mining and agricultural country that fed itself and, when it was Rhodesia, had a booming export industry of minerals, electricity, tobacco and food. The West pressurised for self-government, the country went the same way and now bank note collectors have useless $100 trillion Zimbabwean dollar notes in their collections as a symbol of uncontrollable inflation.

In Zambia, a country with high rainfall, the richest copper mines in the world became flooded and unworkable because there was no money to buy pumps manufactured outside the country. If they perchance could actually purchase pumps, parts were stolen and sold for scrap metal. It didn't matter as there was no electricity to run the pumps anyway. Zambia has one of the biggest hydroelectricity systems in the world and, if you are lucky, you can get power in the two major cities for six hours every second day. Power stations built with aid money are not maintained because, when the equipment fails, more aid money is forthcoming. People are so poor that wiring from the hydroelectricity plants gets stolen and no spare parts, new wiring, generating machinery and other equipment can be purchased because the country is bankrupt. No one knows how to fix major problems at the hydroelectricity stations. No one has been trained in electrical engineering in Zambia and, if Zambians are trained abroad, there is no incentive for them to go back to Zambia. Why go back for no pay and get murdered or die of cholera?

No schools operate. Because teachers were regarded as part of the intelligentsia, they were murdered. Those that survived have not been paid for years and, in order to eat, are working in the fields and trying to survive by growing a few square metres of corn and making sure it does not get stolen upon ripening. Most of the fields now no longer exist and have gone back to jungle. This can happen in two short years. No one can afford to clear the land or purchase seeds. No hospitals operate, no one trained in medicine lives in isolated rural areas because many were murdered, died of a curable disease or left the district. Even if there were medical staff in remote areas, there are no drugs, no surgical instruments, no method of sterilisation, no operating facilities and no electricity.

Surveys by the UN show that 43% of pregnant women are HIV positive. No statistics on community health are kept by Zambia as this costs money. It is not known how many people die of AIDS, malaria, cholera or malnutrition. There is no community health system and those with AIDS just go back to their village and slowly fade away with pneumonia, starvation or some other curable affliction. Some 50% of children do not make it beyond their first year of life but, because most Zambian families have six to ten children, there is a population explosion. Less that 5% of people can write their name so it is probably easier to talk to Martians than to have a family planning education program.

The mining towns have a huge and inefficient workforce. There are few skilled workers, most people do menial manual tasks and no one actually seems to be working hard to produce ore, which would create wealth for Zambia. There are no machines because neither the machine nor the liquid fuel can be purchased. Mine work has devolved from machines doing the hard work to picks, shovels and wheelbarrows. Many mine workers are child slaves who have been kidnapped or orphaned. The workforce is housed in single men's quarters. Frustration, despair and alcohol contribute to daily fights, murders and stabbings. Most men smoke tobacco and chew a hallucinogenic plant (khat) which can cost them their whole daily wage just for one parcel of khat. The men are miles from their home villages and need to earn enough money to feed their extended family of a wife, six to ten children, parents and other relatives, many of whom are orphans who lost their parents to AIDS. Each Zambian worker supports about sixteen people. There is no dole, no Medicare or social security and, in remote areas, no police, no postal service, no telephone system and no hospitals. Nothing. This is the way many other countries were centuries ago. If a miner dies, the family may never know. When a miner coming back to his village with six months pay, he is robbed and killed, no one knows and sixteen people don't eat. Who do you report a missing person to? It happens thousands of times a day.

Prostitutes live in shanty towns around the mines. They are paid in food, alcohol and drugs. AIDS is like a tidal wave and getting bigger and bigger. No miner has a health check because they can't afford a blood test. No one cares. There are no condoms. No one can afford to or bothers to buy condoms. When given them by the World Health Authority, the macho African men says; *"Why do I need to wear a raincoat if I want a shower?"* A condom is against their culture, in some African countries even the role of HIV is questioned, AIDS cannot be seen, people exist for the moment and do not the luxury of thinking about or planning for the future. There is no future.

More than half the workforce is HIV positive. It is very hard to run a mine when semi-skilled people just don't turn up because of illness and death. As soon as new people are trained, they too die. In deep underground mines elsewhere in Africa, the mine fatality rates have risen dramatically. If a miner with AIDS dies at home, then no compensation is paid. If a mine worker dies on the company mining lease, compensation is paid to the family. More and more men are falling down deep shafts, falling under heavy equipment or dying from a high voltage electric shock.

Malaria is the biggest killer in Africa, the virus mutates so quickly that no drug is completely effective and, even if there was a drug to cure malaria, most in Africa could not afford to buy it. Malaria is the biggest killer in the world with four million deaths per annum. The world population increases by two million people a week. Malaria is from mosquito bites, mosquitoes breed in swamps and the breeding cycle can be stopped by the aerial spraying of swamps with chemicals such as DDT. This was done in Asia in World War II by the Americans and they ended up with a fighting force at about 70% capacity whereas the Japanese fought at about 35% capacity. Malaria (ague) has been eliminated from the swampy lowlands of the UK and Europe. Shakespeare made reference to the ague which was common in his time.

Because it was claimed that DDT weakened the eggs of eagles in the USA, there was a massive environmental campaign in the USA to stop the use of DDT worldwide. The World Health Authority banned the use of DDT and hence does not use the easy, cheap, tried and proven aerial spraying to stop malaria in Third World countries. Environmentalists have blood on their hands with at least 50 million unnecessary deaths to their credit. But this does not really matter because black lives are not nearly as important as some common critter in their country. Meanwhile, four million people a year die from malaria, a disease that has been cured in many parts of the world.

The mining and agricultural industries went from profit making to loss making and finally to bankruptcy. They did not become bankrupt because the rich copper ore was exhausted. Mismanagement and corruption bankrupted Zambia. Government officials stole what they could as quickly as they could before it all ran out and then they high-tailed it to live in another country on their stolen cash. Much of this stolen money resides in Europe. With bankruptcy, the country became chaotic and ungovernable, civil trouble broke out and the power gap was filled by warlords. This was easy because the police and army had not been paid for years and, if the warlord gave food and/or money, then the police and army loyalty (plus their weapons) was transferred to the warlord. The warlords had only one law. The person with the greater firepower was in the right.

As a white person, unless you are accompanied by a heavily armed well-paid army, then you would be killed within a day. They might take your money and possessions, do a deal with a warlord and they may kill you anyway. Millions of modern weapons exist. In the towns, leaderless gangs of teenagers and young men roam the streets with machetes and military guns. If you are wearing a pair of shoes, you might be killed because the shoes can be used or sold. If you drive a car, you could be attacked by machine guns or automatic weapons, robbed and then cut to pieces with a machete and left to die. The car will be pulled apart piece by piece and each part will be sold. If you have a house, you need to pay a small army very well to guard you otherwise you will be robbed and killed. If you have a problem, you cannot go to the police. They will also rob and murder you.

Robbery, murder and terror are the way for gangs to get food or enrich themselves. The pattern is the same. Heavily drugged gangsters barely out of their teens visit a target in the dead of night with firearms and razor sharp machetes. Normally only blood and bodies are left behind. Some towns have tried to make the chaos more orderly and have introduced a system of people's justice. If you are caught thieving, the problem is solved easily, quickly and at little financial cost. No police, no courts, no weighing of evidence and no legal appeal. If you are caught thieving, intend to steal or even if your neighbour dobs you in, then the end is swift and brutal.

Commonly the accused (and possible the innocent if there is a dispute with a neighbour) is tied to a defunct lamp post or tree and flogged or stoned to death. Groups of suspected thieves are tied together, wrapped in rubber tyres and burned to death. The village vigilante groups who attempted the people's justice then become a payback murder target for the relatives, friends of the gangsters, thieves or innocent people and more violent deaths follow. The police do not interfere even though they have weapons because the gangsters have bigger and better weapons and outnumber the police. The police use their weapons to find food and enrich themselves and are in competition with the gangs.

If you land a plane on one of the few bush airports which are not overgrown by trees or covered in shanty towns, you will not be able to get fuel, you will not be able to take off unless huge amounts of money are paid and the plane will be destroyed unless massive protection monies are paid to the local gang. Even if this is done, there is no guarantee that the gang will not kill you and then sell everything you have. Wild-eyed gunmen surround a plane as soon as it lands and it is then that you realise that it was a mistake to go to Africa.

Some of these countries actually have governments that hold elections. Such elections work easily and simply. The government, comprising either a dictator, tribal warlord or army generals declares that an election is to be held. If opposition politicians decide to contest the election or an opposition party is formed, then they must do so in public. This is the government's way of finding out who is in opposition.

In the more civilised black African countries, the opposition is jailed for treason. These political hopefuls normally die in prison. If there is actually a court hearing, it is held in secret, no defence lawyers or journalists are allowed, no alibis or contrary evidence are accepted, no press outlet reports the court hearing, accusations are made by criminals who buy their release from prison by lying (only to be killed later to silence them because they know too much) and the court normally rules instant execution. If the court rules detention in prison, then it is generally a long sentence which is not survived as murder and AIDS keep the prison population low. Prisons are expensive to run hence the fewer the prisoners, the lower the costs. If a defence lawyer acts in court or a hearing is reported in the press, then the lawyer or journalist can expect a short life with a grisly end.

Sometimes the opposition leaders have a dreadful accident like falling out of a helicopter, falling from the tenth floor of a building, breaking their neck in prison by slipping on the soap in the shower or having their plane blown up in mid-air. No one, of course, knows how such things happen and, even if there is collateral damage, no one ever faces court or has to pay fines. Except the great masses of the people, they pay dearly and drift into even greater starvation and hopeless health problems.

In the less civilised black African countries, the opposition (who may be a rival clan) are shot and, if ammunition is too expensive, are beaten to death, buried alive in mass graves, hacked to death by machete-wielding gangs, burned alive in a pile of rubber tyres or drowned. In some African countries, it is illegal to speak ill of the army, the leaders or government and, if accused (although not necessarily guilty), penalties range from public flogging, removal of the tongue, limb amputation, public immolation or execution. Not only is the charged person punished, but it is all too common that the whole family is murdered because they too are obviously guilty. If the whole family is murdered, then there is no one to complain if there is a regime change or if there is an opportunity for revenge killing. In some countries, it is illegal to mention the opposition. In some tropical black African countries, it is not possible to drink the river water because of the contamination by rotting human bodies which, of course, attract all sorts of poisonous bacteria, viruses and parasites.

Very little of this is reported in newspapers, radio or television. No reporter would leave such parts of the world if such stories were filed and run. Such stories cannot be told. In pretty well all black African countries, there no free press. In Australia, we do not cherish our freedoms, are quite happy to give away freedoms for some populist cause, we still can criticise politicians, policy and bureaucrats in public and not get beaten to death with a rock or executed with a hammer. How long will Australia have the freedoms of Western civilisation which took 2,500 years to establish? If an African newspaper publishes something the government does not like, then the editor and staff can be hacked to death by government-paid thugs and the offices, printing presses and distribution agencies burned down. No one ever goes to court for killing journalists. Most newspapers, radio and television are owned by the government, warlord, governing clan or army and only lies and propaganda are printed. There is no public opportunity for discussing the news or providing an alternative view and one does not dare discuss politics in private because someone might tell the authorities.

As a scientist, I have been trained to be sceptical and use my trained skills of observation. As one who has seen much of the world, I certainly do not believe everything I read, hear or view in the media. In many cases, as with the gruesome news out of Africa, there is just no real news and the bleeding heart stories are disconnected from reality. In other cases, news is created or one topic may be in vogue. Some networks become an advocate for a cause. The stories might not be untruthful, they just might be giving only one side of the argument. One has to be very sceptical and critical of everything and one must make up one's own mind based on available evidence and, if there is new information, then one's mind may be changed.

Although this is a scene from Africa, sometimes it is better and sometimes it is worse. It depends on local wars, famine and politics. The situation described is by no means restricted to Africa. It has occurred in fundamentalist, totalitarian, dictatorial, fascist, communist and other regimes where power is concentrated, where public criticism is not considered healthy and where dogma and force outweigh reason.

It will happen again, somewhere else. It is our job to make sure that, after 2,500 years of the evolution of Western civilisation, it does not happen in Australia.

If you are feeling like giving money for aid in Africa, undertaking adventure travel in deepest darkest Africa, listening to a politician talking of sharing the wealth or taxing the "rich", experiencing the shutdown of argument rather than open discussion or you are in the market for buying diamonds and other high unit value resources from Africa, then you have been warned.

Those in Australia claiming to be indigenous can thank their lucky stars that Australia was colonised by the British and not the Belgians, Portuguese, French, Spanish or Chinese.

(1980)

The only surviving picture of the plane's crash landing in
Bulong, Western Australia.

Skid marks in the desert

My time was up. Skid marks in the desert after three decades and six years. You don't run out of fuel in a jet at altitude and survive. Six of us did survive and I will never forget the noise of a wheels-up landing with the fuselage of the jet skidding along the red dirt and the thumps as the wings hit saplings. It was not an accident. It was a certainty waiting to happen.

On an earlier trip in the corporate jet from Melbourne to Kalgoorlie, we were descending into Kalgoorlie. I was sitting in the co-pilot seat in a single pilot jet, the pilot asked me where the headframes of the goldmines were and I suggested that maybe he should do a circuit. He replied that he only had seven minutes of fuel left and couldn't. This was not the first time. We had once landed at Kadina with only minutes of fuel and God knows how many other times he had landed with low fuel. The pilot was ex RAF, somewhat psychiatrically damaged and played Russian roulette for his thrills. But he did this with passengers. When he was with the plane on the ground and we were elsewhere, he would often do low-level fuel-consuming trips such that the fuel records did not show that he had been flying with no reserve fuel. He cooked the fuel books for years. He was also arrogant, incommunicative and aloof. Mistake No 1 was to have such a pilot employed, licensed and flying passengers.

On 5th December 1983, we had a dawn start from Essendon airport and were due to land at Adelaide to pick up a couple of others who had come down from Broken Hill. The previous day the pilot had been flying in Tasmania and had refuelled the plane and submitted his flight plan for the next day. The Melbourne Briefing Office told him that there were upper level high winds on the nose between Adelaide and Kalgoorlie and the pilot assumed that the headwind was 50 knots. Mistake No 2. Aviation Safety Investigation Report 198304358 for Cessna 501 Citation 2 VH-BNK shows that the forecast headwinds at 31,000 feet for Melbourne to Adelaide were 90 knots and for Adelaide to Kalgoorlie at 37,000 feet were 100 knots. Such strong headwinds are common when flying from eastern Australia to Western Australia, especially in winter or stormy weather. Big storm fronts were coming in from the west on that day. The pilot's flight plan gave the fuel endurance at 200 minutes ex Melbourne and, after refuelling, 300 minutes ex Adelaide.

A dawn takeoff allowed us to have a short sleep on the flight from Melbourne to Adelaide. The pilot had organised for TAA flight catering to deliver breakfast to the plane and he left a note for the aircraft refuellers to fill the tanks while he was at the Adelaide Briefing Office. Mistake No 3, the pilot should have been supervising refuelling. The pilot's updated weather forecasts required him to have an alternative landing place to Kalgoorlie. The pilot elected for Perth if Kalgoorlie was closed and was told that the fuel endurance to Perth was 302 minutes. If the predicted storms had closed Kalgoorlie we would have been 2 minutes short of Perth and would have crashed in the suburbs. Mistake No 4. The pilot then changed the flight plan and claimed that he had 320 minutes fuel endurance. Mistake No 5, the pilot told the Adelaide Briefing Office a lie yet they did not see that the 320-minute endurance was obviously concocted. Mistake No 6 was when the pilot decided to fly at 29,000 feet rather than at 37,000 feet because the headwinds were less although they were still at twice the velocity of the planned headwinds of 50 knots. Our series of visits and meetings as a due diligence committee would be delayed as we were running late and courtesy prevented us from informing our hosts in a pre-dawn phone call. I doubt if the pilot cared whether we were late or on time and he certainly had no pressure from his passengers to arrive on time.

When the pilot returned to the jet at Adelaide Airport, he found that it had not been refuelled as requested. The refuellers were edgy, they wanted to leave for their breakfast break. Mistake No 7. He claims that he assisted the refuellers and added the anti-icing agent to the fuel during refuelling. This may or may not have happened. What did happen is that the fuel tanks were not filled to capacity. Mistake No 8. After flying for an hour or so, the plane entered cloud, the pilot turned on the anti-icing and continued to fly at 29,000 feet. Operating with the engine anti-icing consumes about 8% more fuel. After about 30 minutes, the pilot climbed to 31,000 feet. We noticed that he was getting edgy and would complain if someone moved around as the trim had to be re-adjusted. I'd had breakfast and settled down to read.

At mid-point between Adelaide and Kalgoorlie, the pilot became concerned that he might not have enough fuel to get to Kalgoorlie let alone the alternate airport at Perth. He did not tell his passengers. If he had, we would have forced him to back track to Adelaide, Port Lincoln or somewhere else where he could get fuel. Mistake No 9. The pilot continued along his original planned track, the pilot had mentally planned to land at Caiguna if the alternate airport requirement was not lifted. The alternative landing requirement was lifted and, although the pilot was within striking distance for refuelling at Caiguna, he continued to fly to Kalgoorlie knowing that he had low fuel and was taking a huge risk. Mistake No 10.

Descent into Kalgoorlie started at 185 miles. I started to read an article in *The Australian* about an aeroplane near Longreach that crashed with no survivors after the pilot became ill and a passenger tried to stop the plane diving. The wings broke off when pulling out of a dive too quickly. At 25,000 feet we were again in heavy cloud and the engine anti-icing was switched on. During the descent, the low-level fuel warning light illuminated. By then there was no alternative airport, no more mistakes needed to be made as we were in a hopeless position, the right engine flamed out with a bang and very soon after the left engine flamed out with a bang. Flaming out by a jet engine is an unforgettable noise. I lifted my head, put down the article that I was reading about the plane crash near Longreach and saw that every light in the cockpit was red. I knew that we had run out of fuel, knew that jets can only glide at a high angle of attack, knew that we could not slow down the plane and knew that aeroplanes are very flimsy. The certainty awaiting to happen had happened.

It was very quiet with the plane gliding like a brick, no one talking and the pilot sending mayday calls to Kalgoorlie. The lady at Kalgoorlie air traffic control freaked out. This was her first mayday and it was a jet, not a slower propeller plane. The pilot didn't use the intercom to tell us that we were coming in and the passenger up the front turned around to tell us that we were going to attempt a forced landing on the Commonwealth Railway Line or mine tailing dams. These I could see were too far away at our rate of descent and it was obvious that we were going to crash in the bush. I knew that jets have a very high stall speed, that crashing in the bush was certain death and was really angry that a risk-taking pilot was going to kill me because of his risk taking. There were no prayers, no thoughts of a supernatural being. Just anger and thoughts of my wife and children. We battened down the luggage, clipped the seats back to the fuselage, stored anything that was loose or heavy and waited to die.

At about 1,000 feet, the passenger up the front pointed out a firebreak, residual hydraulics were used to turn the plane to approach the clearing. There were not enough hydraulics for flaps and there was no point in putting down the wheels. What was incredible was that our angle of glide for the firebreak was perfect for landing and that flaps, if they could have been used, were not necessary. Just before we hit the deck, we went into the brace position. When we hit the ground the noise was deafening, the TAA breakfast residuals scatted around the cabin, seats and luggage were projected forward as we rapidly decelerated and we could feel the wing spars and fuselage twisting backwards and forwards. After skidding for about 200 metres, I lifted my head and thought that I might not die but could end up with dreadful internal injuries as rapid or sudden deceleration can detach or rupture internal organs.

Towards the end of our 400-metre skid, we hit a tree on the port side and the wing was opened up. Although we had run out of fuel, there is always some vapour and residual fuel in the tanks for a fire. We later learned that only five litres of fuel was present in both the port and starboard wing tanks, there was a trace of fuel in the fuel filters and fuel lines and that there were no defects that could have led to fuel starvation, despite the pilot entering the plane after we'd come to rest and recalibrating the fuel gauge. Plane damage was substantial, only the main door would open and the fuselage was so twisted that the emergency door could not open. The pilot did not converse with us, one of the passengers congratulated him on a good landing (but did not comment that he had not filled the plane with fuel) and we were later to learn that he had written off four planes in his career, including three RAF planes and one for his current employer. He certainly had experience with crashing planes and should never have been employed.

Our firebreak emergency landing spot was at *Bulong*, ten kilometres northeast of Kalgoorlie. John Jones, from Jones Mining, owned the station. Every time he sees me now, he wants to charge me for parking a plane on his land and I reply by telling him that the charge for ploughing a 400 metre trench for him is just slightly more than the parking fee. We joke but we both are aware that I should not be alive. If there was no firebreak, we would have been dead with a bush landing as planes and trees are not a good mix. One of the contributing factors to our troubles was a huge summer storm that gave us strong headwinds. The same storm had dumped a large amount of rain on the firebreak and the wet ground meant that we were able to skid rather than come to an abrupt stop.

I knew where we were and walked through the bush to the Oroyo Mine with one of the passengers. When at the mine boundary fence, we were apprehended by mine security who just did not believe that we had crashed in the bush some five miles away. A bit of alpha male behaviour changed his mind and we cadged a lift into the Kalgoorlie Police Station. The police were gobsmacked that there were survivors, a spotter plane had seen the wreckage but had seen no people and police cars were on the way to the site. They elected me as nominated driver to collect passengers and luggage and warned me that if I was caught driving under the influence, then crashing in a jet and surviving was no excuse. We got a lift to the car rental company in a cop car.

At the car rental office, I was told that they had rung the airport to get our ETA and learned that the plane had crashed and all were killed. I pointed out that the first part was correct, the second obviously was not and that we had not cancelled our car rental contract. I was informed that our cars had been rented to others. I was still in alpha male mode and ended up with the car rental office manager's car. I went back to the cop shop to get road directions to the crash site and they told me that they would be bringing in passengers and luggage. I suspect that many police cars went to the site for a sticky beak away from the humdrum of dealing with drunken and drugged deadbeats. We got rid of luggage at the motel, rented another car, had a pub lunch and then went underground.

I could not contact my wife. I wanted to tell her that all was OK and to create some sort of diversion such that the children would not watch the evening news and see that our plane had crashed. She must have been out hunting and gathering. At that time, I played in the police squash team, I rang one of my copper mates, explained the situation and he went looking for my wife around various shopping centres. He found her and, after niceties, he said that he'd just been talking to me and then explained the situation. I am forever grateful for the good training and experience that he was able to put into practice. It was only when the children were in their twenties that I told them because I did not want them to worry every time I was flying somewhere for field work.

Word gets around quickly. While underground, many of the miners wanted to come up to us and touch us such that some of the luck would rub off. There was obvious empathy as there is a great sense of camaraderie underground between miners because of the constant danger and I guess they that felt that there are also dangers at altitude. That night we had a few drinks and the next day rented a plane to go to Meekatharra and Wiluna to continue our work and to get back in the saddle again. One of the passengers did not come and he has never been able to fly since that time.

The trip back to the east at the end of the week was with MMA and then Ansett across the continent as we now no longer had our own corporate jet. By then, I could not board flights unless I was three sails to the wind. I met a geological colleague from Sydney in the lounge at Perth, word gets around quickly, he knew that I was in shock, Ansett had diagonally-striped carpets which I could not possibly navigate in the tired and emotional state that I was in and he physically helped me on to the plane. He must have said something to the crew because I was treated like a king. Some weeks after returning, I was not surprisingly hit with delayed shock and needed help to get back to equilibrium. It actually wasn't shock, it was uncontrollable anger that I'd been placed in this position by my employer, a mining company. Mine work is very safe if there is a culture of safety, if everyone at all levels thinks safety, if people work together and if there is a lack of cavalier behaviour. Accidents are not accidents. They are normally certainties.

I still travel commercially, fly in corporate jets and fly in fixed wing propeller planes with pilots I know. Two of us on that fateful flight regularly fly with the Historical Aircraft Restoration Society (HARS) in their magnificent radial engine seventy year old C47B (the military version of a DC3) and Lockheed Super Constellation planes. Rather than a single pilot, the ground crews who rebuilt the planes are on board as well as numerous pilots with tens of thousands of hours flying with major airlines on a great diversity of machines. On the Connie, HARS normally has a crew of about ten and I often think when flying in it that one could not be in more experienced and safer hands.

The most unsafe aspect of commercial flying is the taxi to and from the airport, especially in Third World countries. However, flying in private planes is a different matter. Forget flying in a single pilot jet. Our pilot was able to make ten consecutive and unnecessary mistakes before the point of no return was reached. A co-pilot would have stopped this. The Adelaide Briefing Office should have been able to see that the flight was not possible in such weather conditions as it was well known about a big storm, headwinds and the dangers of icing up. The company that employed the pilot never should have had him on the books as the company pilot. Whether driving or flying, catastrophes generally do not occur as a result of one mistake in isolation, they occur by a combination of mistakes. I am happy to fly with a single pilot in propeller planes if the pilot owns the plane, conducts his own business using his investment, does not have kangaroos in the top paddock and has not been psychiatrically damaged as a military pilot.

I am one of the very few that have had more airport takeoffs than airport landings and my extra thirty-five years of life I treat as a bonus. Don't put your life in the hand of idiots.

(1984)

Street wise

In my book, Istanbul is one of the greatest cities in the world. Of course it is noisy, polluted, chaotic and elegant. This is its charm. So too are the bazaars, Topkapi, the Horn, the Blue Mosque, the Cistern, the city walls and dozens of other relics from the past. Some parts of Istanbul are downright dangerous, others are very safe. It is a practical city. If the roads are too congested, then it's quicker to drive along the footpath. On the trams, young people give up their seats for the grey-haired, elderly and women. It is a city full of spruikers. Tourists are offered carpets, turquoise, gold, leather ware and trinkets. Frequent travellers are offered contraband, drugs, weapons and women. Spruikers are all ages of the male of the species, affable and have the linguistic basics for selling in half a dozen languages. Spruiking and selling in the summer season is for profit and, in the other seasons, for survival. The more creative non-seasonal selling is accompanied by the smells of roasted corn and chestnuts and kebabs cooked on kerbside charcoal burners or fish from the stoves on the fishing boats at the Horn.

My somewhat battered Renault 12 was often parked outside the Hotel Pamphylia. Normally someone drifted past and requested a contribution to guarantee that the car would not be accidentally damaged. Only a few thousand lira (old lira). Nothing really, but it was important to keep the wheels of the black economy oiled. I was always happy to pay, not for the protection but to make sure that a family would eat that night.

On one occasion, I thought that it was unusual that my fees were not collected. I didn't worry too much, my car was old and battered, known in the district and was not a flash BMW or Mercedes. It even had the Istanbul prefix 34 on the number plate. Couldn't be safer. After wandering through the back streets eating corn and chestnuts and admiring Hereke carpets, I wandered back to the car. Back streets in any big city have a characteristic smell and threatening atmosphere however my bush clothes and a few days growth rendered me an unattractive target.

The car wouldn't open. I walked around and checked the number plates and looked inside. It certainly was my car. The passenger door also would not unlock. I rather stupidly checked that the keys that never left my person were really my keys. I tried the locks again. The key entered the lock but would not turn. I decided to leave the car and find a locksmith in tin-pan alley which was only a block or two away.

A young street urchin, maybe ten years old, came up to me, opened his hand and showed me two car lock barrels and two keys. He was poised to run through the alleys to the locksmith quarter in tin-pan alley. He told me in German that it would cost me DM10 to swap his locks for mine. I roared with laughter at the brazen ingenuity of his street-wise stand-over tactics. He was probably working in partnership with the person who guaranteed the safety of my car. Who knows?

I agreed to pay. Within a second, he took tools out of his pocket and started to take out his income-earning Renault locks and replace them with my Renault locks. Somewhere in the back streets, he probably had a large collection of locks for most makes of cars. His service was fast, fastidious and friendly. He was very careful not to scratch or chip the duco with his tools. He was proud of his workmanship, checked that my key fitted and turned and ascertained that the lock was not sloppy. He oiled the locks and even wiped his oily hand marks off the duco. I only had a green DM20 note. He pulled out a huge roll of bank notes in all the major currencies and was looking for a DM10 note to give me as change. I told him to keep the change as I had DM20 of pleasure from this street-wise urchin.

This young kid was a survivor. He will probably end up jointly owning a carpet shop with his cousin in the bazaar where he will spend his life conning foreigners. Maybe he was the chap some 25 years later who tickled my bank account for $6,500 after I used a credit card in the Grand Bazaar of Istanbul.

(1987)

The view in Paros, Greece, 1987.

Crystal healing

Crystals and gems have been used since antiquity, not only for personal adornment but were considered a safeguard against evil spirits, sickness and injury. Like many ancient myths, the alleged healing power of crystals is enjoying a revival.

The ancient Greeks believed that quartz crystals (*Kristallos*) were a type of ice and believed that amethyst (purple quartz) prevented drunkenness. The Roman author, Pliny, wrote that by wearing amethyst jewellery not only was one was protected from the intoxicating effects of drinking wine but one was also protected from lunacy. Therefore, by wearing amethyst, the pleasures of life such as drunkenness and lunacy were prevented. As a scientist, I have put this to the test many times and excessively yet I can't remember whether it worked or not.

Numerous books have recently appeared extolling the healing powers of crystals. Snake oil merchants are now experts with crystals and many famous mineral collecting localities which represent part of our national heritage have been destroyed by rapacious crystal collectors. I wrote the books *The Mineral Collecting Localities of the Broken Hill District* (1977, Peacock Press) and *Mineral collecting localities of the Broken Hill, Tibooburra and White Cliffs areas* (1997, Peacock Press) to direct mineral and crystal collectors, students and mineral clubs to the third best collecting localities and I have kept the best collecting localities for museums and scientists. In former times, one could take a museum collector along winding tracks into a collecting location and then out on other tracks or cross-country such that they could never find their way back. It is now not possible as almost everyone has a GPS.

Minerals are naturally occurring substances with a chemical composition defined within certain boundaries and a mathematically defined unique arrangement of atoms. This arrangement of atoms is the basis of the crystal structure. The properties of crystals can be explained in terms of the chemical composition (e.g. colour, magnetism, radioactivity, specific gravity etc) and the arrangement of the atoms in the crystal (e.g. lustre, hardness, specific gravity etc). Before a substance can be called a mineral, all the properties must be documented and validated by the International Mineralogical Association.

Nutritionists incorrectly refer to some chemical elements in food as "minerals". Many "minerals" are not minerals (e.g. opal) and some elements have a number of minerals depending upon the packing of the atoms (e.g. hexagonal carbon = graphite; cubic carbon = diamond). Not one naturally occurring crystal displays properties previously unknown to man, all properties can be measured and quantified and all unusual properties can be explained in terms of physics and chemistry. If an electric current passes along the long axis of quartz, the mineral vibrates at a set frequency. This property of piezoelectricity is used in quartz watches. If the long axis termination of a quartz crystal is tapped, it gives out electricity. These properties are simply the conversion of one form of energy (electrical) to another form (mechanical). Energy is not created or emitted outside the crystal, there is no energy field around a quartz crystal and there are no unknown properties of quartz crystals. Sorry to disappoint those readers who are lacking in basic science or a tad unbalanced. You may get over it but not by using crystals.

Minerals are naturally occurring chemicals and every year a few dozen new mineral species previously unknown to science are named after people (e.g. goethite after Goethe), places (e.g. brokenhillite), chemistry (e.g. cuprite), properties (e.g. magnetite) or morphology (e.g. hemimorphite). Discoverers of minerals cannot name a new species after themselves. Most minerals end in the suffix ...*ite* although some old names without the suffix are still used (e.g. quartz, feldspar, mica, olivine, galena). There are now some 10,000 mineral species known from planet Earth and our Solar System. I have the honour of having a new Broken

Hill (NSW) mineral, plimerite ($Fe_4Zn[PO_4]_3[OH]_5$, orthorhombic) named in recognition of my Broken Hill geological research. Further research on minerals may result is the discrediting of a mineral species. Although I may be discredited in circles of those I have annoyed over decades, plimerite has now been found in two places in Australia, one in the Czech Republic and one in Spain and, rather than being discredited, it has been validated. Minerals are normally named after people who are dead hence a whole new debate emerges about plimerite.

Despite reams of textbooks on crystallography and mineralogy over the last 200 years, the myth of mystical powers of crystals is promoted by purveyors of fraud and blindly accepted by those searching the cosmos for delusion. There are daunting lists of natural crystals (i.e. minerals) promoted by "New Age" authors. They claim crystals can be used to cure illnesses. For example, the most abundant mineral on the surface of the Earth (quartz) allegedly can be used to cure kennel cough in dogs. Those in suburbia are sadly kept awake night after night with dogs coughing and my heart goes out to you. As quartz is ubiquitous, one wonders why kennel cough exists at all. No advice is given on how to administer quartz to dogs suffering from this dreadful rampant ailment. In the case of kennel cough, the answer is obvious. Quartz crystals are tapered trigonal crystals and so, as soon as the dog coughs, the crystal should be rammed down the dog's throat. This will stop the dog ever coughing again.

Dioptase, an unusual copper silicate from Tsumeb (Namibia) and the Urals, is recommended for the treatment of animal illnesses and heart burn, weak heart, mental burdens and sleeping sickness in humans. I have had a number of dioptase specimens for decades during which time I have been to the sleeping sickness areas of Africa a number of times. I have never suffered from sleeping sickness. Clearly the dioptase is doing its job.

The rare uvarovite garnet (calcium chromium silicate) is recommended for the treatment of flatulence. This mineral is a relatively recent discovery, it was first described from the Urals and hence flatulence must have been in epidemic proportions before its discovery. I have four beautiful emerald green uvarovite crystals in my mineral collection. The first was given to me in the 1950s. It came from the collection of my great grandfather (H. P. White, FRS; NSW Department of Mines chief government assayer) and he published a scientific report on this specimen from Lucknow (NSW), as I have. The other three I collected in Outokumpu (Finland) in 1977. If uvarovite cures flatulence, then I can categorically state that there must be some mistake.

Crystals in the mimetite-pyromorphite mineral group are recommended for the treatment of marital problems. In this case, the treatment can be lovingly administered by dissolution of some of the hexagonal barrel-shaped crystals in the partner's food or drink. As these minerals are lead arsenic compounds, successful treatment of marital problems is guaranteed.

Tourmaline is a very chemically complex mineral that is recommended for the treatment of unhealthy hair, indigestion, ear trouble, bladder problems, brain problems, epilepsy, laryngitis, melancholy, ulcers, obesity, tonsillitis, weak muscles, loss of smell, weak vocal chords, multiple sclerosis and forgetfulness. Tourmaline can be coloured pink (due to lithium), green (due to magnesium, iron or chromium), blue or black (due to iron) and red (due to manganese). The tourmaline family has the general chemistry of:

$$(Na, Ca)(Fe^{2+}, Mg, Al, Fe^{3+}, Mn, Li)_3(Al, Fe^{3+}, Cr, Ti, Mg, V)$$
$$(BO_3)_3Si_6O_{18}(OH, F, Cl)_4$$

With such a chemistry, no wonder it can be used to cure so many ailments. I doubt if anyone can remember this general chemical formula above for tourmaline hence its ability to cure forgetfulness must be questioned. I have had tourmaline in my collection for the last 30 years of my father's life. He had multiple sclerosis and was surrounded by tourmaline yet it did not seem to do him any good.

The gem ruby (hexagonal aluminium oxide with a trace of chromium) is recommended by "New Age" authors for the treatment of anaemia, low blood pressure, poor blood circulation, constipation, envy, bleeding, wounds, weak physical and mental willpower and the plague. If one has blood problems, bleeding or the plague, it might be better to go to hospital rather than rummaging around in the attic for some ruby in the family jewellery. It is also recommended for increasing strength, for encouraging faithfulness and for cauterising in surgery. While references to blood-related conditions are obviously linked to ruby's colour, anaemia is related to iron in blood hence "New Age" crystal healers don't know that ruby is not an iron mineral. One "New Age" author also recommends ruby for enhancing ESP, thus fulfilling the "New Age" criterion of using one unsubstantiated myth to substantiate another. Believe in one and you must believe in the other, regardless of any proof for either.

A number of the fundamental properties of minerals have been ignored by the "New Age". For example, the most abundant element on Earth is oxygen, followed by silicon. These elements covalently bond very strongly as silicate tetrahedra to form the basic building blocks of the rock forming minerals. These silicate tetrahedra are pyramids and lovingly join in chains thereby giving rock forming minerals inner pyramid power, a strong power of sharing due to covalent bonding, inner strength due to covalent bonding, transparency due to covalent bonding and electrical balance because of the ionic bonding. Why did I have to think of this? Why didn't some "New Age" think of this or do they lack basic chemistry, mineralogy and crystallography?

"New Age" writings acknowledge that many crystals with alleged curative properties are very rare hence treatment cannot be administered by touching, stroking, ingesting or humming to the crystal. Never fear, the "New Age" authors tell us that possession of the crystal is not necessary. One has to only mentally concentrate on this mineral for treatment. If that is the case, why do "New Age" crystal power proponents sell crystals? Why let crystal collecting localities get destroyed by pillagers? Why not just mentally concentrate on the mineral for treatment? For marital problems, do I mentally concentrate on green, brown or canary yellow pyromorphite?

Crystals of minerals are beautiful, they should be treasured and can be used for adornment. Unfortunately, our "New Age" promoters have published that venomous bites can be treated with sulphur or emerald, malaria can be treated with turquoise, venereal disease with zircon, cancer with amethyst and multiple sclerosis with tourmaline. This is criminally irresponsible because the deluded might attempt to administer crystals in life threatening situations when time and a hospital visit are imperative. For example, the contraction and treatment of malaria is extremely well documented and yet to publish that turquoise might in any way help malaria can result in the loss of life. There was a case of crystals being used to assist a difficult birth which went horribly wrong and hence the medical use of crystals is not just a trivial aberration of deluded people.

I have had a scientific interest in crystals for half a century. I have had a very large collection of crystals of minerals for decades yet, like curators of minerals in museums, at times I manage to get sick. This should not happen. I first started collecting crystals in about 1956 and started scientifically studying crystals at Broken Hill in 1968. Since then I have been degenerating. This is proof that crystals have no powers and has nothing to do with the fact that when I first came to Broken Hill there were 32 hotels and 16 licensed clubs. Crystal power proponents lack much basic scientific knowledge of crystals and their conclusions lack any sense of rationality and logic. Their preference for ignorant faith (and wishful thinking) instead of reasoned argument is potentially dangerous to the health of crystal healing's adherents.

(1987)

Resources for 10 billion humans

Many of us like a drink. Or two. Or far too much. Especially at the end of the day. We all know that refrigerators and wine cellars are just not big enough. Most of us have had the misfortune at some time in our lives to run out. What do we do? We either go hunting and gathering at the local bottle shop or pub for more, we can drink less or we can look for some other stimulant. If one is a beer drinker and desperate to keep the levels at high tide and the local has run out of your favourite fluid, then one substitutes this for another brand of beer. If one comes across Slim Dusty's *Pub with no beer*, then one drinks wine, spirits or any rat poison that may be behind the bar. One might even get a taste for a particular brand of rat poison and never go back to beer.

And so too with commodities. If the world resources of zinc start to decline, then there are some pretty simple decisions to make. One can undertake exploration for new resources which is a bit like going down to the bottle shop when the fridge is empty. This takes time and there is a long lead time of about 20 years between the decision to undertake exploration and the production of new zinc concentrate from a successful zinc exploration program. We could, of course, get impatient and invade a country that has large zinc resources either with an army or a cheque book. Because the world's zinc resources and stockpiles decrease, the price will rise and so instead of mining rocks that contain 10% zinc, it may be economical to mine rocks that now have 4% zinc. This is a bit like drinking less if the fridge stock starts to look dangerously low.

If exploration is unsuccessful, then one can use less zinc and perhaps make the layer of zinc galvanising on steel a bit thinner. This has actually happened with many metals used for coatings. For example, most sophisticated electronic equipment now uses layers of gold only one or two atoms thick because gold is the fastest conductor of electricity. This again is a bit like drinking less if the tide gets dangerously low. Because zinc is a sacrificial metal in galvanising, it is hard to recycle but there may be a point where recycling remnant zinc in galvanised steel, tyres and chemicals becomes economically attractive. I don't recommend recycling of alcoholic drinks.

If no new zinc deposits are found, if recycling is uneconomical and there is no future zinc source on the horizon, then eventually the price of the scarce zinc metal will be so high that it may be economically worthwhile to use other elements such as aluminium instead of zinc for coating steel. They might not do the job as well but they are cheaper. Once such businesses are firmly established, it may not be worthwhile to go back to using zinc in galvanising if the price falls due to a big new discovery. This is rather like drinking the rat poison at the *Pub with no beer*, developing a taste and never going back to beer.

We may even think a bit laterally and instead of looking at the traditional zinc sulphide deposits whereby we mine, crush, grind and float the zinc sulphide, we may create new metallurgical techniques using acids, alkalis and ammonia to extract zinc from the many known zinc carbonate, zinc oxide and zinc silicate deposits. We may even get smarter, create new bacteria and persuade it to eat normal rocks that contain small amounts of zinc in silicates and oxides and then harvest the zinc in solution from the bacterial biogeochemical reactions. The bottom line is that we will not run out of zinc. It's just a matter of price and cost and not the geochemical abundance of the metal.

The world's commodity markets work on grade, that is the amount of metal in a rock. Grade is king. There are few copper deposits around the world that have 3% copper in the rock. These are high-grade deposits. The are quite a few more that have 1% copper, numerous deposits that have 0.8% copper and hundreds of unmined copper deposits that have 0.5% copper, generally regarded as low-grade deposits. If there is a shortage of copper, then more and more lower grade deposits are mined, more recycling takes place and costs are reduced in order to accommodate the lower grades.

Considering that about 0.5 tonnes of water are required for the treating of 1 tonne of copper ore, talk of mining in space is an illogical dream because of the lack of water on other planets and asteroids. Furthermore, normally the biggest cost in mining is the crushing and grinding of ores. These processes require huge amounts of energy and such energy sources for mining in space are well into the future and should be kept to the confines of dreaming. Every metal we need on Earth is on spaceship Earth and, over time, the uses, cost structures, recycling and substitution constantly change.

There is no monopoly on mineral deposits. Monopolies and cartels have been attempted in the past (e.g. tin, diamonds) and have failed spectacularly because there is a constant search for substitution, incessant exploration and fierce international competition. As soon as one is a big producer of metals, there is always someone somewhere else trying to push you out of the low cost quartile and trying to take your established markets. It is dog-eat-dog and not the fairies at the bottom of the garden mentality of the environmentalists and doomsdayers.

Not every country has all the commodities in the ground needed to run an economy hence there is international trade of ores, concentrate and metals. For strategic reasons, some major international economies have a strategic stockpile of metals in case of war, cutting of supply lines or international scarcity. For example, the USA does not produce platinoids, diamond, nickel, chromium, vanadium and cobalt and these metals are vital for cracking crude oil, creating plastics, steel making and the electronics industry in an industrialised society and Uncle Sam has a strategic stockpile of these metals. If a major chromium deposit was found in the USA, then Uncle Sam would sell the stockpile as has happened many times in the past.

We are constantly finding new uses for minerals. In my own lifetime, many minerals that were useless rock-forming minerals or mineralogical curios, are now in high demand for the latest technology. We humans use more than 60 elements in the periodic table of 92 natural elements, use synthetic elements (e.g. americium) and synthetic isotopes created in nuclear reactors (e.g. iodine 131, technetium 99) and synthetic minerals (e.g. silica, ceramics) in everyday life. And the list is getting bigger.

A mineral such as crocidolite (blue asbestos) which we now know is carcinogenic has now been replaced by other durable insulating materials such as natural non-carcinogenic minerals or synthetics. Elements that were once chemical curiosities such as the rare earth elements are now substituting the cobalt-nickel-iron magnets in electronics with neodymium-samarium micro magnets that are far stronger and allow miniaturisation of electronics.

To claim that we are going to run out of mineral resources is a public admission of ignorance and a closed mind and an affront to human ingenuity. In many countries, we have run out of common sense but not mineral resources. The same people claim that we will run out of fossil fuels. For thousands of years we have needed energy. We have evolved from using materials such wood, dung and leaves to other sources that emit greater amounts of energy per unit weight such as coal. The discovery of petroleum saved the whales because whale oil and tallow was used for lighting and heating.

We have been threatened with peak oil for 50 years and it did not happen. What happened was a triumph of human ingenuity whereby we can now extract more oil and gas from rocks by artificially creating a greater permeability. We are now aware that there are many rocks that contain gargantuan quantities of gas (e.g. coal) and the gas can be easily extracted.

For almost 100 years, we have known that by breaking large atoms apart (i.e. nuclear fission) or combining small atoms into larger atoms as the Sun does (i.e. nuclear fusion), we create new elements and release energy. This energy we tap in nuclear fission reactors and, until we can master nuclear fusion, we use inefficient unreliable transitional low-density energy such as wind, solar, tidal and biofuels.

Did you know that every year, each person consumes about three quarters of a tonne of food? Soil erosion from this food production is at the rate of five tonnes per person per year, mainly in the Third World. In some parts of the world the amount of arable land is decreasing due to land degradation whereas in other parts, mainly wealthy Western countries, the amount of arable land being used is decreasing because of the expansion of forests, better fertilisers, better herbicides and insecticides, increased atmospheric carbon dioxide and genetically modified crops.

Every year, some fifty billion tonnes of mineral resources are consumed by humans. As an Australian, you consume about 40 tonnes of mineral resources each year. This is a semi-trailer load of coal, petroleum, metal, sand aggregate and cement each year. Virtually none of these commodities are recycled. We cannot go to other planets to mine mineral and energy resources as we have all we need on Earth and the costs of extraction and transport are infinite. Furthermore, our planet has had water for most of its history and almost all mineral deposits form in an aqueous environment whereas there has only been the slight influence of water on one other planet in the Solar System. We are a spaceship, everything we need for the rest of time must come from planet Earth.

In addition, each Australian consumes 180 tonnes per annum of water. Unlike other countries with a far higher rainfall, our water is neither recycled nor reused. By the time water from Lake Constance flows down the Rhine River and gets to the Netherlands, it has been through the human body ten times. In Australia, we generally use water once and let huge volumes of storm water disappear without trace. Water is the most precious commodity on planet Earth and will probably be the cause of much future human conflict.

We demand a certain standard and style of living and resulting in resource consumption. Too often the environmental movement is quick to blame the resources industry and abrogate all responsibility yet they use the latest technology and energy to transmit their dogma. The consumers, people like you and me, are using 50 billion tonnes a year of resources and, as a result, there are secondary environmental disasters mainly in Third World countries because of lack of regulations and lack of wealth.

If one wants to live in the modern world with minimal pollution, then this can only be done when one is wealthy. It cannot and does not happen in poor countries. For some strange reason, wealth appears to be the answer to poverty and with wealth comes a non-polluted environment, health, education and longevity.

I do not worry about the resources we need for 10 billion people on planet Earth. My worry is that if we lose freedoms, we cannot have the creative environment to solve problems, especially if creativity is proscribed and under the thumb of political correctness.

(1988)

Why Australia lost the three-day war with Upper Volta

Contemporary documents from 1988 show that Australia was already aware that there was a crisis in science and education. A total of 167 committees were established during the following decade to establish the short-term electoral implications of this crisis.

The expenditure on research and development in 1988 in Australia as a proportion of gross domestic product was less than half that of other industrial nations at the time (e.g. UK, USA, Japan, France, West Germany) and this expenditure was declining whereas in other countries it was increasing. Very little industry funding was directed towards research and development because it was far easier to borrow funds in Australia for the purchase of foreign technology. Furthermore, a fragmentation of science between the then Department of Employment, Education and Training, Department of Administrative Services, Department of Arts, Sport, Tourism and Environment, Department of Primary Industry, Department of industry, Trade and Commerce and Department of Defence, guaranteed high employment for administrators, competition for administrative funds, repetition of research and equipment and heinous inefficiencies. Ministerial decrees whereby small efficient harmonious research units were forcibly amalgamated into larger monolithic institutions were made despite contemporary information to the contrary. Dawkins Law showed that productivity is inversely related to the distance from the critical mass of the research unit. However, this Law never applied to science administration.

It was decreed that scientists were spending far too much time on creative research and could not be accurately monitored by those who dictated social consciousness. Funding was provided in pre-election times for science however this funding was consumed by appointing administering administrators and with surveys requesting existing information from other data banks. New legislation tied scientists' salaries to productivity which was defined as the number of unpublished internal memos written to Government departments multiplied by the number of committee meetings attended.

Although governments were elected to look after the long-term defence, education, health, environment and social climate of Australia, the user pays principle of the last two decades of the 20th Century enabled the government to abrogate all responsibility for the tax paying community and, coupled with a lack of accountability of senior public servants, resulted in a politicised education system. The education administrators and policy advisers vigilantly maintained their policy of inexperience, expansion, distance and blissful ignorance of reality while using their computer statistics as the font of all knowledge. Uniform course structures devised by policy advisors promulgated replacement of unpalatable segments of history courses with leisure awareness courses.

The science crisis was exacerbated by the lack of returns for excellence. Government data of 1988 showed that, compared with the average weekly wage, the financial returns for scientists and engineers declined in real terms from 1958 to 1988 and, in the year 2015, all scientists and engineers at all levels earned the average weekly wage. Similar data existed in 1988 for science school teachers. These data were ignored as Government opinion was Truth, unrelated to fact and the government edict became the norm (i.e. scientific excellence equals the multiple of political expediency, unsubstantiated opinion and the distance from active scientists).

There was a time in Australian history when real men did science or engineering, and wimps did law, arts, economics and commerce. By 1988, the NSW Higher School Certificate aggregate marks for entry into courses at The University of Sydney and The University of New South Wales showed a different story. Aggregate marks over the preceding decade for entry into science, applied science and engineering, steadily declined whereas those for law, arts, economics, commerce, communications and sociology increased. A quaint method of double taxation called the Graduate Tax was introduced as a Bicentennial present to the Australian underprivileged and high performers. This was a legislative egalitarian sleight of hand and the postgraduate research population disappeared in just three years. Falling enrolments in science and engineering were accelerated and public comment on declining standards was censured.

University entrants were cognisant of the lack of returns for scientists and engineers, but other factors were probably also influential. At that time, science was considered rigorous which was against the popular ethic which stated that anything worthwhile was fun, easy and had no tomorrow. The words sacrifice, hard work, respect and rigour were expunged from the language and self-gratification was regarded as morally superior to anything the past taught us. This proudly uneducated society demanded to have the right to borrow for the purchase of the latest technology which was feared. There was also unanimous support (through video key-in surveys) for the Freedom from Knowledge Movement which espoused that it was an Australian birthright not to understand the basics, implications, costs and responsibilities of technology. The environmental movement grew into a city-based fundamentalist foundation representing the service economy, the unemployed and welfare recipients and political activists. The "Industry Employment is Evil Policy" (which commenced in 1972) and gained a firm foothold in the 1990s and successfully contracted Australia's industrial base. In the early 1990s, the Foundation electronically simulated and pre-recorded all environmental field studies from their studios and, in order to promote their message for maximum electoral impact, deemed that no interdependent or multidisciplinary science should colour their facts.

The Australia society of the 1990s was tightly structured. The intellectual elite comprised the service economy who used their creativity to avoid taxation. The service economy paid no tax hence these caste members were not required to carry identity cards. A number of poorly paid intellectually-limited technicians provided the new and the real wealth to the economy and a few creative vestigial ageing scientists were kept warm by the valves in their electronic equipment. Scientific research had to provide immediate financial returns greater than bank interest rates. Society and experimental politically correct social engineering was directed by a lethargic caste whose members could only be third generation Canberra permanent residents. The caste satisfied their greed by holding the exchequer keys.

Scientific research progressed for far longer than expected under this policy of exploitation of the excellent, productive, curious and keen. The inquisitiveness, motivation and dedication of poorly paid research scientists was undertaken in a hostile environment using antiquated equipment. Use of the words rigour, standards and excellence encouraged instant social banishment. This was used as proof that science had such a low electoral image that, on moral grounds, it could not be financially supported.

At the beginning of the millennium, Australia's economic malaise became a tragedy. The country was then totally dependent upon export earnings from primary industry, had no secondary industry and had 117 service economy employees for every primary industry employee. The economy had halved, Asia, Europe and the Middle East purchased raw materials from more reliable suppliers such as Bolivia, Burma and Liberia. The Australian commune was bewildered when pitiful agricultural production (resulting from prolonged land degradation) and exhaustion of mineral resources (resulting from the cancellation of mineral exploration) created deep economic depression that could not be solved by multiple Sky-channelled social awareness committee meetings.

Australia was a signatory to the Tepid Mother Earth Treaty requiring closure of all thermal power stations by 2010. This contribution to decelerate the global climatic change was followed by similar action by Iceland and Yemen. For decades, the Australian commune knew that electricity generation by nuclear fission or fusion was morally indefensible. Australia therefore, did not build nuclear power stations and even the tiny research reactor at Lucas Heights (NSW) was not replaced after its 50-year life. Despite population increases and an increase in per capita energy consumption, hydroelectric power generation in Tasmania and the Snowy Mountains remained static for over 40 years because no new dams were built. A pre-petroleum exploration tax and changing Middle East trade facilitated exhaustion of Australian petroleum resources in 1999 and all diesel power plants became idle later that year. Petroleum products could then only be used for official travel between government committee meetings. Solar power was available for the 143 residents of White Cliffs (NSW). Because of the lack of basic background scientific information and technological lead times, the energy crisis of 2010 resulted in the closure of more than 95% of Australia's industry, cessation of primary industry exports, cancellation of international borrowing rights, mass social disruption and a successful fourteenth military coup d'état.

The military entertained themselves for years by playing with the knobs and looking at the flashing lights on their transistorised equipment purchased in better times from High Voltage (formerly Upper Volta but transformed and renamed after a massive research effort which created dynamic secondary industry based on electronics). Because of a lack of basic science, the military were unable to understand how their equipment operated, were unable to repair equipment failures, were unable to manufacture equipment and yet were dependent upon technology. The only option was eventually taken. Invade High Voltage to acquire the scientific and technological background to feed and clothe the children of Australian military personnel.

The adjacent Olifant Republic was invaded by mistake because of a failure of antiquated equipment.

(1989)

Peter Black, (Blackie), Mayor of Broken Hill from 1980 until 1999.
photo taken in Broken Hill, 1988.

A bender with Blackie

He was going to give it up on Monday, The demands of being both Mayor and school science master were too much to keep it up and it had started to get a hold of him in recent years. He wanted to show that he could shake it off unaided but he wanted to go out in style. This was his swan song. However, Australian swans are black. The attraction of escaping for a weekend from home pressures, children and telephones was inviting as was the prospect of visiting new terrain with an old friend. Old friends don't judge and they are not worth votes.

A loose arrangement was made a month or so earlier when attempting to out-talk each other while fishing. He claimed that he knew how to fish and was a better fisherman than me but he was on my patch. I didn't tell him that in the lake the baited hook needs to be 6 inches off the bottom. In the surf, he cast into the first gutter and I had surfers carry my tackle into the deeper second gutter. I caught fish. He caught nothing.

The loose arrangement was confirmed on Wednesday. When I got to the Hill, some 130 litres of diesel was taken on 15 minutes before the appointed time. He surprisingly appeared from Council on the dot of 5 pm, the arranged Friday meeting time. Normally he is up to 3 hours late and his punctuality expressed the seriousness of the situation. The tension could have been cut with a knife and his escape from the matrimonial home in less than 5 minutes was inordinately long.

I gave him the keys as I had already driven 1,300 kilometres that day. I was relaxed, he had his own Landcruiser and was an experienced bush driver. Impecuniosity forced him to call in at the Masonic Club, cash a cheque and wash it down with a few. Once cashed up, the next stop was the Mulga Hill and eight dozen were taken on board to keep us going for the outward trip. He laid down the ground rules. No drinking until out of town. I attempted to remind him that I was to meet John and his son Richard at Tibooburra that night, some 350 kilometres north. Acquired aural deficiency was now on automatic pilot. I already could see that we might not make it that night, although Blackie swore that we'd arrive at 2 am. He didn't tell me where we'd arrive.

In three minutes, we were out of the Hill. The ice-free esky had consumed two dozen, the remainder were warming up on the seat between us for emergency easy access. The first can hardly lasted 5 kilometres and we bemoaned the fact that the Stephens Creek Pub was now closed. Some 30 kilometres up the track at Yancowinna Creek at the *Corona* turnoff is Yanco Glen. It was firebombed a few years ago by a disgruntled thirsty patron but trade still continued in a back shed, the only building in what was a town. It took us three cans to get to this esteemed establishment. The previous two publicans had been shot by disgruntled patrons. There was a time when only travellers could get a drink on Sundays hence there were pubs on all the roads out of the Hill at a distance whereby one was legally a traveller. Yanco Glen was one such place.

Blackie reckoned he needed to see the good folk of Yanco Glen because some of them might actually vote for him. He was driving and I could see the onset of disaster. Another can had to be consumed quickly as it is bad form to walk into a pub holding a can. After the second stubbie at Yanco Glen, I managed to extricate him as he could see that they blindly voted for him drunk or sober and he vowed not to have another before Salt Hole Creek. Kennedy's Tank is 3 kilometres from Yanco Glen and Salt Hole Creek is a further 2 kilometres. The dry Salt Hole Creek runs every five or ten years or so and it is a landmark because it is the only bridge on 350 kilometres of road. A pause enabled him to wax lyrical about the beauty of the red dirt country and open spaces. This was followed by an impressive demonstration of exploding clay when hit by warm body fluids. The seal was broken. He was gone.

Abusive endearment and the opening of another gave him the strength to drive further. I suggested that the windows be closed tight and the fan blasting to raise the internal pressure, a simple matter of physics, when we passed the occasional vehicle. Automatic pilot was locked and such bush practice was totally ignored in preference to wallowing in billowing clouds of hot dry red bull dust which, of course, had to be washed down.

The next call was the deserted *Bijerkerno* homestead, a distance of eight cans. Arthur still owned the shearing shed and his son Morris had amalgamated *Poolamacca*, a former Kidman property, with the adjacent *Bijerkerno*. Both were poor runs set in hilly country. Both of us have a long association with *Bijerkerno*, the original mine office last century of the Mt Euriowie Tin Mining Company. Since Morris had removed the walls and the roof of the homestead and the roof, walls, cladding, struts, noggins, floorboards and bearers of the outhouse, the place was looking a little on the bleak side save for a lone bougainvillea and two chimneys over old shafts.

Blackie lamented the passing of Lindsay, the last of a breed of old time prospectors. The old boy had spent his last decades in a collection of humpies at the old Trident Mine on Caloola Creek with generations of dead vehicles, compressors and a collection of aeroplane propeller blades. Dear old Lindsay, he was besotted by the potential mineral treasures of his pegmatite mine. He had rare tin, lithium, caesium and beryllium minerals, he had a very keen eye for minerals which no one would buy at that time. Blackie was one of two folk at Lindsay's funeral in town, 80 kilometres away. The other was a long-lost nephew who appeared out of nowhere to claim the mining leases as there was increasing interest in high tech metals. The Trident had been renamed the Christine Judith Mine by Lindsay after his two daughters. I wonder if they ever knew?

Our memories were fluidised by a few more and our senses were re-awakened when we realised that we hadn't shut the gate. We'd only come on a short reminiscing visit and there was not a sheep in sight over the 400 square kilometre view. We drove across the gibber down the slope, shut the gate and left *Bijerkerno* to continue north.

Abusive tirades about the depths of my ignorance, dust prevention, the 19th Century *Corona* stage coach track and the density of saltbush on the plains of *Sturts Meadows* were interspersed with the percussion of ring pulls. Despite *Sturts Meadows'* Peter Bevan being at the opposite end of his political spectrum, Blackie reckoned that he was a pretty good sort of cove. Blackie was relaxing. He was not on public show, he had someone to abuse and someone who understood. Upon approaching *Fowlers Gap*, there were some discussions as to whether we should call in. However, we both couldn't for the life of us work out why we should go in now that John Reynolds had left. We had a few to clear our thoughts and stopped at the Gap to admire the setting sun over the infinite vista. Blackie attempted to persuade me why the broad sweeping nothingness was morally and ethically superior to the waterfront where I lived at that time. Although I felt he was right, I was duty bound to take the contrary position. The pointless argument continued on this wonderful 38°C summer evening with a clear sky and a gentle breeze which forced the flies to abort their landings.

Our traverse through *Fowlers Gap* property was accompanied by slurred ramblings of a hazy history of the various bores, tanks and double-posted gates. There was an anthropological story on the various middens which, throughout the diatribe, appeared to change positions. Miscellaneous disjointed information continued to flow about a rare species of bat in the creek and a red river gum somewhere out there that Sturt had blazed in 1844.

The road across the Fowlers Gap flats crosses a huge featureless clay pan which provided a clear demonstration of his superior natural bush skills. At this stage he was at least twice the legal limit, clasping refreshment in his right hand, extolling the virtues of Tally Ho while rolling one in his left hand and steering the Tojo at 110 km/hr with his knees and yet remaining perfectly straight in the wheel tracks of the corrugated dirt road across the flats. And this was in the fading light of sunset! These skills are all but dead in the bush and it warmed the cockles of my heart to see Blackie perform quite naturally and with excellence. This was one of the most incredible feats of an evolved hominid that I have ever had the pleasure of witnessing. Blackie is a man of principle, one of which is that real bushmen drive without a seat belt. Such principles are common in the real outback. Many from Sydney go to wineries at Mudgee and Orange and think that they are in the bush because they are out of their comfort zone. I can assure those Sydneysiders that, on a quiet night, one can hear the surf in Mudgee which is more than 1,000 kilometres from the real outback.

Two score and five years of hitting it hard takes its toll and the watering stops for him were now more frequent. Once the seal's broken, it's the end. Disaster struck after *Fowlers Gap*. The esky was empty. It was refilled and those less than body temperature were selected like diamonds for instant consumption. We had a few while we watched the evening pastel greens and pinks in the eastern sky lose focus and disappear. Further up the track in the sand dune country, bladder pressures and thirst quenching enabled us to cement a number of views about the wonderful Southern Hemisphere night sky in a warm atmosphere gently scented with the subtle aroma of salt bush, blue bush, everlastings and lemon grass.

A mobile purposeless debate ensued regarding whether it was 20 or 40 kilometres to *Packsaddle*. The senses of each party were questioned and creative abusive explanations for the apparent sensory damage were generously offered. Blackie had relaxed to the point where he was now actually enjoying himself. The heights of this slurred conversation were interrupted when *Packsaddle* suddenly appeared from beneath its protective sand dune. Wisdom prevailed and the driver felt that we should eat as well as have a few at this lonely fuel pump with a tree, tin shed with a veranda and a bar. The veranda is 200 kilometres from the nearest town and has a view across God's own scrubby red sand dunes and a clay pan.

The company at *Packsaddle* can be desperate and the food worse. Copious lubrication facilitated the descent of a tepid sterile glutinous pie that was a prime candidate for condemnation by health authorities. We continued north at a slower pace, not because it was dark and kangaroos abounded, but because he now claimed that there was a likelihood of spilling some of the precious amber fluid barely warmed by the extinct Esky. The next vague hour was somewhat uncertain which clearly must have been due to the change from Central Standard Time to Eastern Standard Time. He now had some difficulty in locating the track which he claimed kept moving and the consumption of warm fermented fluid (a pagan English habit) was becoming increasingly difficult.

The turnoff track to *Mt Arrowsmith* prompted speculation about the health of its owner Bill Evans, cockies' daughters and the rundown state of the adjacent *Pincally* run by Bill's dysfunctional nephews. *Pincally* homestead had lost its internal walls to accommodate a full-sized billiard table, one corner of the structure had boxes of used plastic plates and cutlery and the opposite corner contained unused plastic plates and utensils. At times the nephews would butcher a bullock on the concrete path into the homestead and one had to kick away dead hooves to enter the building. The nephews liked to go out shooting and the safest place to be was not in the homestead or the shearers' quarters but in the windscreen-less truck with them. The non-drinker nephew had been banned from the Milparinka pub, the drinker nephew had not. We must have passed the tracks to *Kayrunnera, One Tree* and *Mt Browne* homesteads without noticing.

Travellers to Tibooburra drive north after *Mt Browne* but Blackie's excitement mounted as he turned westwards off the track to cross Evelyn Creek before driving south to Milparinka. It was then I knew that we would not get to Tibooburra that night. Milparinka consists of an institute for imbibing and stone ruins from a gold rush in the late 19th and early 20th Centuries.

Milparinka was alive with the ruins from this Century. A number of shearing crews had arrived from outback or beyond and a few miners had escaped from town for a forgetful weekend. Entry to the bar wasn't accompanied by the normal pall of silence and top-to-toe inspection that one experiences in bush pubs. Drinkers had better things to do, serious business was in progress and a number of strangers didn't make any difference. With digits pointing to the heavens, he ordered. The publican's daughter and the governess were serving. The daughter was somewhat cool after a life of isolation dealing with over-thirsty desperate barely-evolved male hominids whereas the governess was high spirited and feigned insult at the body language order of drinks. After a few thirst quenchers, we were chastised as a method of finding out who we were. A local miner immediately advertised who Blackie was and then purloined me for half an hour to trumpet about how he had once travelled the South Seas and that he was drinking to celebrate his retirement as an underground timekeeper. I had escaped identification.

He had moved into the circles of shearers and was now in full swing with these thirsty gentlemen, drink for drink. Their forbears a century ago were the founders to his Labor Party. Towards midnight, I saw an opportunity to retreat from hard-drinking miners and shearers, escaped to the back of the truck, laid out my swag and had a kip. I vaguely recall later in the darkness his bovine bellow and driving around in circles. I kept my head down as my thirst had abated. He was physically incapable of walking so he had to drive to the shearers' bush camp on Evelyn Creek and, in order to get to know these noble gentlemen, spent 10 minutes struggling to remove a case of warm canned fluid from the truck. He left me sleeping and continued the session with the shearers.

At piccaninny dawn I saw the battlefield, the ruins of humanity, a rough camp and the residuum from a hard night. He was unconscious bolt upright in the passenger seat of the Tojo. Here was a chance to get to Tibooburra at dawn. Drunken unrecognisable protests erupted from him as I drove from the camp because we were deserting his honourable mates in their hour of greatest need. It appeared that after my retreat the previous evening, some poor coot of a shearer had hit a sober kangaroo and the shearers towed the wrecked vehicle back to Milparinka pub. To placate him, I drove back to the pub to inspect the damage however, there was no one to be seen near the pub, the town ruins or the moonscape.

The remaining journey to Tibooburra started with a cacophony of complaints about leaving his poor mates followed by his collapse into unconsciousness between the gear stick and the seat. It was a long way to drive in third gear. Dawn and Tibooburra came concurrently and I went and woke John and Richard who were camped on the edge of town. Immediately after introductions, he opened a warm one and continued to keep his levels up. John diplomatically suggested that he should have something to eat and so coffee and cereal were served. He poured a warm can into his plate to make his breakfast cereal more palatable, he appeared more stable on his feet and we went bush to achieve the original aim of the trip. We filled up the truck and Richard did a quick calculation to show that, since the Hill, we had consumed a similar volume of liquid as the vehicle.

He was very slow across the hills. Electric signals from his brain did not transmit to his legs, which were valiantly trying to climb through fences. This phenomenon, well known in the outback, is probably due to some unknown kind of electromagnetic interference induced by fences oriented in a north-south direction. He had our attention while sermonising from a hill that this rock sequence looked like the Corona, the Torrowangee, the Adelaidean and the Koonenberry. Our attention was not directed towards the confused stratigraphic picture but we marvelled at his energetic chaotic body movements and the lack of spillage of a single warm drop of liquid bread.

We headed west along the Corner track, the *Gum Vale* track and then along a sequence of creeks towards the old Pioneer Mine. He was the only one consuming and it would be many hours before the sun would reach the yardarm. Inspection of an old open pit just to the north of the Pioneer had Blackie explaining the geology of a retaining wall and then he desperately searched for a way out of the shallow open pit. He had to be led out of the pit as he was totally bushed. This was new ground for him, nevertheless, we got lengthy explanations and tirades of abuse about my ignorance on matters geographical, geological, chemical and anything else that was caught in the residual filters of his mind.

At Pioneer, he was knackered. The temperature had risen to the high 30s and he was still drinking it warm. To our amazement and admiration, he was still standing and only partially incoherent. He sat dejectedly at the base of a collapsed headframe, can in hand, van Nelle rollie in the other. We left him, climbed the hills to look at some of the subsidiary workings, he made a pathetic attempt to follow us and, after a wavering tortuous 50 metres, he turned back. Upon return, we found him unconscious and asleep in the back of the truck.

It was a long drive down Waratta Creek. He woke and appeared marginally better because he was groaning about the beauty of the river gums, the wildlife and the contrast between the red dirt and the cloudless clear blue sky. Proof of further recovery was when I suffered abuse about my driving prowess and choice of directions, he argued about whether we should drive down the dry sandy creek or on the bank and whether we should drive north or east from a defunct windmill. We kept driving south. These were good signs. However, he was totally incapable of appreciating that I had driven cross-country in this area a number of times previously and actually knew my way on my patch.

Once on the main track, we headed further south for the Mt Browne Goldfield. The only way was ominously right past the Milparinka pub. The Evelyn Creek camp was in its pristine state and we bumped into the police stock patrol inspecting an old grave. A drunken shout instructed me to stop and reverse. This I did. He wound down the window and bellowed at the sergeant *"You fucking miserable old bastard. What are you doing here? Don't answer, just shut up, turn around and come and have a drink."* I'm sure the sergeant used this occasion to show his young constable how to bond with the locals when not catching cattle duffers. We again visited the Milparinka imbibing institute.

The friendly face was again serving. He greeted her with six skyward-facing digits which were taken in good humour. She proudly showed me an old school science assignment set and marked by Blackie. She had kept this for over a decade. John and Richard, who had seen the evils of drink since dawn, chose soft and the rest of us had high octane. A few comments were passed from the other side of the bar about his performance last night, was I the person he claimed I was and how on earth did he get voted in as Mayor. Years later after 19 years as Mayor, he was the Labor Member for Murray Darling in the State parliament for 8 years and after that was a councillor again for a while. We consumed some abominable partially frozen pastry-meat-gelatinous fluid mixture, had one (or maybe a few more) for the road and went to Mt Browne.

It was 20 years since he'd been to Mt Browne with Eva who, he assured us, besides being a bit of all right, she knew a lot about the history of the area. He couldn't remember anything about the history of the area but assured us that it was Eva who knew everything about the history of the goldfield. This was of great use to us, of course. I didn't have the heart to tell him that not only did I know a lot about the history of the area but I also knew a lot about the history of Eva. Maybe he forgot that I lived in the Hill 20 years ago. Now he was driving and insisted upon cross-country travel up to the top of the highest hill to take in the 360° view of the endless never-never. It's a case of spot the plant in this part of the world. We looked at the more recent gold workings near the Good Friday Mine and tried a few dishes at an old dam just to get the thrill of finding a few colours. This was poor man's country, prospectors reckon the goldfield was hungry and they could never made wages during nearly a century of work here.

At stumps, we retreated and once again had to as through the thriving metropolis of Milparinka. At this stage, he claimed that he was feeling a little off colour. We were not sure whether it was because he had been drinking non-stop for 24 hours or whether he had some sort of real internal problem. We reckoned it was the former. He had a few therapeutic fluid intakes to calm down his insides and he then relaxed enough to entertain us back to Tibooburra with licentious drinking songs and poetry. Drunk or sober, he was a man of kulcha.

At John's camp in Tibooburra, he couldn't go on. It was shock and horror when he actually accepted our sympathetic suggestion that maybe he should have a kip. He chose the shade of a ghost gum and provided a cacophony of snorts, grunts, exhalations and groans in his unconscious hour. An hour and a half after our arrival in town, we were in the back parlour of the two storey, one of the two institutions in town. Three jugs induced his appetite but, because he wasn't feeling well, he required some more fluid therapy. A jug or two for dessert and we were ready to go to the front bar.

The cook collared him on the way through and said how she never missed his Monday wireless program, what a wonderful voice he has and how disappointing it was to meet him in the flesh and see his face. He was in such as state that he interpreted her comments as a compliment. She added that she knew he was a dreadful pisspot but that she'd vote for him next time anyway. Tibooburra was worth nine votes to him and every one counted. He promised to give her a cheerio call on his next program.

It was hell in the front bar. A mass of warts, hair and sweat beneath holey blue singlets encircling the bar in upright, prostrate and reclining positions. John and Richard guessed that another hard night was on the way and, like cowards, walked back to their camp. We had a jug or two passed through the window, tippled the contents while supporting the veranda posts and later drove into the donga to find a place to spread our swags.

A mile or so out of town, we negotiated our way around a ute left in the middle of the track. Lights on, engine running, door open and the poor driver slumped unconscious over the steering wheel. Must have been something the poor chap ate! We did the charitable act for a colleague in hops, checked that he was not dead, strapped him into his seat, shut down all systems on his vehicle and left him to continue his kip. It would have been rude to disturb this unknown chap as it appeared that he'd also had a pretty stressful weekend. I kept driving down the track until I met a gum-lined creek bed and turned up into it. I opened the door to help Blackie out with his swag, he fell like a sack of spuds onto the sand and there he stayed unmoving, unconscious and inert until morning. This was a five-star hotel for me, I picked a flat patch for my swag some distance from the vehicle to reduce disturbances from nocturnal emissions and warthog impressions. With night temperatures of 38°C, neither clothes nor bedding were necessary. I stretched out in the warm summer evening to view the infinity of our Universe.

Come dawn, I had some difficulty in waking him. He was starting to look a very sad sight and I actually felt sorry for him, especially as he seemed to be plagued by intestinal problems. A hearty fluid-less breakfast followed by an inspection of the Nuggety Hill field stimulated and revived him and we adjourned to the Family at Tibooburra for a liquid lunch. Famous passing artists such as Clifton Pugh have painted murals of local scenery, orgies with contemporary local personalities and various odd sods and bods. The locals barter for refreshment with gold and solid food is totally forgettable. Most locals keep some gold on their person in small medicine bottles but such sights are never seen by strangers as there is no knowing who collects tax nowadays. Whenever it rains, locals find gold nuggets in the gutter of the main street.

A generous volume of cold supplies was purchased for the southward return trip. First stop was to pay our respects to all and sundry who we remembered or didn't remember at Milparinka. Our welcome just didn't seem to wear out at this esteemed establishment. A couple of parched aviators landed on the gibber strip adjacent to the institute, quenched their thirst more than once, took a six pack or two for the rigours of altitude and continued their flight northwards. After a few friendly cleansing refreshers, we continued south down the track in the searing heat of an outback summer afternoon. After Milparinka, we overtook an indigene couple in a beaten up vehicle totally unsuitable for the bush. They had three punctures and were driving very slowly on the rims in a desperate run for help at *Packsaddle*. We couldn't do too much to help as we had different-sized wheels and this time we both agreed that *Packsaddle* was not far, some 15 kilometres onward. In an act of great Christian kindness, Blackie gave them liquid supplies for their arduous journey and their spirits lifted immediately.

Packsaddle was normal. Surly service of condemned ersatz dog food and cool liquids. The heavy depressive atmosphere was too raw, we had supplies on board so we left after the first. Cold supplies kept us going until the old Fowlers Gap Hotel, razed in a fire in 1912. Probably an insurance job. We were able to focus enough to inspect the cellar, discussed the local hallucinogenic flora brought in by Afghan cameleers a hundred years ago, marvelled at the inner strength of the pioneers and made room for the warmer cans. We were now on the final lap to the finishing post and were quite happy to continue south in silence amid friendship and the forgiving privacy of the red dirt country.

Yanco Glen was full of low life commuters from the Hill. We had one for the boundary gate and drove the last 30 kilometres in silence. Upon arrival in the Hill, we both retreated to bed. I left early the next morning. I didn't see Blackie for a while although gossip in the Hill about the old Black Mayor tells me that he gave it up. For a while.

A short while.

(1989)

Select company of the few people who have had minerals named after them,
Leoben, Austria, 2010

Aleşehir

Western Turkey has experienced stretching which resulted in the sliding down of huge uplifted blocks from the basement. Continued stretching has produced a series of seven flat-bottomed graben valleys separated by rugged mountains of older basement rock.

I was attracted to these graben because, in the long ago in this area, King Croesus built a fabulously wealthy empire based on gold. His city of Sardis is still well preserved. The King's gold derived from the alluvial sediments on the floor of the valley and elaborate sluicing treatment works had kept thousands of slaves employed, fed and watered. In those times, rainfall and temperature was higher than now and there was more water for sluicing. There was presumably little gold left in the valleys as slave power is very cheap, very efficient and, in relative terms, the price of gold has not changed for thousands of years. A troy ounce of gold for the last thousand years has been worth a week of a carpenter's time. The gold mined by King Croesus undoubtedly originally came from the hills but which hills.

After some investigation, it became clear that the gold derived from dissected terraces of older partially consolidated gravels draped half-way up the walls of the graben. These gravels were once flat lying sediments on the valley floor, now they were steeply tilted well above the valley floor as a result of very rapid land rise.

In tectonically active areas, the geological processes are very rapid and the land rises and falls quickly. For example, on the southern coast of Turkey, subsidence has drowned ancient Lydian cities that are now a few metres underwater whereas the famous port city of Efeses is 15 kilometres inland as a result of uplift. There can be no understanding of sea level change without an understanding of land level changes which can be very rapid.

The gold had come from the source area of gravel and the cobbles and boulders in the gravel immediately told me where to look. The source area for the gold was composed of fractured limestone masses perched high above the valley floor at the boundary between the graben and the basement rocks. It was here that hot acid gold-bearing fluids had chemically reacted with limestone and precipitated gold in rocks. This gold is normally invisible and grows into larger grains in alluvial sediments.

I climbed up donkey tracks to the part of the scarp that I though was shedding gold into the valley during aeons of uplift, weathering and erosion. I knew I had come to the right place because there were hundreds of old pits, an abandoned crushing and mercury distillation plant, and large dumps of waste that had been roasted to volatilise mercury. A village had been built on the area flattened out by the old mercury mining and distillation activities. For some decades last century, the village was able to feed itself as a result of the employment in the mercury mines. The village probably provided the mercury needed to detonate the shells for the Turkish defence of Gallipoli.

The village dwellings were made of mercury-bearing stone. The tracks were cobbled with mercury-bearing tailings and the village well was an old shaft used for extracting the mercury-bearing ore. The village had its normal quota of ferocious-looking cowardly wolf dogs, elderly men sitting in the sun, old humped women carrying the firewood and doing the heavy work, deep mud and dung, and pens constructed from sticks and stones for the goats and sheep.

As per usual, one must seek an interview with the village mufti and explain why one is in the area and what will be done. After the necessary niceties, the village mufti instructed a young boy, no older than eight years old, to be my guide. No guide was necessary as I was looking at rocks in a five square kilometre area around the village but my arrival presented a commercial opportunity for the village.

My guide was a charming child. He was a typical village boy with a shaved head, ear-to-ear smile, ill-fitting mud-caked hand-me-downs and plastic shoes with no socks. He knew every one of the old mercury mines in his playground and he took me to every shaft, pit, costean, ore dump and prominent outcrop. He knew his patch well.

My child guide had severe brain damage, typical of congenital mercury poisoning. He was constantly shaking, had slurred unintelligible speech, deformed digits and ears, and constant salivation. He showed passing interest in my maps, compass and satellite-based ground positioning system and was absolutely fascinated with my Estwing geological pick. He would keenly watch how I would select partially silicified limestones, break off a number of chips, place these rock specimens in a cloth sample bag and label the bag with an ink pen.

He indicated that he would like to collect my samples for me, I gave him my hammer and, after attacking every rock within sight, I managed to coerce him into sampling only the rocks which I considered were of geological interest. Far too many samples were collected and, as it transpired after analysis of the samples, none of the specimens were of interest. This is not unusual.

Some of the mountain streams were fascinating. Long tapering ice crystals had grown in from the banks to the centre of the stream. Water flowed under the ice and only in the centre of the stream. Because I had often seen the same texture in quartz veins which formed from silica-saturated hot fluids flowing along fractures in rocks, I took a number of photographs.

My little guide then took me to every icicle, every ice waterfall, every ice-laden stream and indicated that these sites were far better for photography. I wanted to photograph an analogue of a quartz vein in rock and he thought I was interested in photographing ice. He was a lovely kid. We had lunch together next to an ice-laden stream in the sun and out of the wind. He was highly complimented when I took his photograph.

When back at the village, I paid the mufti for the boy's services and gave my little guide the same amount of money. Custom required me to have a çay with the mufti and senior village men using what was mercurial water. Boiling water to make tea does not get rid of mercury. The young boy was dismissed. Upon my departure after just one cup of tea, I asked the mufti to find my guide for me. He was again presented to me, I offered him my geology pick as a present which he took with a high-pitched yelp of joy and ran off down the village road swinging my pick around his head.

He was happy. The village will continue to look after my little guide for the duration of his shortened life.

(1991)

Kücükyenice

As Ömer and I drove up the track from the river, we could see a solitary miner working in an open pit at the top of a hill. Our rather poor maps recorded no mines in the area but we had been attracted to the area because of its geology, also derived from poor maps. The sandy, limey and salty sediments of an old lake bed had been cut by a sequence of 20 million-year old volcanic rocks. The ancient lake had formed by the stretching and subsequent sinking of the crust. Sinking occurred in fault-bounded blocks that went from Balya to Bergama in western Anatolia. It was along these faults at Balya that lead and silver had been mined since antiquity and gold had recently been re-discovered near Bergama.

The old miner was very happy to stop working and let us look at the rocks in the pit face. He was mining yellow antimony oxide on a tribute basis for an antimony smelter near Gönen. The antimony oxide mineral cervantite just looks like a mixture of yellow iron oxides and clays which are common in all weathered rocks. It was clear that we were dealing with an experienced miner who knew his stuff. He had to know his stuff because there was no old age pension, social security or medical benefits in Turkey. He may have been 50 or he may have been 70. It's hard to estimate the age of someone who has had a hard life in the open doing back-breaking physical work. Even at his age, he had to work to live, all he knew was mining and if he didn't physically exert himself in an open pit, then he didn't eat. Mustafa was poor and proud.

I was interested in the host rocks. They were altered limestones. Alteration had occurred from hot antimony-bearing fluids passing through a porous permeable reactive rock such as limestone and deposited opaline silica, clays and the bladed silvery-grey antimony sulphide called stibnite. It is a very easy mineral to identify in the bush. If a match is rubbed along the face of a stibnite crystal, the match catches alight. No wonder it is used on the sides of matchboxes.

Mustafa the miner had a collection of picks, pelican shovels, sledge hammers and drill rods. It was all hammer and tap and no explosives were used. Boiling water was produced from a fire and a billy-full of water was poured into the drill hole rock to try to make the rock crack. This was one of the mining techniques used by the Romans. There were wooden wheelbarrows and leather bags for collecting ore. He was dressed in thick tattered muddy clothes for working on the northern side of the hill in winter. No hard hat. No safety boots. No gloves. No mask to filter out the deathly silica dust. Just a green woollen cloth cap and a pair of cut down Wellington boots which probably leaked. It could have been a scene from the goldfields of eastern Australia in the 1850s. I took photographs of this living history and offered to send prints to Mustafa the miner. I asked him to write his name and address in my field book for the despatch of the photographs. He changed his mind and said he really did not want the photographs after all. It was then I realised he could not write. I should have been more sensitive and I lobotomised myself for my stupidity.

We were given a conducted tour of all the small pits, shafts and open cuts in the district. We went to inspect çakmak hill, the original reason for our visit. Çakmak is the Turkish word for flint that was used by the locals to describe a great diversity of silica-rich rocks. Because çakmak could mean a great diversity of rock types, all çakmak locations in volcanic settings were inspected. The most interesting locations of çakmak were normally steep rocky pinnacles and old place names such as gümüs (silver), altin (gold), şap (alum) and bakir (copper) gave clues about what might have been mined at that place in antiquity.

The collection of silica-rich rocks I sampled suggested that we were in a place where very acid hot springs had repeatedly and explosively boiled. At times, the hot springs had exploded and the çakmak had been broken into sharp angular pieces, slivers and needles and re-cemented by silica from a new influx of silica-rich waters. This jigsaw of fragments could be put back together showing that the fragments had only moved centimetres. This also showed that boiling was explosive, the energy to convert water into steam came from the water itself which then instantaneously cooled and precipitated dissolved silica. Some geological processes take aeons whereas what I was looking at took less than a second.

I could see remnants of an old land surface that told me that the hot springs had boiled close to the surface and, from experimental studies and work on the New Zealand hot spring systems, I deduced that any gold would have been precipitated at a depth of about 200 metres. Traces of gold, silver, mercury, antimony and arsenic should occur at the old land surface. This was confirmed by the texture of the opaline silica in the çakmak, the presence of ruby red crystals of the arsenic mineral realgar and a large surrounding bleached zone where acid steam had converted the hot volcanic rock into flinty clay. I was getting geologically excited which, as all geologists know, can be dangerous and expensive.

My experience and knowledge of natural systems gave me all the clues I needed but I needed rock chemistry to validate my observations. I knew that I would be back in the area. All the rocks in the area had that smell of gold. Some time in the future, I had to work nearby. By then, all samples would have been processed and chemically analysed. I could then be armed with greater knowledge and have another brief look at the area as part of planning the logistics for the next summer season's exploration.

The sample results were, not surprisingly, encouraging and I passed through Kücükyenice again on my way to another field area to the north. My intention was to do a brief compass and tape survey of the antimony mines before starting the exploration season in earnest. My survey started on a ridge where the rocks had been slightly hardened by silica hence underwent less weathering and erosion and stood out as high ground. There were a number of old open pits, an old two-compartment shaft and a disused adit. One open pit had recently been reopened and the same Mustafa the miner was extracting stibnite ore. When he caught sight of me, he downed tools and sprinted out of the pit. Mustafa hugged me, thanked me for sending the photographs and wanted to stop work and take me to the çay house.

Prints of the photographs I had taken were enlarged and sent from Australia and I just addressed the airmail package to Mustafa at Kücükyenice village in western Anatolia. Very few village people receive post, mainly because most village folk are illiterate, and the Turkish postal system must have thought that this delivery from Australia was very important. It was a credit to the Turkish postal system that he actually received the photographs that had created great interest in the village. Not only was the status of Mustafa the miner greatly enhanced, but also an air of intrigue had developed about the mystery photographer from far away. In order to finish my survey, we agreed that I would meet Mustafa at the çay house at dusk.

When I came down from the hills to the village, it was clear that Mustafa the miner had reached the çay house well before me. Business was as usual for the village women who had their coloured washed clothes spread out on rocks and hawthorn hedges to dry. Other women were cooking the daily bread in the village's communal oven and others were sitting around in a circle on the ground grinding wheat by hand into flour.

A group of children stood on the road that bisected the village school from the bread-making activity. They would not let me past unless I took group and individual photographs. These were absolutely delightful kids. The boys with crew cuts, ill-fitting hand-me-downs, open plastic shoes and no socks. Some had a few front teeth missing which made their smiles even more beautiful. The girls were too young to wear chadors and were draped in cotton print pantaloons, pinafores, blouses and jackets. All smiles and a lot of noise but they kept their distance from this stranger with white hair and blue eyes. A number of the children had rounded faces, copper-coloured hair and aqua blue–greenish eyes.

These are Turkmenistani features. One particular girl stood out from the crowd. She was taller than the rest, had a long shock of almost iridescent copper-coloured hair and piercing aqua blue-greenish eyes. I took a few rolls of film of the group and individuals and promised the children that I would send the photographs to the village school, the kücück eskola.

At the çay house, there was the normal pall of smoke and numerous idle, smoking, talking tea-drinking men. In most villages the women do the hard physical work as well as bearing children, cooking and washing. At the çay house, I was warmly welcomed individually by every man and was directed to sit down at the head table. Everyone wanted to honour the guest with a glass of tea and, after about ten small glasses of the sweet tannin-rich çay, I laid my small thin aluminium spoon horizontally across the top of the glass indicating that I wanted no more. I explained who I was and what I wanted to do in the summer season in the hills overlooking the village. The village was to be my base, I would employ a few chain men to help me and I would employ Mustafa the miner to clean out the abandoned adit so I could go underground and map the rocks.

The teacher from the one-teacher kücück esloka, Ibrahim, insisted that I talk English with him. In the field, I always carried an English-Turkish/Turkish-English dictionary with me, despite having a working knowledge of Turkish. Ibrahim had brought with him a tattered dictionary from his school. He needed it as much as I needed mine. We conversed using nouns separated by the frantic searching for words in our dictionaries. Our conversation was very slow, had many misunderstandings and amused the onlookers crowding around our table. The teacher challenged me, in English, to a game of backgammon. It was on.

Backgammon is played everywhere in Turkey, especially in the çay houses. In the big cities, it is tea drinking, smoking and backgammon that are the main activities in bazaars, back streets and shops. It is a game I knew well from my previous geological work in Iran and from social occasions in Australia. I accepted Ibrahim's challenge because I thought that I was a better than average backgammon player. It is a Persian game that was given to the Raj of India. On a state visit, the Raj of India gave the game of chess to the Shah of Persia. For the return visit, the Shah asked his intelligentsia to invent a game that, unlike chess, was a game of both skill and chance. A game with no complicated pieces. A game more like the game of life. A game that anyone could play, even an Australian in Turkey. The game invented and presented to the Raj on the return visit was backgammon. Even Persian prisoner slaves from the Punic Wars chained underground in the Lavrion silver mines of Greece had cut backgammon boards out of the limestone and made dice and counters from clay.

It is an international game thousands of years old. It is a game I enjoy. A fast game is a good game. I started to play this game of chance and skill against Ibrahim and, much to the enjoyment of the onlookers, Ibrahim's skill was far greater than any chance given to me by throwing the dice. I could not win a single game. I tried playing skilfully, recklessly, conservatively and randomly and just could not win a game. The crowd discussed my every move and, after a while, realised that I needed some help. When I went to move a counter, an anonymous gnarled guiding hand from the encircling crowd would stretch out over the board, grip my hand and make sure that my counter ended up in the correct spot. I then started to have a few wins. We must have played thirty games before I threw in the towel. I was looking forward to coming back for a summer field season.

Enlarged photographs of the children sent from Australia preceded my next visit. I drove slowly from Ivrindi to Kücükyenice along the battered dirt roads in order to understand the lie of the land and to get to know the geology better. Road cuttings, local road base, stone walls, stone buildings and piles of rubble in the fields are invaluable clues to the local geology. No one is going to cart stone from miles away to build a stone wall around a field. These walls were obviously made of stone collected from the field that was surrounded by the wall to make ploughing easier. As I drove up the track from the river, I saw a new pile of fresh rocks.

These clearly had not come from a new mine as the rocks were rounded fresh volcanics that had been carried up the hill from the river. I stopped and saw that a new well was being dug for the village.

The well was more than twenty metres deep and access was down some very flimsy frayed rope and spiralling wooden ladders. Materials were hauled using a counter-balanced battered bucket and steel kibble with a somewhat worn rope over a pulley. If the load shifted or fell, anyone underneath would have been killed. Safety is a luxury we wealthy westerners enjoy. The shaft had been dug by hand to well beneath the water table. During digging, the shaft had to be kept dry by continual bucketing out of the inflowing water using the bucket and kibble. The well was now being filled with large round boulders from river gravels to stop the walls collapsing and to make the water accessible. At the bottom was my long lost friend, Mustafa the miner. I greeted him and came down because I was interested to look at the fresh rock in the bottom of the well.

He hugged me, we sat at the bottom of the well and ate some bread. It appeared that once the new village well was finished, Mustafa had no work because the London Metal Exchange price of antimony had slumped due to the dumping of antimony on the market by the Chinese. The excess antimony on the market probably came from the Dachang tin-lead-antimony mines near Guilin that I had visited a few years earlier. Mustafa could no longer eke out a living as a tribute miner and he was at the mercy of the international metals and money market beyond his ken and so far away. He was an innocent bystander who ate or starved depending on matters beyond his control in far off lands. Mustafa was relying on my return such that he could eat over summer.

After we made arrangements for the dewatering and cleaning out of rubble from the old two-compartment shaft and the connecting adit in the hills behind the village, I made the dangerous climb to daylight and my vehicle. I continued the drive up to the village and, at the edge of the village, was met by the normal mangy dogs, the odd free-range goat and old women walking back to the village doubled up under a load of oak firewood that they'd just cut. I stopped in the town square in the late afternoon sun between the çay house and the mosque and was immediately surrounded by a crowd of children who appeared out of nowhere. They clearly were very pleased to have received photographs of themselves and, for most of the children, it would have been the first time they had seen their own photograph. I was later to learn that in some of the village huts, my photographs took pride of place on the wall.

The children were dancing around me and squealing with excitement. It was like a scene of the encircling Willis' midnight dance from Adam's *Giselle*. These will-o'-the-wisps were silhouetted against the mosque, swarming in the dusty hazy light like butterflies and encircling me with flashing cabalistic colours. School had just finished, we gave the children some boiled lollies and tried to quell their excitement. A few lolly papers were dropped in the town square, my backgammon-playing teacher Ibrahim appeared, chastised the children and instructed them to clean the whole town square. This they did. The teacher placed the oldest child, the tall girl with copper-coloured hair and the aqua blue-green eyes in charge of cleaning the square. This was the way Australia was when we were poor.

My work kept me in the village for two months. A routine developed. An early morning gathering of the chain men and miners I employed would disperse to our various chores, we would all meet on the dumps of the old mine for lunch where someone was employed to keep a fire going and another person was employed to make tea and at sunset we would drift back down to the village çay house. I now had a special table for the plotting of maps, downloading of data and organising the next day of activities. Every morning when I left the village to work in the hills, the copper-haired girl was waiting for me. Every evening I returned, she would be waiting for me outside the school that was on the outskirts of the village. She would warmly greet me with smiling eyes. What was she thinking?

Every night at the çay house, Ibrahim the teacher would ask me to come to his school the next morning to have a cup of coffee. Every invitation I refused because my field work in the hills was not finished, the first snow falls had come and I was aware of how long it took to partake in the simple act of drinking coffee or çay in Turkey. Maybe the Protestant work ethic some of us have in Western democracies is a blight on our lives?

At the end of the field season on my last day in Kücükyenice, I agreed to come to the school at 9 am for a cup of coffee. When I arrived at the village school on the slope overlooking the village, there was a school assembly in the snow-covered school yard. I was the honoured guest, Ibrahim the teacher formally welcomed me in front of the assembly and the children saluted me. It reminded me of my post-war primary school days when straight lines, silence, undivided attention, marching, the singing of a hymn and the saluting of the flag was the normal morning ritual at assembly. I'm sure it did me no harm.

There was only one school room and one teacher for all the village children of all ages. A barn-like room with a worn knotted oak plank floor, a wall slate, a central potbelly stove, benches for all the children and a front desk for the teacher. It was entry into a 19th Century Australian bush school house. As soon as I entered the class room, I knew what was meant by coming up to the school and having a cup of coffee. On the slate was drawn the outline of the continent of Australia. Tasmania, as per usual, had been expunged. It was clear to me that I was to give a lesson about the land I came from and that the children had been primed.

These are the challenges I enjoy. I spent the morning in the class room providing an illustrated lesson on the geography and history of Australia, including Tasmania. I drew and labelled in Turkish the mountains, cities, agricultural and mining regions on the wall slate board. The children furiously copied everything I drew and wrote on their own smaller slate boards. As a result of my one and only lesson at the kücük eskola at Kücükyenice, whenever I now work in impoverished countries, I bring along scores of pens stolen from hotels and notebooks to distribute at the local school. A heart-starting Turkish coffee was served at recess and a cleaned slate allowed me to draw aspects of the vegetation, climate, wildlife, fisheries and reefs.

I didn't mention the war. I wonder if these children knew that we Australians invaded their country in 1915 during World War I? I wonder if these children knew that the first act of Islamic terrorist killing in Australia was done by two "Turks" and took place in Broken Hill on 1st January 1915? I didn't mention the Ottoman genocide of Armenians in 1915. These were not matters for children of this age, especially when linguistic difficulties could easily lead to misunderstandings. During my time in Turkey, older people had sometimes come up to me and told me that they are looking after our young men buried in their country. These people never told me that Turkish casualties in 1915 were four times those of the Allies.

It was then question time and this involved the rapid use of my Turkish dictionary. The first question was from a little crew-cutted boy who wanted to know the religion of Australia. This was an Allah-given opportunity to demonstrate the multicultural nature of Australia and the fact that we have Christians of numerous denominations, Jews, atheists, Hindis, Shiites and Sunnis all co-existing in peaceful harmony. I hope he understood that Australia had no state religion and that it is a secular society with all institutions underpinned by the basics of Christianity. Other questions indicated that the children had been stimulated by this foreigner from a far-off land. As expected, there were questions about crocodiles, snakes, sharks and spiders and surprise that we didn't have wolves and bears. I hoped that one day, if there is a great change and Turkey becomes a fundamentalist theocracy, that these people might remember the foreigner who gave them a lesson. He was not all that bad, was he. Maybe they won't accept xenophobia, maybe they might develop some religious tolerance, maybe they might even try to understand other cultures or maybe they might not take up arms for some spurious nationalistic, religious or ethnic cause.

The copper-haired girl was the class monitor. She was given the jobs of making and serving coffee, adding wood to the pot belly stove, disciplining and organising the smaller children, cleaning the class room, providing me with chalk and cleaning the board. She was being trained to be a village wife and mother. This she will do well but it was just perpetuating the past. She probably will spend the rest of her life in Kücükyenice or an adjacent village doing what her mother and grandmother did.

I wondered if she had her appetite whetted about the world beyond or whether her mind had been opened?

I will never know, but I tried.

(1991)

Professor Ian Plimer
Head of Department
1985 - 1991

Once in academia, portraits were diverse,
such as this one for the University of Newcastle.

The flautist

The Anatolian Fault has been active for more than 100 million years. It is an east-west structure that can be traced from the Pyrenees to Kazakhstan. The sliding of one block of the crust past another has produced a long history of earthquake and volcanic activity in Anatolia and has led to the opening of the Marmara and Black Seas. Major earthquakes occur roughly every 300 years and multi-storey buildings are re-built along the fault scarp to replace those destroyed by previous earthquakes.

A recent rotation of stresses changed fault movement from a sliding motion to stretching which led to crustal extension and the pulling apart of the crust. Great blocks of the crust were thinned, broke off from the surrounding rocks and sunk with the inevitable associated earthquakes, volcanism and geothermal activity. It is this stretching of the crust that allowed the intrusion of lavas into limestone at Sebepli. Sediments and small coal layers were deposited over the blocks of crust that had sunk. The cooling molten rocks intruded during thinning released huge amounts of hot acid gold-bearing waters. These geothermal fluids moved along fracture systems and chemically reacted with limestone.

In summertime, the line of sight in the oak-forested mountains of Sebepli was less than twenty metres so we decided to put in a grid in late winter after all the leaves had fallen. Oaks are one of the last deciduous plants to lose their leaves in winter. Once we had established a grid, we could use the spring for mapping and sampling and, if targets of interest were delineated for a 3-dimensional look, then drilling could be undertaken in summer.

Winter time is certainly no time to be doing field work in alpine Turkey.

The thick snow and biting wind made conditions somewhat unpleasant and there are just not enough hours of daylight to achieve a good day's work. We decided to work in winter because we would have had a greater line of sight for surveying.

Our plans for detailed investigation of the site were devised in Australia. Like all well made plans, they came unstuck by an unexpected fundamental flaw. Sebepli was at the ridge crest between the Biga Peninsula and the Marmara Sea. In winter the cold land mass met warmer moisture-laden air driven inland from the sea. In winter, the area was shrouded in a pea-souper fog day and night. The line of sight was only ten metres rather than the twenty metres in summer.

Our days that winter were spent blindly stumbling on the precipitous slopes over jagged rocky outcrops of quartz, silicified limestone and limestone. We were most aware that our presence disturbed the villagers' activities in the mountain forests. There was the distant chopping of wood for cooking and heating fires, the tinkle of sheep bells and the occasional shepherd's shout.

Crib time was spent at the datum peg on the rocky peak of Sebepli Mountain. Crib is an old-fashioned underground miners' abbreviation for the 17th Century English board game of cribbage. It was played on a board with match sticks in semi-darkness in underground openings cut out to serve as the miners' lunch room. The miners carried their crib (or lunch) down underground in a sealed metal tin (crib tin) to prevent rats enjoying their lunch. In the crib room, tea was drunk, cribbage was played, lies were told and, after half an hour, work started again. A routine at Sebepli was established. My job was to try to get the saturated oak to burn, Kiwi Mike cooked a steaming hot stew for lunch, Neddy prepared the billy of tea and Okan did the housekeeping with the downloading of data.

Our lunch spot was used to store pegs, equipment, excess clothing, cooking equipment, food and water. Like all isolated country areas, whether Turkey or elsewhere, items left in the bush are neither interfered with nor pilfered.

Every lunchtime, a few shepherds just happened to drift in from the thick fog to stand around our fire and warm themselves. They carried their thin ekmek wrapped in newspaper for lunch and they never rejected our invitation to drink piping hot çay with us. They enjoyed the company of strangers and our conversational attempts were greeted by toothless smiles.

One little shepherd boy, no older than twelve years old, was too shy to come in close to the fire. He was poorly clothed, poorly shod and often had no food. He always greatly admired our field boots. We would regularly give him a hot lunch which he would then take away from the fireside-populated comfort and eat alone. We never heard or saw him disappear back into the foggy forest to tend to his sheep.

One lunch, Neddy asked whether we had heard the sound of a flute drifting up the mountain through the fog. The three of us had been at the other end of the grid and had heard nothing. We suggested that maybe Neddy should drink less raki, a potent local firewater which occasionally made Neddy hallucinate.

The next day, Mike, Okan and I also heard the flautist's melodies. Upon questioning, the shepherds told us that the flautist was the little shepherd boy who comforted his sheep with music. In the thick fog, the sheep could not see their guardian shepherd. The boy's sheep kept within the safe earshot of the flute and the shepherd could also hear his sheep's distinctive bells.

We tried everything to try to get the boy shepherd flautist to play for us over lunch. He was too shy and too self-conscious to play in front of an audience. He was clearly pleased that we enjoyed his music. We did notice that he now spent much more time herding his sheep in proximity to the grid which enabled us to hear music all day. The music was evocative and hauntingly beautiful. The melodies drifted in and out of tonality and were all an unfamiliar blend of Asian and European phonics. Thick snow, defoliated forest, interesting rocks and simple melodies drifting through the fog over Sebepli Mountain gave us an unforgettable time of interesting geological field work set to music.

At times, one of us needed to drive in to town to despatch our samples and get provisions. On one trip, Kiwi Mike made some purchases and presented the boy with a new flute and a pair of field boots. The boy took the gifts and quickly vanished into the foggy forest. We couldn't see him but he thanked us by serenading us with his whole repertoire during our lunches at the datum peg at Sebepli.

Our young flautist had never been to school. He'd not had formal music training. He probably couldn't read or write. Why would he need to? He had never been more than five kilometres from his home village. He had been entrusted with the villagers' sheep and probably will have a stable fulfilled life comforting the village sheep entrusted into his care with music from his flute. His sheep would never know how lucky they were. He will never experience a prosperous or totally destitute life. He will do the same thing year in, year out all his life. It will be simple life. Will the 21st Century even have an impact on him? Will he ever hear a symphony orchestra? Will he ever hear the hauntingly beautiful flute music of Mozart such as the passionate andantino movement of the Concerto in C, K.299 or *Die Zauberflöte*? I suspect not.

The last time a year or two later I was in that neck of the woods, I made a diversion to pass through Sebepli *en route* from Izmir to Istanbul. I went to Sebepli Mountain and tied my field boots to the top of our old datum peg.

I know that he will know where the boots came from.

(1991)

Şapdağ girl

She was well aware that in a matter of years, she would die a slow horrible death as others had before her. All her childhood had been spent knapping ultrapure silica into cobbles for use as grinding blocks in ceramic works.

Agricola knew that working in an environment of silica dust produces irreparable lung damage within months and coughing, silicosis and death at a very early age. Sharp spicules of silica pierce the lungs to produce bleeding, lithification of lung tissue, loss of lung expansion and a painful death by drowning in your own blood. Agricola wrote:

> "...some mines are so dry that they are entirely devoid of water and this dryness causes the workmen even more harm, for the dust, which is stirred and beaten up by digging, penetrates into the windpipe and lungs and produces difficulty in breathing...it eats away the lungs and implants consumption in the body."

Even if she had read Agricola's 1556 AD book *De Re Metallica*, it was too late. She probably couldn't read and she certainly would not have had access to this classic volume in Latin or English. Hoover and his wife translated the book from Latin to English. Edgar Hoover worked as a mining engineer at the mines in Broken Hill (NSW), Gwalia (WA), various places in China and at Bawdwin (Burma). He later became President of the USA and, although not an outstanding President, he could read, understand and translate Latin unlike those Presidents who followed.

She would not have been aware of Calvert's Holland's 1843 AD description of the working conditions of cutlery grinders in Sheffield who used silica for grinding and polishing:

> *"The dust, which is thus every moment inhaled, undermines the vigour of the constitution, and produces permanent disease of the lungs, accompanied by difficulty of breathing, cough, and a wasting of the animal frame, often at an early age of twenty five. Such is the destructive tendency of the occupation that…many sick clubs have an especial rule against the admission of dry grinders, as they would draw largely on the funds from frequent and long-continued sickness…Grinders' asthma in its advanced stages admits neither of cure nor of any material alleviation."*

Large volumes of silica-laden steam some 20 million years ago moved up fractures in the volcanic rocks of Western Anatolia. The fluid stripped material out of the volcanic rocks and left pipes of porous silica behind. Small amounts of alum (şap) and gold-bearing crystalline silica were also deposited. The silica was so pure, so hard, so even-textured and of ultrafine grainsize that it was prized as the grinding blocks for clay in ball mills at ceramic factories.

The silica mines were perched beneath the alum cliffs of the mountain called Şapdağ. Mining was by drilling, blasting and sizing by sledgehammer. This was done by men. Drilling used water to cool the drill bit. This water also served to keep down the dust and, as a result, the men did not inhale silica dust. A group of teenage girls and women sat in a circle on boulders on the edge of the cliff underneath a bamboo and reed gunyah knapping the sized boulders down to small cubic blocks with a hammer and chisel. Knapping produced dust and sharp fragments of excess silica.

We went to the pine slab hut and had çay with the foreman. The hut had a pot belly stove in the centre for cooking, making tea and warmth and around the pot-belly stove were a number of four-gallon drums for seats, wooden benches and a warped trestle table. Pinned to the wall were three home comforts. The statutory photograph of Karmel Ataturk, last year's calendar from a ceramic company in Bursa and a large faded colour

124

photograph of all the mine workers.

One face on the photograph had been cut out. There was just an oval hole in place of the face of a woman. It appears that she was a young married woman who had the misfortune to be looked at by another man. That man was not her husband. Her head was lifted high enough for another man to look into her eyes. She now no longer works at the mine and all memory of this sinful woman had been erased. Another face in the photograph attracted my attention. It was that of a strikingly beautiful teenage girl, maybe eighteen years old who, even in a photograph, had a sense of presence. Her cotton print pantaloons were tied at the waist and feet, she had a floral blouse and was partially covered by robes. In my mind, I called her the Şapdağ girl. Her head was covered with a chador which made her even more attractive.

After a few cups of sweet çay, we climbed the cliff to inspect the geology of the silica mine. I asked the foreman if I could take photographs and the men in their dirty ragged work clothes posed for a still life photograph of them swinging sledgehammers. Such still life photographs could have been taken in the goldfields of California or Victoria in the mid-late 19th Century. The miner's clothing, footwear and lack of safety equipment were no different. No steel-capped boots, no hard hat, no gloves, no dust masks, no eye protection and no spats for leg protection.

The women looked on while the photographs were taken, talked, laughed and tried to avoid eye contact. Many of the knapping women had a rasping cough and I noticed that the Şapdağ girl was among them. She too had the cough. She was still in the same clothes from the photograph in the cay hut, she was a little taller and older, maybe in her late teens or early twenties. She was even more beautiful than in the photograph and her poise suggested that she was just not aware of how beautiful she was. She was confident and challenging and her brownish skin was covered in grey silica dust. A young mineworker only had eyes for the Şapdağ girl but she didn't seem to or didn't want to see him.

To my surprise, the foreman suggested that I photograph the women.

One of them must have quietly asked him and, because I was no threat to the social stability of the village and their women, he gave me permission. Some of them didn't want to be photographed and the rest wanted a group photograph. The Şapdağ girl not only wanted to be photographed with the group but to my astonishment asked to be photographed alone. She removed her headscarf for the photographs and actually looked into my eyes. She smiled. Her greenish-brown eyes were piercing me, they followed me round like the eyes of the Mona Lisa. They never left me. I wonder what she was thinking? Did she realise that she was doomed? It was fortunate that there was some employment for her within walking distance of her village and the money would have kept her extended family fed. The Şapdağ girl had to work otherwise a few people would not eat. Marriage would have been arranged but not to the young mineworker who admired her and, if she didn't die in childbirth, then the silica dust in her lungs would leave young orphans to repeat the cycle. She probably knew this and accepted that this was her future and a portrait photograph would be her immortality.

I returned to the Şapdağ silica mines after an absence of some years. The photographs I took of the workers were also hanging in the çay hut and the pit had advanced one more bench into the cliff. There were still young women knapping silica into cobbles. Some of them had the same rasping cough I heard on my previous visit.

The Şapdağ girl was not there. She would have been if a watery mist for dust suppression was used or if she had worn a cheap dust mask.

(1991)

Gümüsler

In the spring time, the nomads bring their flocks of sheep from the valleys to the emerging grasslands of the high Taurus Mountains. They travel long distances to graze their ancestral pastures. They always travel the same route, graze the same pastures and camp at the same springs. Wooden picket sheep enclosures are constructed at the camps for protection at night time and their dogs have metal-spiked collars to prevent them having their throats ripped out in a fight with a wolf. Each day the shepherds bring the flocks from the pens to the grasslands and back.

After the departure of the shepherds last autumn, we surveyed in a very large grid. Each point was defined by a marked wooden peg. Such pegs are ideal for the construction of sheep pens, fire wood or carving into crooks. We had experienced this before and were in the habit of asking the locals not to remove our grid pegs until we had finished our surveying work and the winter snows had melted. Once they knew what we were doing, then the only pegs that were disturbed were those pushed over by sheep trying to scratch themselves.

We kept track of the shepherds as they came through Niğde to Gümüsler. The Turkish word for silver is gümüs and, because the maps were so poor, we had to use ancient place names to give us a clue about the geology and old mines. We knew why we were in the right area but did the shepherds know? As the caravan of shepherds and their flocks ascended through the gridded areas, it was explained what we were doing and why we needed the wooden pegs in the ground over summer. They were happy to have company on their ancestral mountains and the chief invited me to visit them once they had established their alpine camp.

The Taurus Mountains snake their way through southern Turkey. They formed as a result of the twisting and pushing associated with the opening of the Mediterranean Sea as northward-moving Africa collided with Europe. Large kilometre-thick slices of older rock had been pushed or thrust over younger rocks. These thrusts once contained broken rocks that were now cemented together with quartz. These thrusts were at altitude and draped themselves over hill and dale. It was here that we found the gold. Well, not really. It had been discovered in pre-Roman times.

We certainly were not the first to be attracted to the area. The thrusts had numerous small pits which had been sunk for gold. The workings were minor, very little tonnage had been removed and they were possibly of Hittite age. The miners knew what they were doing. The pits were at the intersection of fractures in the thrust where the gold had been remobilised and grew as coarser grains. Glacial gravels shed from the high peaks had been mined on a massive scale on the grassed alpine plateaux and Roman relics were still present. It was fortunate that at that time the planet was considerably warmer than at present and the Romans were probably able to work their mines all year round. Unlike the Carthaginians, the Romans did not explore for minerals and invasion was commonly to acquire areas that had previously been mined for lead, silver, copper, tin and gold. So too with Gümüsler. The silver and gold were probably originally discovered and mined by the Hittites which gave the Romans good enough reason for invasion. The home of the Hittites, Cappadocia, was not too far away. Hittites were miners and it was quite possible that they worked the high Taurus Mountains in times when the climate was far more hospitable.

High in the Taurus Mountains, I wondered whether the average suburban Australian was aware of the influence that Hittite miners had on their lives. Although not an expert on the culture of nanology, I am aware that the humble garden gnome was used in the underground iron and copper mines of Cappadocia. In this land of phallic hills, strange monuments and cave dwellers, the garden gnome at a cave dwelling or underground mine entrance was a necessary protection against evil spirits and devils.

Like many good ideas, it was stolen by others. The gnome entered Teutonic mythology with the exploitation of metals from the mines of central Europe in the Middle Ages, of which the best known characters are Snow White and the seven vertically-challenged. The area of ancient mines in Saxony and Bohemia centred around the Erzgebirge also required gnomes to ward off evil spirits and devils, despite the deeply Christian population. There are some in this life who have been called to be gnome specialists. The purist gnome specialists tell us that a gnome can be no greater than 68 centimetres high, must have a grey-white beard and must be dressed in a red bonnet (*Zipfelmütze*), a green apron and over-sized shoes. Next time you look at a humble garden gnome, please treat it with far more respect as it is a relic from thousands of years of superstition. And they work. No one in suburban Australia with garden gnomes can prove that they've ever been visited by evil spirits and devils!

Traverses through the alpine grasslands and across the spine of the Taurus Mountains were necessary to map the shape of the thrust surfaces. On one such traverse, I came across the shepherd's camp. Their tents were circled around a spring and the water ran down slope across the fresh alpine grasses into a number of picket sheep pens. The white tents were a hybrid between a yurt and a tepee. Most of the shepherds were out in the hills tending their flocks in the alpine meadows and the chief came out to welcome me.

A visitor is a gift from Allah. A large red carpet was laid out on the grass in the sunshine for the chief and his visitor. A circle of onlookers developed and we were waited on by a number of women. My field boots were removed, I was given an embroidered cushion to sit on and I was welcomed with a drink of cold curdled sheep's milk. This was followed by another drink, eyran, made from diluted yoghurt and some ekmek (a local bread). The chief discussed the quality of the grazing lands this summer and I was able to explain in detail about our exploration activities.

The chief was inquisitive about the other lands I had worked in and a number of times commented upon my white hair and blue eyes. The onlookers pressed closer for a full facial view of their visitor. It was clear from the quality of my clothes, my field vehicle and the equipment that I used that I came from affluent circumstances. The chief asked me about my homelands.

Where was your homeland? How did people live? What did they eat? Was there enough food? How did people dress? Did the young go to school? Did the snow also cover the grazing lands for half the year? What was the religion of my homeland? Who was my leader? Why did I need to leave my homelands? Did I have any sons? Explanations were not constrained by language but by the size of one's world. I pulled out my field book and drew a map of the world for the chief. I showed where his lands were and where my lands were. I was able to tell him that I lived a long distance from him, more than 1,000 days walk or 5,000 days walk with a flock of sheep. I drew a map of Australia and, with various coloured pencils, drew the mountains, cities, the various agricultural activities, the mining centres, the forests and the deserts. I showed him the population distribution, the breakdown of the various religions in Australia and drew a picture of the average modest suburban house with its 2.2 children. I tried to explain that children went to school and that my land had adequate resources for its population.

He was interested in Australia's sheep. By using *Kalabity*, a 778 square mile property in outback north-eastern South Australia that I know well, I sketched out what a large outback sheep station looked like. Because of the fences and the lacks of wolves, he recognised that shepherds were not necessary but couldn't understand why we didn't use the milk from sheep. He was not aware that in the 19th Century before pastoralists could afford to fence outback properties, shepherds looked after flocks and protected them from dingoes and aborigines.

After two hours of paying my respects. I decided that it was time to get moving and bash a few rocks. The chief quietly spoke to one of the older women who returned with a young woman. The chief asked whether I would like this woman and whether I could take her back to my land to work for me. The chief was a pragmatic altruist. The plump brain-damaged teenager was a burden to nomadic shepherds living on the bread line and she would certainly have a far better life in those strange lands where they were so affluent that sheep's milk from huge outback stations was not used.

It was difficult to explain that the chief's proposal was just not possible. I did not attempt to explain the basics of immigration and visa conditions. I did not attempt to explain that in my far-off land there are many forgotten abused kids and mentally disturbed people on our city streets. I did not try to explain that the young woman would be far better off with her own family rather than transposed into an alien culture and family. It was just all too delicate and difficult. I stated that my chief only allows his own in my lands and that the chief's daughter would not be allowed to enter my chief's lands. At that time, Bob Hawke was Prime Minister of Australia.

As I was driving away from the camp, I looked in the mirror and saw that the young brain-damaged woman was running after the vehicle, pleading and crying.

(1991)

Outalpa Springs 1995

Outalpa Springs

The Adelaidean is characteristically barren, cold and windswept. In winter, the freezing lazy wind can't be bothered to go around and cuts straight through. There is very little outcrop and rare dead finish tries to grow on the calcrete coating. The Adelaidean rocks have a great story to tell. Written in these rocks is evidence of two massive ice ages when the Australian continent, somewhat smaller than its current size, was at the equator yet Australia was covered by ice. There were kilometre-thick ice sheets at sea level and at the equator.

There were numerous ice advances and ice retreats in this part of the world around 700 million years ago. When the ice advanced, sea level dropped and the oceans were covered by sea ice. There was no continental shelf. Ocean water circulation was stopped and the cold dark ice-covered oceans became starved of oxygen. Iron dissolved in this oxygen-poor water. On land when the ice advanced, it scraped the land surface clean, masses of boulders, cobbles, pebbles and rock flour were transported great distances and these ice-entrapped rocks polished and then scratched the bare rock surface. These scratches give the road maps for the direction of ice flow.

When the ice retreated during an interglacial, glacial debris was left covering the land and this debris was permeated and flushed by glacial melt waters. Because there was no continental shelf during glaciation, sea level must have risen at least 600 metres because shelf sediments are seen in interglacial sequences. Glaciers calved icebergs that floated out to sea. As the icebergs melted, they dropped boulders picked up by the advancing glaciers. Rocks were dropped onto the sea floor marine muds which ended up containing boulders of all sizes. There are sand trails and splash marks from ice-rafted stones hitting the sea floor 700 million years ago. In today's world, every time there is a surge of glaciers, the same thing happens.

As the ice retreated and seawater warmed, the sea ice started to break up. Ocean water circulation started again, the oceans dissolved oxygen from the atmosphere and the dissolved iron precipitated as iron oxide muds on the sea floor. There are extensive sequences in outback South Australia of iron-rich mudstones containing drop stones. The message written in the rocks is about climate changes far greater than anything measured in the modern world.

Over the last 100 million years, Australia has had an exciting history. The continent of Australia was at the South Pole yet the climatic conditions were temperate to tropical. Volcanoes were active, vegetation was prolific, dinosaurs ruled yet needed big eyes because half their life was spent in polar darkness and Australia was still joined to India, Antarctica, South Africa and South America in a giant polar southern supercontinent. Australia and India stretched away from Antarctica, a large rift basin covered by the Southern Ocean formed and Australia drifted northwards at 12 centimetres per year. During this voyage, India separated from Western Australia and charged towards the Asian continent. India collided with Asia resulting in the wrinkling of the crust to form the Himalayas and the Tibetan Plateau.

Australia slowed down to drift northwards at 7 centimetres per year and collided with southeastern Asia to give Indonesia earthquakes and volcanoes. Australia also got rid of New Zealand about 100 million years ago and gave them their well-deserved earthquakes and volcanoes. Once South America drifted away from Antarctica some 34 million years ago, a circum-polar current isolated Antarctica and it froze. By that time, Australia had escaped well north and had a temperate to tropical climate. Once Antarctica froze, inland Australia became arid and coastal areas remained temperate to tropical.

A long history of high rainfall, tropical vegetation and deep leaching of soils is well preserved all over Australia with the maximum tropical conditions around 30 million years ago. Soils were leached to impoverishment, endemic plants adapted to survive on nutrient-poor soils and the landscape was ground down to flattened plains with sluggish meandering muddy rivers.

While Australia was enjoying tropical conditions, the escape of India, the opening of the Tasman Sea and the collision with Indonesia produced stresses in inland Australia. Old weaknesses were re-activated and blocks rose and fell. In eastern Australia, the Great Dividing Range started to rise, changed the course of rivers from easterly to westerly and climate was tempered. In the outback, ranges of mountains were pushed up and basins formed from subsidence. This process is still taking place. For example, the Flinders Ranges are still rising with regular earthquakes and earth tremors around Copley whereas Lake Eyre is sinking.

Some six million years ago, it all changed. Glaciation followed a long period of global cooling and the alps of southeastern Australia and Tasmania were covered by ice. The same sort of glacial debris that was left over Australia 700 million years ago now covers much of Tasmania. There were five glaciations and five intervening periods (interglacials) when the climate was warmer and wetter. In the interglacials, many areas of inland Australia that are now salt lakes were fresh water lakes surrounded by lush vegetation. In inland Australia during glacial times, conditions were very windy, cold and dry. The red sand, typical of the outback, was blown by the cold dry winds into dunes. The winds bought salt air from the oceans, lakes dried and left salt and the winds in inland Australia spread salt which still troubles us today.

Inland Australia has poor soils resulting from millions of years of tropical leaching with remnants of tropical vegetation that are covered by a blanket of dune sands and salts resulting from past glacial times. When there is water, the dune sands are wonderful agricultural soils as any outback garden or Murray-Darling Basin farm shows. The water and air circulation patterns are such now that inland Australia has low and sporadic rainfall, mainly as a result of cyclones. It is only when Australia is finally stitched onto Asia as part of the EuropeIndiaAsiaAustralia Supercontinent that we can expect a different inland climate.

The rare permanent springs of the outback are sites of what must have been gushing spa waters in former tropical times. One of these is Outalpa Springs, located in contorted Adelaidean rocks which have the story of past climates written in stone. Outalpa Springs, a soak at the headwaters of Doughboy Creek, now consists of a well, defunct yards, a collapsed stone dwelling and a pile of rubble, possibly an old shearing shed. There may even have been a vegetable garden on the flats.

It was an old shepherd's camp. In the 19th Century, large sheep stations were unfenced and did not run merino sheep. It was far cheaper to use shepherds to tend to the flock rather than to fence in large areas for the small sheep. Shepherds would take the flock into the harsh rocky hills for saltbush and blue bush pickings and return to the camp to water the flock with saline water and pen the sheep for protection against dingoes and spearings. Water from the springs was used by humans, sheep and wildlife.

On the barren prickly flat down the hill from the house was a cemetery with thirteen graves, most of which suggest a high infant mortality because of the grave size. There must have been quite a few people that lived at Outalpa Springs suggesting that it was a permanent water supply. Adelaidean mudstones with drop boulders have been piled into mounds at the grave sites and only one grave had a complete headstone. The headstone, also with glacial drop boulders showing the history of past climates, has a poignant inscription in capital letters of recent human history beneath a cross:

JOHN PARY DEAD JANUARY 1866 SON OF EMANUEL PARY OLD 2 YEARS 4 MONTHS

Who was Emanuel Pary? It's an Irish name. Did he come to Australia because of the 1844 potato famine which resulted in the death of a third of his country folk and the immigration of another third? Did he come to the New World after serving in the Crimea War? Why did he come to Australia and not the United States of America? He was certainly better educated than many of his contemporaries because he could write. He must have loved his infant son John to spend many long hours carving the inscription to give his infant son John some semblance of dignified immortality in the harsh unforgiving outback. Emanuel Pary knew it was January 1866 but not the exact day.

Was there a Mrs Pary or was John Pary's mother a common-law wife? Did John Pary have siblings? How did the women cope in such a hostile environment, especially in child birth? Were the cassia, acacia, everlastings and Sturt desert peas used to decorate the humble Pary tent or house and put on John's grave? Did the lemon grass get used for tea or insecticide? Was one of the unmarked graves that of John Pary's mother? How did the Pary family travel from Adelaide, some 400 kilometres distant to Outalpa Springs, when there were neither roads nor railways at that time? Did the Pary family get attacked by aboriginals who clearly must have inhabited the area because of small soaks of permanent water, petroglyphs, paintings and tools?

Was John Pary born at Outalpa Springs? Did the poor-quality spring water kill baby John? Was death by gastroenteritis, typhoid or cholera? Or was it by drowning after torrential rain? Maybe a snake or spider bite, an infected wound or a horse accident? In those days there were more people on a *per capita* basis killed from horse accidents than in today's world from car accidents. What would have become of John Pary if he had lived his designated three score and ten years? Would he have been one of those that worked on the 5,400 kilometre-long dingo fence, the longest fence in the world? Would John Pary have fenced the adjoining properties of *Outalpa*, *Plumbago* and *Bimbowie* in the 1880s? Would John Pary have built some of the grand homesteads in the outback in the 1880s? Would he have sought a fortune in the declining goldfields of Victoria or the Broken Hill mines, discovered in 1883 and only 150 kilometres away? How would he have eked out a life in the 1890-1891 depression, a depression that hit Australia far harder than the Great Depression of the 1930s?

Would John Pary become a small land-holding squatter only to be financially destroyed by the rabbit plague and depression of the 1890s? Would John Pary's sons have been gassed and killed at the Somme? How would the elderly John Pary have subsisted in the Great Depression of the 1930s? Would the elderly John Pary have seen a flying machine, heard a wireless or spoken on the telephone? Did John Pary have any siblings who would now have teenage great great grandchildren?

The Outalpa Springs are a sobering reminder that past generations had a far lower standard of living and quality of life than we now enjoy. Our wealth, infrastructure, social security, health and education benefits today were built on the shoulders of unknown giants like Emanuel Pary. In Pary's time, the choices were simple. Starve or work. Tending stock, droving, clearing and working on the land, building fences, factory work, digging up minerals or transporting goods kept food on the table and often required very long periods away from family. Travel for months was normal, somewhat unlike the generous conditions of today's fly-in fly-out workers. There were very few shiny bum or intellectual jobs. Work was physical, hard and for long hours. There were no unions, no rights, no minimum wage, no equality and no fringe benefits. There was only hope underpinned by Christianity. People survived.

They, like us, also suffered crippling pain upon the death of one of their children. Food and water were scarce and not very nutritious and the average longevity was about half that of today. Reading and writing was a luxury, very few people owned property, work was backbreaking and there was no social support structure. If there was a proximal family, there may have been very limited support during periods of illness. If there was a debilitating injury or fatality at work, then it was bad luck. At those times, as long as each day bought no injuries or death and one square meal, half a bed and a bit of a roof, then everything else in life was a bonus. In those days, there was not an obesity epidemic.

The outback gives us stories of the past written in stone. Stories of climates, continents and catastrophes and answers to some of the profound questions of natural science. In the isolated outback, one often finds a solitary grave and place names such as Dead Man's Hill that could tell a story.

The writing on a headstone at a lonely outback grave site at Outalpa Springs was a human story for which an infant's death produced only questions but no answers.

(1993)

On the Camino, Spain 1988.

The environmental impact of creation

In the beginning, God floated the idea of creating Heaven and Earth. He was immediately served with an injunction by Greenpeace to prevent any creative activity whatsoever as He had not undertaken an environmental impact study and had no permit to work.

At the hearing, God was cross examined and asked why He wanted to undertake this massive project, especially as it appeared that it was extremely unlikely that any social benefit would derive from His venture. The Wilderness Society reminded God that His Bible stated that "*the earth was void and empty and darkness was upon the face of the deep*" hence the area where He wanted to creatively meddle could be classified as a pristine wilderness. God successfully argued that unless Earth could be seen, it could not be classified a wilderness area. Upon further questioning, God revealed that by Him saying "*Let there be light*" the wilderness area could be seen for assessment of its environmental value.

This created pandemonium in the courthouse. How could God create light without burning something that would pollute the Universe? Had He considered the smoke, thermal and optical pollution that His creation of light would produce? What would be mined to produce all this energy? Would the mining be open pit or underground? What was God to do with the tailings and waste? Was God aware of the dangers of greenhouse gases and nuclear energy? In order to seek compromise, God argued that He would create a pollution-free thermonuclear powerhouse however, at the mention of the word nuclear, the masses at the court hearing broke into histrionics. God faced aggressive questioning from the assembled environmental movements. Would His giant thermonuclear power generator really work? Could the safety of thermonuclear fusion be guaranteed? What about Chernobyl? In order to allow his proposal to proceed, God suggested that instead of thermonuclear energy, He would create solar energy. A warm inner glow entered the hearts of those in the courthouse, the assembled detractors agreed that solar power would be far better environmentally than thermonuclear power and some of the more sensitive souls were so touched by God's environmental concern that they actually wanted to shake His hand and compare sandals.

The remaining hard core continued to question God on His alternative energy proposal. Wouldn't precious energy be wasted if light were emitted from the Sun all the time? God had a brilliant idea and, in order to conserve energy, God suggested that He divide light and darkness and He would call the light Day and the darkness Night. The assembled environmental masses thought that this was an inspired zero emissions, carbon-neutral, energy-saving proposal and grudgingly acquiesced to this creative step.

However, the next creative step had God in a spot of bother. When God was asked how Earth would be covered, He answered *"Let there be a firmament made amidst the waters; and let it divide the waters from the waters"*. Greenpeace, the Australian Conservation Foundation, Friends of the Earth and miscellaneous other environmental lobby organisations voiced strong objections. If God created a firmament, would not the mining industry pillage the firmament for minerals? God tried logic and argued that a firmament was necessary in order to produce the 210 tonnes *per capita* of water, food and minerals that would be consumed by Western people at the end of the second millennium AD. The gag was applied, the court adjourned and God was refused permission to continue argument on the firmament. After the adjournment, God was given permission to make a brief statement. He stated that homelands and sacred sites could not be annexed unless there was a firmament. The gathered masses wanted to voice objection to this obvious apartheid yet embraced the idea of compulsory partitioning of homelands to allow the tangible expression of their inherited guilt. God was given permission to create a firmament. Questioning then shifted to His creation of waters.

Neither Greenpeace nor Save the Aquatic Fauna wanted God to create the oceans because this would tempt the petroleum industry into offshore drilling. It was feared that fishing and tourism where people have fun might take place. It suddenly dawned on God that logic was His worst defence and He started to invent arguments which would seem plausible. Rather than discuss the necessity of oceans for climate, resources and survival, God insisted that His creative venture must have oceans. God argued that the oceans would allow the sustainable harvesting of organic salt and that natural kelp may eventually be a cure for cancer. Without oceans, God argued, there would be no habitat for dolphins and whales. The court room erupted into cheers, people struggled to pat God on the back, environmental leaders announced that the god of nature would be named Gaia, God signed numerous autographs and a warm ambience settled over the tear-stained masses. However, because so few at the hearing had faith in God, He was instructed to apply for the necessary permits from the appropriate local government, maritime, shipping, agricultural and water commissions before undertaking this creative step. Those in court were pleased that there was the potential for greatly increasing the size of the bureaucracy.

When God tried to explain that the barren firmament should be environmentally enhanced with vegetation, there was a vigourous objection on the basis that the flora might be commercially exploited for profit. God was now well aware that it was totally pointless to argue that flora would be the key to survival and so He stated that He would only create species native to planet Earth. He strengthened his argument by suggesting that if the firmament was covered by abundant vegetation, then all could be vegetarian. The vegans in court tried to cheer but they just didn't have the energy. God's popularity was increasing and the environmental leaders now privately felt that God was good however, as a matter of ideology, they were committed to objecting in public to every creative step God wanted to make. Environmental leaders showed commercial pragmatism. How could they keep the wheels of public donations spinning if they were not seen in public to object to everything? It was eventually agreed that, subject to the Noxious Weed Board and Forestry Commission permission, that if God vegetated the planet with only native species and not genetically-modified species, then He would be issued with a permit to say *"Let the earth bring forth grass, the herb yielding seed and the fruit tree yielding fruit."*

In order to win over various New Age movements, astrologers, UFO watchers and the Lunar Cycle Birth Movement, God announced to the court that He wanted to state *"And let there be lights in the firmament of the heaven to give light upon the earth"*. The various New Age movements were asked to voice their objections however, because their answers required the construction of sentences and the use of words of more than two syllables, they could only look bleary-eyed at God, monotonously chanted *"God is cool"* and fondled His long flowing robes.

Some disquiet was expressed about God's plan to have only native flora without soft cuddly environmentally sensitive fauna. A passionate discussion ensued with some suggesting that if there were animals on the firmament then they would be hunted, killed and eaten whereas others wanted soft cuddly objects to allow them to have publicity about the plight of these animals in order to raise donations such that they could keep being paid. The question of methane emissions from animals was raised. It was unanimously agreed that, in the absence of evidence, that methane emissions were bad. However, a compromise was struck. If God could create domesticated sheep and cattle that emitted no methane, then the indigenous native wild animals could democratically decide whether they choose to, or choose not to emit methane. The gathered masses felt good, especially as God had declared He'd create only vegan cattle and sheep. On the condition that God adhered to the various statutes of the Native Flora and Fauna Protection Act, various National Parks Acts, the Fisheries Acts and observed the RSPCA regulations, God was given permission to say *"Let the waters bring forth abundantly the moving creature that hath life, and the fowl that may fly above the earth"*.

The proposal to create man met insurmountable ethical and political difficulties. The vivisectionists were concerned about the morals of rib transplant on a sleeping patient without the required documentation, the Women's Electoral Lobby would not agree that man was to be created before woman, animal liberationists were incensed that man was to have dominance over animals, the gay lobby did not want woman created from man yet the transexual lobby were delighted, the right-to-lifers argued that rib tissue had inalienable rights and ASIO insisted that, before people were created, they first must have security clearances. God now had the measure of His opponents and announced to the court that He would not only create indigenous people and that He would set aside a special week for indigenous people, another for women, another for left-handers and another for those with in-grown toe nails. Opposition evaporated, there were excited suggestions about having a special year dedicated to indigenous people and, after no thought, it was decided that these matters were aired at a subsequent public hearing, then God may be given permission afterwards to say *"Let us make man in our image, after our likeness, and let them have dominion over the fish in the sea, and over the fowl of the air, and over the cattle, and over all the earth"*.

Despite the onerous conditions laid down by the court, God was willing to adhere to all these conditions and, at the end of the hearing, He was asked when He hoped to commence His creative project. Great consternation arose when God stated that He wanted to complete the project in six days. The unions would not agree, too many bureaucrats would have to work too fast to an exacting budgeted deadline with no time for taxpayer-funded yoga sessions. This was unprecedented compared with all previous attempts at productive creativity which had been prevented by prolonged industrial action. God was advised that the EIS and necessary permits have an application period of 90 days followed by a public viewing period of 60 days in each capital city. Upon receipt of all of the information, the granting bodies required a minimum of 180 days to review the applications prior to the public hearing. If there were no appeals arising from the public hearing, the process would take at least 36 months from the time of application before God was permitted to commence His creative venture.

God became positively catatonic. To His horror, God suddenly realised that He had only focussed on creation of the heavens and Earth and had forgotten to create the rarest commodity on Earth – common sense. The red, black and green tape of the regulatory processes were such that it was not possible for God to create Earth in the proposed six-day period.

God fulminated "*To Hell with My project*" and Earth, as we know it, was then created.

(1993)

Goosestepping for God

In the book *Finding inner peace and strength* (Doubleday, 1982), the well known American television evangelist Jerry Falwell stated:

> *"The Bible is the inerrant word of the living God. It is absolutely infallible, without error in all matters pertaining to faith and practice, as well as in areas such as geography, science, history, etc"*

So writes an extremely popular religious fundamentalist. Do we really only need one book for our passage through this life? Should we ignore such a simplistic view of our world or do Falwell and followers represent a threat to society?

If we analyse such a statement, it is clear that it is nonsense. The geography of the Bible is highly equivocal. Even in our own lifetime, place names (e.g. Leningrad) and the names of countries (e.g. Rhodesia) change. Those of us who spend much time using maps can show that almost every modern 1:250,000 map contains a geographic error. Does the Bible tell us of the location of Mt Ararat? Certainly not. In fact, the biblical resting place of Noah's ark (Mt Nisir) was probably replaced in the Dark Ages by Mt Ararat. The Bible of the 3rd Century AD cited the resting place of the ark at the geographically unknown Mt Nisir. The word Ararat entered the Armenian language in the 12th Century AD and, because near Mt Ararat (Kücük Agri in SE Turkey) is a 300 x 50 cubit boat-sized block of rock in a mountain mass flow debris, the ark location and dimensions may have entered the Bible in the last millennium.

As for the science of the Bible, did the biblical scribes really know about continental drift, the effect of gravity on light, the double helix structure of DNA, the behaviour of sub-atomic particles, the nature of disease,

Newtonian laws and Einstein's relativity. I think not.

The biblical compilers and scribes recorded the observations of the day and attempted to interpret natural phenomena. Natural phenomena which held as fascination were generally catastrophic events such as meteor showers, earthquakes and floods. Many observations of unusual phenomena were verbally handed down from generation to generation, were transposed incompletely across cultures and languages and then finally written in Hebrew only later to suffer multiple translations with variable interpretations and cultural bias such that the various individual Bible translations vary significantly.

However, the Bible is the foundation of Western Civilisation and is a literary masterpiece. In Pygmalion (George Bernard Shaw), Professor Higgins advises Eliza Doolittle: *"Remember, you are a human being with a soul and the divine gift of articulate speech: that your native language is the native language of Shakespear[sic] and Milton and The Bible."* Even the avowed atheist Richard Dawkins concedes *"a native speaker of English who has never read a word of the King James Bible is verging on the barbarian."*

The science of the Old Testament is fascinating. There is no doubt that scanty observations of natural phenomena are recorded. What I find interesting is that primitive nomadic peoples thousands of years ago attempted to interpret these natural phenomena. These interpretations are at variance with interpretations today. However, we can see the evolution of knowledge and thought.

To claim, as Jerry Falwall does, that there can only be a literal interpretation of the Old Testament belittles all biblical scholarship. Because much of the Old Testament is contradictory, it could be argued that literal interpretation damages Christianity as the Bible becomes the object of mockery.

If the Bible is inerrant, then the science of the Bible makes a farce of this perceived inerrancy. For example, the Earth was formed out of water (2 Peter 3:5), the Earth rests on pillars (1 Sam. 2:8), the Earth does not move but stands still (1 Chron. 16:30), the Earth has ends and edges (Job 37:3) and the Earth has four corners (Isa. 11:12; Rev. 7:1).

Do we really believe as a matter of literal inerrant truth that our flat Earth formed from water, stands on pillars and that the Sun rotates around the Earth? Does the sky have water above it, does the firmament support the Sun, moon and stars and does the firmament have windows (Genesis 7:11)? If one is to have a literal belief of the Old Testament, then this must be the scientific view of the Solar System and the Universe.

Does modern biology agree with the inerrant biblical biology which states that bats are birds (Lev. 11:13, 19; Deut. 14:11.18), some fowls have four feet (Lev. 11:20-21), camels do not have cloven hooves (Lev. 11:4), a mustard seed is the smallest of all seeds and grows in the greatest of all plants (Matt. 13:21-32), turtles have voices (Song of Sol. 2:12), some four-legged animals fly (Lev. 11:21) and a foetus can understand speech (Luke 1:44)? The concept that the world's languages didn't evolve slowly but appeared suddenly (Gen. 11:6-9) has no linguistic, historical or anatomical basis.

In I Kings 7:23, an altar from Solomon's Temple was ten cubits across and thirty cubits around. This means the mathematical constant pi (π) is exactly 3. All school children know that π is not 3 but 3.14159 etc and there is nothing to suggest that the Hebrew author was approximating. If π is exactly 3, then no machine, aeroplane, ship, motor vehicle etc could be designed or would operate. The Bible's mathematics is consistent and in II Chronicles 4:2, we also read that π is exactly 3.

Astronomy has always held a fascination for humans and biblical astronomical interpretations all reflect the science of the day. The literal view of the Universe is that the Earth is fixed, immovable and non-rotating (Joshua 10:12; I Chron. 16:30; Psalm 93:1; Psalm 96:10 and Psalm 104:5) and such a view was used in the Holy Writ to convict Galileo of heresy.

In Ecclesiastes 1:5, we learn that *"The sun also riseth, and the sun also goeth down, and hasteth to the place where he rose"* which can only be interpreted to mean that the Sun rotates around a flat earth. We still today talk of sunrise and sunset suggestive of a flat Earth. Flat earthism is a basic concept of biblical cosmology.

The ancient Hebrews were clearly flat earthers and in the Genesis creation story we learn that the Earth is covered by a vault and that celestial bodies move inside this firmament. Such geometry is only possible if the Earth is flat. In Daniel 4:10-11, Daniel *"saw a tree of great height at the centre of the earth, reaching with its top to the sky and visible on the earth's farthest bounds"*. Simple geometry shows that such visibility would only be possible on a flat Earth. Such a view is confirmed in the New Testament (Matthew 6:13) when Satan took Jesus to the top of a mountain from where they could see all the kingdoms of the Earth. If the Earth were indeed flat, then jet lag would not exist.

The biblical view of the Universe is somewhat different from our views, unless one has a belief in the inerrancy of the Bible. Again, this view is a reflection of the times. The Universe was three storied with a cavernous underground Hell, a flat Earth supported by pillars, and an astral dome from which the Sun, moon and stars were attached At times, stars fell and, because there was a real danger of the sky falling in, the firmament was supported by pillars and above the firmament were waters.

Such a view was an attempt to explain the biblical world in terms of volcanic eruptions, distance to the horizon, basic building skills, rain clouds, meteor showers and the blue sky (Genesis 7:11, 28:12; Exodus 20:4; I Kings 8:35; Job 11, 7-8; Psalms 78, 23-24; 138:8; 148:4; Isiah 7:10; 14, 13-15; Ezekiel 26: 19-20; Amos 9:2; Matthew 11:23; Romans 10: 6-7; Philippians 2:10). One admires the observations and ingenious explanations of our Universe by tribal people thousands of years ago. However, in today's space age, one can only treat those who take a scientific literal view of the Bible with incredulity.

The biblical story of creation is convoluted and contradictory. There are more than two hundred documented contradictions in the Bible. Does it really matter if the Genesis 1 and Genesis 2 versions of creation are different? I don't really think so as it is clear that the older view of creation (Genesis 2) would be different from a younger one. The two creation stories are first pass scientific explanations thousands of years ago by nomads living on a very small part of the planet. Our modern view on the origin of the world around us is somewhat more sophisticated. It is based on a voluminous amount of repeatable scientific evidence.

Our view of the evolution of the modern world is not correct and our modern view will be refined with more scientific evidence. The biblical creation stories are beautiful accounts by primitive nomads struggling to understand the world around them. They are neither right nor wrong but do form an interesting part of our evolving culture. Why should we be forced to accept only one literalist view as the absolute truth?

The expansion of knowledge since the compilation of the Bible is exciting. Scientific knowledge now doubles every seven years. The interpretative framework of the biblical compilers is clearly unsupported by the substantial repeatable scientific evidence collected over the last two thousand years. For fundamentalists in the 20th Century, whether Christian, Hindi, Islamic or Buddhist, to blindly cling to the knowledge base of thousands of years ago as objective truthfulness defies credulity. Furthermore, for someone like Jerry Falwell to use applied modern science such as television to transmit this message and yet to adhere to biblical science is absurd.

In the fundamentalist, there is a hunger for certitude driven by a deep psychological unease. Surely there must be more to life than ambiguity and paradox? Many people move to fundamentalist religions but become restless because they are still knee deep in the real world despite an inner voice that says that this is the way, the truth and the light. As a scientist, I am excited by the unknown.

Although a rational person can easily dismiss fundamentalism as the shibboleth of simplicity, the fundamentalist mind is tortured with fear, inconsistency, contradictions, and guilt and lusts for power and authority. Fundamentalism regularly raises its anti-intellectual head in Judeo-

Christian, Islamic and Hindu communities. Fundamentalism grows in periods of uncertainty, deprivation, warfare and social stress. Christian and now Islamic fundamentalism has grown very rapidly in recent years, especially in the US and Middle East respectively. I suspect that it is a response to uncertainty and rapid change. We live in such times today and, because of the internet, we are living in a period of time where change and instant communication have never been so rapid.

Fundamentalism can drift towards totalitarianism as we have seen in many cultures, especially in the Islamic world. However, Christianity has provided a powerful force against totalitarianism as shown by Lech Walesa and Pope John Paul II who were instrumental in changing Catholic Poland from communism to a democracy. The church has had significant roles in changing the political landscape, for example, by pushing for the abolishment of slavery which is still alive and well in many African and Islamic countries.

Are we really certain that we will be employed, supported and in good health for the term of our natural life? Do we really know if, in our lifetime, we will be destroyed by unseen nuclear, chemical and biological weapons? Do we really know what the next great technological advance will be, especially when we are struggling to keep up with the last generation of technological advances? Can our offspring cope with a decrease in educational standards thereby allowing them to solve problems? Can the world cope with rapid political, national and economic changes in the former eastern bloc countries and the Middle East? Can a humanitarian world cope with Africa or countries that appear to have no hope? Can a country change when self interest has been replaced by national interest thereby threatening democracy?

The fundamentalist mind cannot come to terms with such uncertainty and the possibility that we humans are a purposeless accident on planet Earth. Christian fundamentalists have an impoverishment of imagination and appear to have no necessity for exercising the mind. Body exercise is regarded as healthy but, by contrast, mind exercise is fearful, unnecessary and possibly even sinful. This has been my experience in more than a decade of dealing with creationists, who represent the educational wing of fundamentalism. As soon as discussion requiring argument, synthesis and critical analysis arises, the fundamentalist retreats into dogma regarding the authority of the Bible. Such discussion is the antidote to scholarly inquiry and demonstrates the theological Cyclopean nature of fundamentalism. Entry into the Kingdom of the Blind is comfortable. It is especially comforting because an open mind could possibly create uncertainty and fears. By retreating to the dogmatism of fundamentalism, one has the spiritual endorsement for the turning of a blind eye to honesty and free inquiry. The fundamentalist now has the foundation for the acceptance of religion based on bigotry and ignorance.

Because God is accessible to all, including those of even the most modest and impaired cerebral power, the rigour of using intellect in probing Christianity is non-compulsory. One recalls Voltaire when questioned *"Do you believe in God?"*, he argued that the most confusing answer one can give is to say *"Yes"*.

Nevertheless, the fundamentalists insist that the Bible is literally true and infallible, that the Bible has no contradictions and that it is in all of its parts divinely inspired and divinely guaranteed. It is this approach to the Bible that is the only legitimate Christian approach for the fundamentalist. In contrast to previous times, the fundamentalist is not happy with the label fundamentalist. The required image is that of academic respectability and the fundamentalist label is not acceptable for this image. Once the brain is in the fundamentalist mindset, it is not possible to see the contradictions and the lack of logic.

In the fundamentalist press and preaching, the savage intolerance and illogical criticism of Christians who do not embrace fundamentalism is indeed a revelation. Those profoundly professing fundamentalism regard themselves as exclusive and theologically and morally correct and superior amongst Christians. Some even regard themselves as chosen people. In fundamentalist writings and churches, the fundamentalist's prime aim is to impose his understanding of the Bible. The Bible is somewhat like a legal statute book for which absolute obedience is the required answer. The commander is the minister or pastor and absolute obedience to his fundamentalist interpretation of the Bible is synonymous with absolute obedience to a commander. As a measure of the fundamentalist follower's insecurity, this obedience is willingly given. This obedience and the resultant certainty is most appealing, especially to young and emotionally battered people searching for some meaning to their lives. The fundamentalist follower in the flock immediately knows with certainty where they stand with their God. Unfortunately, this God is an idol in the mind of the fundamentalist.

With fundamentalism, all the rules are known. It provides a safety net. There is a kind of security with one's own authoritarian God telling you what to do and think. No difficult choices. No weighing up of pros, cons, advantages, disadvantages and consequences. All pre-ordained and written down. With this view of life, you always know where you stand with your God and those around you.

Guilt has a special place in the fundamentalist mind. It is the fuel that drives the machine. If there is no guilt, then there is no fervent fundamentalist flock. The commander must saturate his flock with guilt in order to maintain his power as commander. Fundamentalist church services are solemn occasions punctuated with guilt-ridden self-abasement during which the commander deems to be the medium for forgiveness. Such actions allow the commander to be superior to and authoritarian with his flock. The commander's self-congratulation of having avoided wrong doing is a technique to allow the commander to maintain control of the flock. Even the Jimmy Swaggert's of the world can continue unabated if they are forgiven because, after all, we know that the Devil made Jimmy do it.

The place of women is firmly fixed. There are no female ordained fundamentalist pastors. Women have their place: Kinder, Küche und Kirche. Such a place in life for women is replete with scriptural authority

(I Timothy 2:12): *"I permit no woman to teach or have authority over men: she is to keep silent."* Fundamentalist men impose this view on their chattels and, because of insecurity, the women allow themselves to be placed in such a position. The biblical family comprises a repressive power structure in which the male is dominant. The husband is very clearly the unquestioned head of the house. The wife willingly submits, accepts her place in the home, accepts her role of supporting her husband and bringing up her children in fear. The wife has been trained to be totally spiritually, financially and emotionally dependent. If she was already insecure or emotionally damaged, then marriage to her fundamentalist head of the household can only exacerbate her plight. If the wife has an opinion of her own or does not submit to the power structure, then she must be fearful of the Lord's displeasure and her children are commonly turned against her because she has wilfully wandered off the well signposted path into the clutches of Satan. Remember Eve. Remember Lot's wife. In extreme cases, the wife will lose her children or be murdered.

In many ways, fundamentalism is a patriarchal protest movement. Feminism is a tool of the Devil, the result of evolution or one of Satan's clever tricks because it appears to challenge the biblical basis of the traditional family unit with the man as the head of the house. Mention of sex, or even worse, homosexuality, bisexuality or transsexuality, launches apoplexy to galactic heights. Such a response is somewhat unusual because the Old Testament is embellished with much uncomplicated sex. In contrast, idolatry is regarded as a cardinal sin. However, in fundamentalist circles, idolatry is quite normal and sex and nakedness invokes feelings of guilt and fear. It is possible that the fundamentalist is frightened of good healthy sex because it requires coming to terms with one's own identity without the support of accoutrements such as clothing. It is possible that the fundamentalist is more at ease in defining what he is not rather than what he is?

The thread that unites fundamentalism is self-righteous power. Many fundamentalists are driven by the lust for power, money and gratification of basic hormonal drives. Despite the fundamentalist's inward and small view of the world, the dominant motivating force is the hunger for power, authority and the trappings of power. To be a medium for purveying the absolute and literal interpretation of the Bible is an expression of the fundamentalist's perceived power and authority. Fundamentalism allegedly supported by scriptural authority has created numerous theocracies based on power and authority however such theocracies are more difficult to establish in the secular democratic world that is underpinned by Christianity. As second prize, the fundamentalist establishes a theocratic church, family and educational structure.

It is the role of fundamentalism in education that is of great concern to me. Some years ago, the fundamentalists gained control of education in many theological colleges. Once the insecure or emotionally damaged material for brainwashing was selected, these were set upon the Christian community to breed like rabbits. In the public education system, the rise of creationism (or creation "science") and the burgeoning of "Christian" schools is a reflection of this rise. This rise is commensurate with the increase in popularity of the charismatic, evangelical and Pentecostal churches who, on the surface, provide a far greater sense of belonging than the conventional churches in the absence of theological scholarship. This rise is coincidental with the massive technological boom that we are currently experiencing. This rise is rooted in insecurity.

The fundamentalist has been brainwashed and sees the role of education as brainwashing. Woe betide the child in a "Christian" school who questions sacred cows. Public education, whether in State or "Christian" schools, must be open to rigorous scrutiny because it receives public funding. The major denominations schools are exposed to such scrutiny, the Catholic schools have their own scrutiny body (Catholic Education Office). The permeation of science and history curricula with biblical pre-suppositions is a perpetuation of the fundamentalist's own brainwashing, the best example of which is creation "science". The proponents of creation "science" argue that there are two equally valid scientific views to explain the origin of life. Epistemology is ignored. What is not stated is that the science of creation "science" is fraudulent or unsustainable.

This is the entrée – the exposure of every school child to the narrow bigoted views of Protestant religious fundamentalism. It does not seem to matter to fundamentalists that we live in a pluralist secular country and that some parents might wish to guide the religious education of their children. The main course is the control of the education curricula and systems and this has already happened in some parts of the USA. Creation "science" thrives on the scientific illiteracy of the community and that in a democracy there is also enormous tolerance.

Because it has been shown many times that creation "science" is not science and that it is the political face of fundamentalism, the tactics have now changed. Creation "science" is now no longer touted as an alternative view to evolution, possibly because it is overtly religious. The choices now being promoted by those fundamentalists who wish to control education about the origin of life are now intelligent design (i.e. redressing of creation "science" [good guys]) or evolution (integrated interdisciplinary science [bad guys]). The overt religious nature of creation "science" has changed to the more covert intelligent design which is commensurate with the rise by stealth in the teaching of creation "science" in our schools. The fundamentalist sees his greatest opportunity for corporate growth in our schools.

In the USA, the killing of medical practitioners (e.g. Gunn, Britton) who undertake abortions was by fundamentalists who considered that they were ordained to practice an eye-for-an-eye. As Rev. David Trosch stated: *"Members of the American Civil Liberties Union will be placed high on the target list. Members of the National Organisation of Women, members of Planned Parenthood and other pro-abortion or choice organisations will be sought out and terminated as vermin are terminated. It will be seen as a necessity for the defense of innocent life."*

This is the friendly face of fundamentalism. Fundamentalists have created a god in their own image. Their god is vengeful, punishing and unforgiving. Conversations or interviews with fundamentalists are a revelation because such people do not appear as raving lunatics talking gibberish. There are no vestigial doubts about their position. They are certain.

Jewish, Hindu and Islamic fundamentalism regularly rear their ugly head. The comments about Christian fundamentalism apply equally to other religious fundamentalists. For example, in Pakistan the death sentence was ordered by a Court for a fourteen year-old boy. Furthermore, this child was ordered to do two years hard labour before being executed. The Pakistani penal code was amended in 1992 and now has provision for anybody who directly or indirectly defiles the name of the Holy Prophet, whether visibly or by innuendo. The penalty is execution. A person can be convicted of blasphemy on the word of a single witness. Neighbourly disputes take on a deathly new face. Religious fervour leaves minorities vulnerable, as was the case with the fourteen year-old boy. The boy, with two other suspects, had been accused by his village imam of throwing scraps of paper containing blasphemous remarks into a mosque. Two of the suspects were murdered by zealots before a court hearing. During the hearing, it was shown that the fourteen year-old boy was illiterate. Nevertheless, he received the death sentence.

To see fundamentalism as the preserve of the mullahs, the illiterate and the obscurantists is to misread its influence. All Pakistani politicians, motivated as much by personal political ambitions as ideological conviction, have pandered to its strictures. All have indulged in *pro forma* denunciation of Western secularism. They are able to have it both ways, appeasing the masses by passing the death sentence and then appeasing the international community by commuting it to a long prison sentence as a gesture of clemency.

The appeal of fundamentalism is that it is a totalitarian approach to life that imposes an immovable conformity. This is my objection to fundamentalism. Fundamentalism is a major frightening threat to civilisation. It undermines the epistemological basis of knowledge, the independence of thought, the freedom of the individual and the freedom to practice the religion of one's choice.

(1994)

Malice in wonderland

Heat, bushfires. Just another Australian summer, some hotter, some wetter, some cooler, some drier. As per usual, the Northern Hemisphere freezes and the blame game is in overdrive. At the 2005 Montreal conference, Greenpeace's Steven Guilbeault stated: "*Global warming can mean colder, it can mean drier, it can mean wetter, that's what we're dealing with.*"

It is that simple! If it's hot, it's global warming, if it's cold, it's global warming. Demonstrators in sub-zero temperatures in Montreal chanted: "*It's hot in here! There's too much carbon in the atmosphere!*" The same apocalyptic Guilbeault states "*Time is running out to deal with climate change. Ten years ago, we thought we had a lot of time, five years ago we thought we had a lot of time, but now science is telling us that we don't have a lot of time.*" Really!

In 1992, Greenpeace's Henry Kendall gave us the Chicken Little quote "*Time is running out*", the *Irish Times* of 1994 tried to frighten the leprechauns with "*Time running out for action on global warming, Greenpeace claims*" and in 1997 Chris Rose of Greenpeace maintained the religious mantra with "*Time is running out for the climate*". We've heard such failed catastrophist predictions before. The Club of Rome on resources, Ehrlich on population, Y2K and now Greenpeace on global warming.

Over the last 30 years, the US economy grew 50%, car numbers grew 143% and energy consumption grew 45%. There were decreases in air pollutants of 29%, toxic emissions of 48.5%, sulphur dioxide levels of 65.3% and airborne lead of 97.3%. The world is becoming a better place. Most European signatories to the Kyoto protocol had greenhouse gas emissions increase since 2001, whereas the US emissions fell by nearly 1%. Furthermore, carbon dioxide (CO_2) credits rewarded Russia, (east) Germany and the UK who had technically/economically backward energy production in 1990. By the end of this century, the demographically doomed French, Italians and Spaniards may have too few environmentalists to fund Greenpeace's business.

So what really do Greenpeace want? A habitable environment with no humans left to inhabit it? Destruction of the major economies to prevent a computer projected catastrophe that suggests that that the planet will warm by 0.07°C over a few decades. A look at past computer projections of climate shows that the computer models and measurements are unrelated. The computer models got it wrong and yet we are expected to entertain the idea of changing global economies based on the same computer models. Pull the other one.

Does it matter if sea level rises a few metres or global temperatures rise a few degrees? No! Over time, sea level changed by up to 600 metres, atmospheric temperatures by some 20°C, carbon dioxide varied from 20% to 0.03% and our dynamic planet just keeps evolving. Life still keeps doing what life does. Greenpeace dogma, contrary to scientific data, implies a static planet, as do the creationists. Even if sea level rises by metres, it is probably cheaper to address this change than reconstruct the world's economies based on a speculated sea level rise.

For some 80% of time, Earth has been a warm wet greenhouse planet with no ice caps. When Earth had larger ice caps, climate was far more variable, disease depopulated humans and extinction rates of other complex organisms were higher. Thriving of life and economic strength occurs during warm times. Could Greenpeace please explain why there was a pre-Industrial Revolution global warming from 900 to 1300 AD? Why was sea level higher than at present 6,000 years ago?

There is no debate about climate change, only dogma and misinformation. For example, is there a link between hurricanes Katrina and Rita and global warming? Two major hurricanes hit the Gulf Coast six weeks apart in 1915, mimicking Katrina and Rita. If global warming caused recent storms, there should have been more hurricanes in the Pacific and Indian Oceans since 1995. Instead, there has been a slight decrease at a time China and India increased emissions of CO_2 astronomically. The impact of hurricanes might seem more severe because of the blanket instantaneous news coverage and because more people now live in hurricane-prone areas on more expensive houses hence there is more property damage and loss of life.

Only a strong economy can produce the well fed who have the luxury of espousing with religious fervour their uncosted impractical impoverishing environmental policies. By such policies, Greenpeace continues to exacerbate Third World grinding poverty. The planet's best friend is human resourcefulness with a supportive strong economy with reduced release of toxins. The greenhouse gases, H_2O, CO_2 and CH_4, have been recycled for billions of years unrelated to human politics.

Climate change has taken place for thousands of millions of years. The extraordinary hypothesis that humans cause climate change must be supported by extraordinary evidence. It has not been shown that any measured modern climate change is different from past climate changes. In the past, climate has changed due to numerous processes and these are still driving climate change.

Past global warmings have not been driven by an increase in atmospheric CO_2 and, during the time that humans have been in Earth, there has been no correlation between temperature change and human emissions of carbon dioxide. Without correlation there can be no causation. The underpinning assumption is that human emissions of CO_2 drive global warming and, in order to arrest the warming trend, human emissions of CO_2 must be reduced.

Which part of the 130-metre sea level rise over the last 14,400 years is human-induced? To reduce a multi-component chaotically variable natural process like climate change to being due to just human-induced CO_2 emissions is pseudoscience, especially as the sum total of human emissions is only 3% of the total annual emissions.

Emissions of CO_2 from human activities are from the production of energy, metals and cement; land, air and sea transport; and heating and cooling. Despite very generous research funding from the public purse, it has yet to be shown that the human emissions of CO_2 actually drive global warming. If it could be shown that the human emissions of CO_2 drive global warming, then it would also have to be shown that the natural emissions of CO_2, 97% of total annual emissions, do not drive global warming. This has not been done.

Natural emissions are mainly from oceanic degassing and mantle degassing via millions of submarine volcanoes, mid ocean ridge volcanicity and ocean floor fractures with less voluminous emissions from mantle degassing via terrestrial volcanoes, mountain degassing, fractures, earthquakes and respiration.

In past times when the Earth's atmosphere had hundreds of times the current CO_2 level, there was no runaway greenhouse, no irreversible warming and no climate catastrophe. In fact, there were ice ages. Can Greenpeace explain this?

The erroneous assumption that the dominant driving force for global warming is the emission of CO_2 by humans has been made in the absence of considering the effects of the Sun, plate tectonics, the Earth's orbital oscillations, oceanic oscillations and extra-terrestrial radiation.

The oceans remove most of the CO_2 from the atmosphere. What is rarely considered is that CO_2 is plant food, it is rapidly removed from the atmosphere and it has an atmospheric life of about 7 years. Soils and rock weathering also quickly remove CO_2 from the atmosphere. There is an underlying assumption that once humans emit a CO_2 molecule, it stays in the atmosphere for a very long time or even forever. Any CO_2 emitted by humans is part of the carbon cycle that involves recycling of CO_2 through the atmosphere, life, water and rocks.

The human-induced global warming ideology is underpinned by

the perception that the planet is static and that dynamic change only occurred once humans started to emit CO_2. Nothing could be further from the truth.

The Industrial Revolution in Europe and the USA triggered a great increase in human emissions of CO_2 from the use of fossil fuels. This also led to increased prosperity, health, longevity and the rise of the middle class, many of whom now object to the use of coal.

The planet has been warming over the last 300 years since the Maunder Minimum and it has not been shown that any part of this general warming trend is of human origin. Furthermore, during this general warming trend, there have been both cooling and warming events.

Another Industrial Revolution is taking place in Asia, fossil fuels are bringing people out of poverty and the rate of emissions of CO_2 from burning fossil fuels has accelerated. However, there is no correlation between the emissions of CO_2 by humans and temperature. In fact, the increased content of CO_2 in the Earth's atmosphere has led to the greening of the planet and increased agricultural productivity.

If only human emissions of CO_2 drive global warming, then there should have been no warming and cooling events before the Industrial Revolution. However, pre-Industrial Revolution climate changes were fast and numerous events of cooling led to depopulation.

The arguments to support human emissions of CO_2 drive global warming are based on models wherein the principal variable is CO_2. Measurements and observations do not support this hypothesis. Past natural warmings have had a delayed effect on increasing atmospheric CO_2. This is the exact opposite of the populist catastrophist mantra. If climate models are run backwards, past events of cooling and warming are not seen.

We have now had more than two decades of climate models and these models have not predicted what was measured. Without correlation of CO_2 with temperature over time, there can be no causation hence there is only one conclusion: Human emissions of CO_2 do not drive global warming. This shows that complicated models in a multi-component chaotic dynamic system are an unreliable and naïve attempt to understand Nature.

Models, research and energy policy are underpinned by the fallacious assumption that human emissions of CO_2 drive global warming. Such ideology thrives in a dumbed-down educational environment where there is little knowledge of history and geology.

The policies of Greenpeace impoverish and kill people in the Third World and are a huge financial strain on Western countries. Is that what Greenpeace want?

(2006)

The long history of climate

For 80% of time, planet Earth has been a warm wet greenhouse planet. Polar icecaps are rare, plants have only been on Earth for 10% of time and 99.99% of all life that has ever existed is extinct. Global atmospheric CO_2 and CH_4 have been variable over time and have decreased over time whereas O_2 has been in the atmosphere for 50% of time, has greatly fluctuated and has increased over time. There have been five major and numerous minor mass extinctions of complex life. Extinction opens new environments for colonisation and, because former terrestrial animals have become extinct, we humans now have a habitat. It is claimed that we are in a period of mass extinction but the evidence is to the contrary. Sea levels have risen and fallen thousands of time by up to 600 metres, land levels constantly rise and fall and massive rapid climate changes have derived from supernovae, solar flaring, sunspots, meteorites, comets, uplift of mountain ranges, pulling apart of oceans, stitching together of land masses, drifting continents, orbital changes, changes in the shape of Earth, ice armadas, changes in ocean currents and volcanoes.

The major components of the atmosphere have been added by volcanicity and other components are added by life, principally from the organisms that have ruled and continue to rule the world (bacteria). The messages written in stone show that the lithosphere, hydrosphere, atmosphere and biosphere are constantly interacting on our dynamic evolving planet. There is no evidence to suggest that the future of planet Earth will be significantly different from its past. However, planet Earth is not a spaceship and some great environmental changes in the past have been related to rocky and icy visitors from space.

In the long ago

Planet Earth condensed 4,567 million years ago (Ma) from recycled stardust. Since that time, the continents have been enlarging, Earth materials have been constantly recycled and the Earth and all associated systems have been dynamically evolving. The Earth has not stopped being an evolving dynamic system just because humans now live on the continents.

During the first 800 Ma of planetary history, Earth was bombarded by large asteroids, one of which broke off a mass to form the Moon. Volcanic activity was degassing Earth. The main gases emitted from volcanoes were and still are the greenhouse gases H_2O, CO_2 (carbon dioxide) and CH_4 (methane) together with minor helium, nitrogen compounds, sulphur compounds, acids and rare gases. The earliest atmosphere probably had a high ammonia and sulphur dioxide composition and these gases were quickly scrubbed out of the atmosphere by rainfall. The main greenhouse gas on Earth is H_2O. These volcanic gases accumulated to form a primitive O_2-deficient greenhouse gas atmosphere. Early accumulations of water in oceans were vapourised by large asteroid impacts. The intensity and frequency of impacting has decreased over time and now only 40,000 tonnes of extraterrestrial material is added to Earth each year.

As soon as there was liquid water on Earth, there was life. This early bacterial life thrived, the O_2-deficient atmosphere was hot and CO_2- and CH_4-rich. Rain was extremely acid. Early Earth was very warm and wet however there is some evidence to suggest that there were minor periods of local glaciation. The origin of these climate variations is unknown. Bacteria slowly diversified and, by the time the Earth was middle aged, one group of bacteria had emitted such large quantities of O_2, that the atmosphere became slightly oxygenated. Some of this excess O_2 was trapped in rocks by weathering, most dissolved in the oceans resulting in the precipitation of iron oxides. It is these iron oxides that form the great iron ore fields of planet Earth (e.g. Pilbara, WA). Life, the atmosphere, the oceans and the rocks interacted, a process that has been occurring for at least 2,500 Ma on our dynamic evolving planet.

For at least the last 2,500 Ma, the continents have been pulled apart and stitched back together. Every time the continents are pulled apart, huge quantities of volcanic H_2O, CO_2 and CH_4 are released into the atmosphere. When continents stitch together, mountain ranges form. Mountains are stripped of soils, new soils form and remove CO_2 from the atmosphere, these soils are stripped from the land and the CO_2 becomes locked in sediments on the ocean floor. Because of the inverse solubility of CO_2, events of glaciation remove CO_2 from the atmosphere whereas CO_2 is added back to the atmosphere during interglacials.

The origin of the greatest climate change on Earth is an enigma. Between 800 and 600 Ma, there were two major glacial events and numerous smaller events. This sequence of glacial rocks is very well displayed in the Flinders Ranges of Australia. Sea level changed by up to 600 metres and interglacial sea temperatures were +40°C. Furthermore, glaciation was at sea level and equatorial. Bacterial life survived, which is no surprise, because we now know that bacteria live in O_2-poor or O_2-rich conditions in acid and alkaline hot springs, in highly radioactive water, deep in the Earth in cracks in rocks, in volcanic rocks in mid ocean ridges, in clouds, in ice and in every environment on Earth. Bacteria always have been the dominant biomass of Earth and yet their role in interaction with the atmosphere is unknown. Bacteria some 400,000 years old have been resurrected from the Greenland ice sheet and from salty liquid inclusions of water in the 250 Ma salt beds of Texas. After glaciation, the atmosphere had some 20% CO_2 and bacteria thrived and diversified in the warm oceans. After a failed attempt (Arkaroola Reef), multicellular life appeared (Ediacaran fauna, first discovered in South Australia), there was a mass extinction of the Ediacaran fauna, life diversified and used the CO_2 to make shells and skeletons. This explosion of life (and predation) from 543 to 520 Ma gave us all of the major life forms currently present on Earth.

Plants appeared at 470 Ma, there were numerous minor mass extinctions and there was a major mass extinction of multicellular life at 430 Ma. Vacated ecologies were quickly filled and life continued diversifying. More minor mass extinctions followed and there was another major mass extinction at 368 Ma. Between 368 and 251 Ma, massive coal deposits formed, there was a major 50 million year period of glaciation and the atmosphere was blessed with a very high CO_2 and O_2 content. Life continued to diversify. Minor mass extinctions continued and, at 251 Ma, the biggest major mass extinction on Earth took place. Some 96% of species became extinct, evidence for impacting is weak and the smoking gun is volcanicity in Siberia. Massive volcanic activity over a very short period of time exhaled huge volumes of CO_2 into the atmosphere inducing a greenhouse and this was counterbalanced by the release of sulphur compounds that reflected heat and light. The resultant climate was cooler, acid rain may have destroyed large tracts of vegetation thereby creating a collapse of terrestrial environments and the seas may have become acid for a very short period of time. Life diversified quickly to fill the vacated ecologies.

Another major mass extinction took place at 217 Ma. A swarm of asteroids hit the Northern Hemisphere, a continental mass was fragmented, large volumes of lava were released and the Atlantic Ocean formed. The planet was still a warm wet greenhouse planet with the normal cycles of rising and falling sea levels, rising and falling land levels and changing climates. The record written in stone by fossils in the period 520 Ma to the present shows that the planet is a warm, wet, greenhouse, volcanic planet with the normal cycles of rising and falling sea levels, rising and falling land levels and changing climates.

The day before yesterday

Some 120 million years ago, Australia was at the South Pole enjoying a temperate climate. There were minor glaciers in the highlands, volcanoes were active and dinosaurs adapted to the long periods of darkness by evolving enlarged optic nerves. Global sea level was more than 100 metres higher than at present, the sea surface temperature was 10 to 15°C higher than now and many continents were covered by shallow tropical seas. Planet Earth was a warm wet greenhouse paradise and thick vegetation covered the land masses. Atmospheric CO_2 was about 1% when the world's major coal deposits formed 368 to 251 million years ago. It is currently 0.04%.

From 251 to 120 million years ago, the global CO_2 content varied greatly and increased to a peak 6% CO_2 120 million years ago. This derived from intense volcanic activity associated with continental fragmentation. Thick vegetation covered the land masses. The atmospheric O_2 content greatly increased to 35% at 300 Ma, decreased and then increased to 27% at 150 Ma. It is currently 21%. During times of high atmospheric O_2 content, there was spontaneous combustion of the atmosphere, global bushfires and increased erosion. Australia started to pull away from Antarctica at about 100 Ma. It drifted northwards at 7 cm/year, the Tasman Sea opened and the Indian Ocean opened with India starting to drift away from Western Australia.

The opening of the Tasman Sea produced the rise of the Great Dividing Range, the diversion of the major river systems and changes to the climate of eastern Australia. A minor mass extinction of life 90 million years ago was the result of volcanoes in the Indian and Pacific Oceans belching out CO_2 and other gases into the oceans and atmosphere. The oceans may have become acidic for a geological instant, some 26% of advanced life became extinct and there were warm times until volcanism waned. Volcanic emissions of CO_2 are common. In 1984 and 1986, burps of CO_2 from the volcanic crater lakes of Monoun and Nyos respectively killed thousands and added CO_2 to the atmosphere. Near Mt Gambier, CO_2 is commercially extracted from rocks, one small hot spring on Milos (Greece) contributes to 1% of the planet's volcanic CO_2 and huge quantities of CO_2, the planets second most common volcanic gas, constantly leaks from at least 3.5 million unseen submarine volcanoes.

An extraterrestrial visitor at 65 Ma impacted Earth but the major mass extinction of life at that time probably derived from a huge volcanic event in India with the associated release of CO_2, CH_4 and sulphur gases into the atmosphere. Ancient soils, vegetation and rock chemistry show that conditions were tropical. Another minor mass extinction at 55 Ma was caused by a Caribbean volcano. There was a rise in sea temperatures by up to 8°C for 100,000 years, atmospheric CO_2 was 10 times that of today, the oceans became acid for a geological instant, the oceans lost dissolved O_2 and the ocean floors released CH_4 into the atmosphere. During these warmer times, plankton sucked up the atmospheric CO_2, mammals thrived and life filled the vacated ecologies. Atmospheric CO_2 decreased from 3,500 to 700 parts per million (ppm) within a million years, stayed low until 47 Ma and went up and down to about the present level (380 ppm) at 40 Ma.

India collided with Asia at 50 Ma. Uplift produced the Tibetan Plateau that started to scrub CO_2 out of the atmosphere. The Tibetan plateau is still rising and CO_2 is still being scrubbed out of the atmosphere. The Drake Passage opened as South America drifted from Antarctica, a circum-polar current developed and Antarctica refrigerated at 34 Ma. Changes in submarine topography along the Tasman Rise, the closing of the Mediterranean Sea, the onset of polar glaciation and the flow of polar bottom waters formed climate zones, a feature that had not previously existed during the previous long periods of warm wet tropical climates. There were a number of minor mass extinctions, comet and meteorite impacts and sea level changes. For example, the Murray Basin became a large sea, retreated and then advanced again only to start its final retreat at 5 Ma.

Warm currents in the Indian Ocean were deflected and drifted through the Great Australian Bight and up the Pacific coast of Australia. Southern Australia from 17 to 14.5 Ma was again tropical with mid-latitude temperatures 6°C warmer than today. Atmospheric CO_2 was 180 to 290 ppm. This warming occurred when atmospheric CO_2 was 30 to 50% lower than today! Land changes closed the Straights of Gibraltar at 7 Ma, the Mediterranean Sea again dried and because there was less salt in the oceans, parts of the oceans froze. Both the ice and salt reflected sunlight and the planet cooled further. By 5 Ma, Earth was so cool that very slight orbital wobbles now had a bearing on climate with climate cycles every 41,000 years. At 1 Ma, this changed to 100,000-year cycles characterized by 90,000 years of glaciation and 10,000 years of interglacial. We are currently in one of those interglacial periods. Cooling changed forests to grasslands and primate extinction and diversification to upright bipeds took place. By 2.67 Ma, central American volcanoes had closed the seaway between the Pacific and Atlantic Oceans, explosive volcanoes in Kamchatka had added dust to the atmosphere, dust reflected sunlight and the planet cooled further. The Northern Hemisphere polar ice cap formed.

The penultimate interglacial was 128,000-116,000 years ago. *Homo erectus, Homo neanderthalensis, Homo floresiensis* and *Homo sapiens* coexisted, sea level was at least 6 metres higher than at present and the planet was far warmer and wetter than now. We live in unusual times when only one species of *Homo* is on Earth. During this interglacial, there was more vegetation than today and atmospheric CO_2 was 78% of today's concentration. After warming, the atmospheric CO_2 and CH_4 content increased suggesting that atmospheric temperature rise drives an increase in atmospheric CO_2 and CH_4 contents. Orbital-driven cooling commenced, the eruption of Toba (Indonesia) produced dust that reflected sunlight, sea level dropped and glaciation continued. Three species of *Homo* became extinct and we, *Homo sapiens*, were reduced to 4,000 breeding pairs. We very nearly became extinct. During the history of the latest glaciation, armadas of ice were released into the sea every 7,000 years resulting from the physical failure of thick ice sheets. These had a profound effect on climate. Short cool periods occurred every 1,100 to 1,300 years.

The zenith of the last glaciation was 20,000 years ago. Sea level was 130 metres lower than today, polar temperature was 10 to 15°C lower than today and there were very strong cold winds. The northern hemisphere was covered by ice to 38°N with more northern areas such as Scandinavia covered by more than 3 kilometres of ice. The loading of the polar areas with ice changed the shape of the planet, the planet's rotation changed and as a result ocean currents distributing heat across the Earth were changed. Humans lived very short lives around the edge of ice sheets. Australia was buffeted by anti-cyclonic winds that deposited sand dunes and carried sea salt spray that was trapped in the inland basins such as Lake Frome and Lake Eyre. Tasmania and parts of the south eastern highlands of Australia were covered in ice and sea level was so low that Aboriginals walked to Tasmania from mainland Australia. Rainforests disappeared and the Amazon Basin consisted of grasslands and copses of trees. Coral reefs were stressed and disappeared in colder conditions when sea level was lower.

Yesterday

The northern polar ice sheet started to melt 14,400 years ago. There were very rapid and major temperature fluctuations, sea level rose and fell and the total sea level rise over the last 14,400 years has been at least 130 metres. Land masses previously covered with ice started to rise. For example, Scandinavia is still rising and has risen more than 340 metres over the last 14,400 years. As a counterbalance, the Netherlands, southeastern England, Schleswig-Holstein and Denmark are sinking. The breaching of dams of melt waters filled the oceans with cold surface waters 12,900 to 11,700 and 8,500 to 8,000 years ago resulting in changed climates, an increase in sea level and changes to ocean currents. After these intensely cool periods, temperatures rose by 5 to 10°C in the space of a few decades. Sea level rise resulted in the breaching of the Mediterranean into the Black Sea Basin some 7,600 years ago and is probably the origin of the Sumerian, Babylonian and biblical stories of a great flood.

One of the consequences of a massive sea level rise over the last 14,400 years is that the West Antarctic Ice Sheet was no longer unpinned by the land. Two thirds of the West Antarctic Ice Sheet collapsed into the oceans and sea level rose 12 metres. The final third of the West Antarctic Ice Sheet has yet to collapse to produce a 6 metre sea level rise as part of the dynamic post-glacial climate on Earth. Climate changes induced by changes in ocean currents cooled North Africa, grasslands changed to desert, humans migrated and the great Mesopotamian cities were established.

Sea levels were 1 to 3 metres higher in the Holocene maximum 6,000 years ago. It was a few degrees warmer and there was 20% more rainfall. Cold dry periods, glacier expansion and crop failures between 5,800 and 4,900 years ago resulted in deforestation, flooding, silting of irrigation channels, salinisation and the collapse of the Sumerian city states. Long periods of El Niño-induced drought resulted in the abandonment of Middle Eastern, Indian and North American towns. About 1460 BC, Thira (Santorini) exploded and threw 30 cubic kilometers of dust into the atmosphere. The tsunami, ash blanket and destruction by Thira greatly weakened the dominant Minoans. This led to the rise of the Mycaeneans and Greeks. One volcano changed the course of western history.

Global cooling from 1,300 to 500 BC gave rise to the advance of glaciers, migration, invasion and famine. Global warming commenced again at 500 BC, there was an excess of food and great empires such as the Ashoka, Ch'hin and the Romans grew. Contemporary records of crops, lake sediment proxies and Roman clothing shows that conditions were some 5°C warmer than today.

In 535 AD Krakatoa exploded, as did Rabaul in 536 AD. The Earth passed through cometary dust in 536 AD. The dusty atmosphere reflected heat and light and darkness prevailed and, as a result, the climate cooled and there was famine and warfare. Changes in solar output resulted in the Medieval Warm Period from 900 to 1300 AD. The first to feel the change were the Vikings who were able to navigate the northern waters, colonised Newfoundland and Greenland and established extensive trade routes as far south as the modern Gulf States. On Greenland, there were grain crops and livestock and Eric the Red invited settlers to come to

Greenland because of its booming agriculture. Such agriculture would not be possible today. The warmer wetter climate of Europe produced excess crops and wealth that resulted in the building of castles, cathedrals and monasteries. As with previous warming events, there was great prosperity, fewer wars and less starvation.

In 1280 AD, volcanic eruptions on Iceland, weakening solar activity and a change in ocean currents started the Little Ice Age. The North Sea froze in 1303 and 1306 to 1307, there was massive famine in 1315 and the plague pandemic attacked the weakened population in 1347 to 1349. There was massive depopulation and it took Europe 250 years more to reach the population of 1280 AD. During the Little Ice Age, there were warmer periods associated with sunspot activity. During minimum sunspot activity (1440-1460, 1687-1703 and 1808-1821), the intensely cold conditions were recorded by the Dutch masters and King Henry VIII was able to roast oxen on the frozen Thames. There were food shortages. Short cold dark periods occurred after the eruptions of Tambora (1815) and Krakatoa (1883) respectively. In fact, 1816 was known as the "year without a summer". This was the time when Turner painted stormy oceans and skies full of volcanic dust, Mary Shelley wrote *Frankenstein* and Byron wrote *Darkness*.

Today

There has been warming for the last 300 years since the end of the Little Ice Age. The twentieth Century and early 21st Century AD are times of natural post-glacial rebound. Ice sheets, a rare phenomenon in the history of time, still exist. Sea level is relatively low, as are global temperatures and atmospheric CO_2. Between 1920 and 1945, there was a period of slight warming, then a period of cooling and warming again commenced. In 1976 to 1977, global temperatures in the lower atmosphere jumped 0.3°C, sea surface temperature in the equatorial Pacific jumped 0.6°C, sea surface temperature during upwelling increased 1.5 to 3°C but there was reduced upwelling, the heat content of the upper 300 metres of the world's oceans increased, there was increased wave activity in the North Sea and the length of the day changed. The stepwise increase in temperature in 1976 and 1977 shows that there was a major re-ordering of the ocean heat transport coinciding with an orbital change expressed as a change in the length of the day and solar changes. Maybe global warming of the 20th Century is just a measure of the variability on a dynamic evolving planet?

To put such measurements into perspective over the history of time, changes in atmospheric temperature in the 20th Century can only be considered small and slow. A >20 year global coverage of satellite atmosphere temperatures shows only modest warming in the Northern Hemisphere, a slight cooling in the Southern Hemisphere, a slight greening of the planet and increased crop productivity. Temperature measurements from balloons agree with the satellite measurements for the period of overlap. Because greenhouse warming is a phenomenon of the atmosphere and irregularly-spaced and adjusted ground temperature measurements are considered unreliable, significant changes should have been recorded. They have not.

Et moi

Science is married to evidence and bathes in modest uncertainty. The nature of science is scepticism and science encourages argument and dissent. Scientific evidence is derived from reproducible observation, measurement, experiment and calculation. Evidence in geology is interdisciplinary, terrestrial and extra-terrestrial and shows the complex and fascinating intertwining of evolving natural processes on a dynamic planet. Scientists engage in healthy argument about the veracity of evidence. On the basis of evidence, an explanation called a scientific theory is constructed. A scientific theory is the best available explanation of evidence, it may change with new evidence and it must be coherent with the existing body of knowledge. Scientists also argue about scientific theory. Scientific theories are testable and once the scientific theory has been tested over time, it becomes accepted into the body of knowledge. The word belief is not used in science because belief is untestable. This process of science has not taken place with the construction of what is popularly called the greenhouse effect, global warming, climate change or any other erroneous label. Furthermore, science is unable to make judgments about what is good or bad. These are judgments which vary with time and are based on contemporary politics, religion, aesthetics and culture.

Underpinning the global warming and climate change mantra is the imputation that humans live on a non-dynamic planet. On all scales of observation and measurement, sea level and climate are not constant. Change is normal and is driven by a large number of natural forces. Changes can be slow or very fast. However, we see political slogans such as "*Stop Climate Change*" or government publications such as *Living with Climate Change* demonstrating that both the community and government believe that climate variability and change are not normal. We have always lived with climate change and, whether we have governments or not, climate change will take place. By using the past as the key to the present, we are facing the next inevitable orbitally-driven glaciation yet the climate, economic, political and social models of today assess the impact of a very slight warming and do not evaluate the higher risk of yet another glaciation. Geology, archaeology and history show that during glaciation, famine, war, depopulation and extinction are the norm. Geologists are the ultimate climate scientists. They use integrated interdisciplinary science in the light of past climate changes and, from long experience, are sceptical of futuristic models. The validated geological history of the planet shows a different story to the incessant catastrophic predictions. It's no wonder that geologists think that human-induced climate change is nonsense.

In 1831, Admiral Sir James Robert George Graham had the Union Jack hoisted on a volcanic landmass that suddenly appeared near Sicily. It was called Graham Bank and was claimed by England. It was also claimed by the Kingdom of the Two Sicilies who called it Isola Ferdinandea, the

French (L'Isle Julia) and other powers who variously named it Nerita, Hotham, Scicca and Corrao. In the subsequent dispute over ownership, France and the Kingdom of the Two Sicilies almost came to war and England and the Two Kingdoms of Sicily had a diplomatic row. During the intense diplomatic dispute, the island quietly slipped back underwater. In 1987, US warplanes thought the dark mass 8 metres below sea level was a Libyan submarine and attacked it with depth charges. In February 2000 when the volcano again stirred, Domenico Macalusa, a surgeon, diver and the Honorary Inspector of Sicilian Cultural Relics, took action. He persuaded Charles and Camilla, the last two surviving relatives of the Bourbon Kings of the Two Sicilies to fund the bolting of a 150 kg marble plaque to the volcano at some 20 metres below sea level. The plaque pre-empted ownership if the volcano ever again rose above sea level. It was placed underwater in September 2001, by November 2002, person or persons unknown had smashed the plaque into 12 pieces.

This rock is worth nothing, is of no use as a territorial possession and is of no scientific interest and yet the French and Bourbons nearly came to war 170 years ago and the English and Italians are still in dispute.

Graham Banks serves to show that whatever political decisions we humans make, the land rises and falls, sea level rises and fall and climates change as they have done since the dawn of time.

(2007)

Rasp Mine core shed, Broken Hill, 2001

One volcano can ruin your religious ideology

In Iceland, one can have one foot in Europe and one foot in North America. The volcanoes of Iceland result from the pulling apart of the Atlantic Ocean. This process, rifting, depressurises hot high-pressure rock beneath Iceland. Water, carbon dioxide and other gases migrate to these depressurised zones, act as a flux and the mantle of the Earth beneath Iceland partially melts. These gases dissolve in the molten rock which buoyantly rises as a basalt melt. Water can be added to near surface molten rock from ice, ground water and seawater, as is happening in Iceland. As the molten rock rises, the weight of the overlying rocks decreases and a point is reached where gas dissolved in molten rock is explosively released. The same occurs when a warm bottle of carbonated drink such as champagne, beer, cola or soda water is opened.

In a volcanic explosion, a huge plume of expanding and cooling gas blasts through molten rock which instantaneously solidifies to particles of very fine-grained razor-sharp glass. This is what is commonly known as volcanic "ash". It's not ash, nothing was burned. This plume of "ash" is blasted high into the atmosphere by superheated gases, mainly water vapour and carbon dioxide. Volcanoes also emit sulphurous gases, the main ones being sulphur dioxide and hydrogen sulphide ("rotten egg gas"). It is water vapour and carbon dioxide that drive volcanic eruptions and, since the beginning of time, volcanoes have been adding greenhouse gases to the atmosphere. The reason why the Earth's atmosphere has been decreasing in carbon dioxide since the beginning of time is that there has been at least 2,500 million years of natural sequestration of carbon dioxide into carbonate minerals, sediments, soils and life. This process still takes place today. Over the last 500 million years, atmospheric carbon dioxide has decreased from 0.7% to 0.04%. We have a crisis of carbon dioxide – there is not enough of it.

Volcanoes are rare. Most molten rock rises because it has dissolved huge amounts of water vapour and carbon dioxide and becomes lighter than the surrounding rocks. As these gases boil off the molten rock, the crystallisation temperature of the melt rises hence most molten rocks from deep solidify as solid rocks within 15 kilometres of the surface. It is unusual when molten rocks erupt at the surface. The Earth's crust is constantly leaking gases and most of these derive from degassing and cooling melts at depth.

Basaltic volcanoes emit large amounts of carbon dioxide compared to the felsic volcanoes that occur in the Pacific Ring of Fire and the Mediterranean-Trans Asiatic Belt. There are at least 1,500 active terrestrial volcanoes and more than half of these occur in the Pacific Ring of Fire. Small amounts of carbon dioxide dissolve in terrestrial volcanic lavas whereas huge amounts of carbon dioxide dissolve in basalt. A recent estimate suggested that there are at least 3,477,403 submarine basaltic volcanoes off axis from the mid-ocean ridges. These volcanoes and associated gas vents and hot springs emit monstrous amounts of carbon dioxide. Most of the world's volcanoes are basaltic and occur in submarine environments where they are unseen, non-explosive and are no threat to humans. Massive eruption craters have only just been recognised on the floor of the Arctic Ocean and for eruptions to occur at such depths, the molten rock must have contained at least 13% dissolved carbon dioxide. Some eruptions only emit carbon dioxide and many deep water hot springs are surrounded by pools of liquid carbon dioxide. All new submarine basaltic rock is cooled by circulating seawater and the process of pumping seawater through basalt can actually produce heat. Most ocean water heat actually derives from both the Sun and submarine volcanoes.

The eruption of Eyjafjallajökull in Iceland is a very small eruption. Just a modest belch from a small Icelandic volcano has caused chaos with international air transport. There was a bigger eruption from the same vent in 1821-1823. The Icelandic volcano of Laki had an even larger eruption from June 1783 to February 1784 which produced "ash" and a massive haze of dry sulphuric acid clouds over Europe. The air was acrid, there was difficulty in breathing, deposition of white sulphate films, destruction of plants, crop failure and famine. Mortality rates increased and the following summer and winter were gloomy and cold.

Only about 3% of the annual carbon dioxide emissions are of human origin. The rest come from volcanoes, life, oceans, rocks and soil. It has yet to be shown that this 3% of annual emissions drives modern climate change. In the past, the six major ice ages were initiated at times when the Earth's atmosphere had up to 1,000 times the current carbon dioxide content which suggests that carbon dioxide has not driven past great climate changes.

To claim that we humans should seize stewardship of carbon dioxide emissions ignores natural processes such as ocean degassing, volcanism and planetary degassing. The energy emitted by a volcano is far less than that of the energy transfer in the atmosphere that drives climate.

When environmentalists, lobby groups and politicians can turn volcanic eruptions on and off whenever they please, then they can have a go and trying to twiddle the dials and change global climate. Don't wait up.

(2008)

Camping, Plimer style, Shoalhaven Gorge, Tallong, NSW, 1966

Sea level rise

Is sea level rising? Yes and no! The answer is written in history, archaeology and geology.

What seems like a simple question is not simple because Nature is complex and fickle. What appears to be a sea level rise may be the sinking of land, the sinking of a measuring station or an actual rise in sea level. Now don't say *"Who knows?"* because there are ways of knowing.

Sensationalist headlines tell us that Pacific Ocean atoll island nations are being inundated because sea level is rising. There is neither evidence nor logic to support this view. The next illogical step is that this alleged sea level rise must be due to climate change. The final illogical step is that someone or something is to blame. Radical activists go one step further and claim that sea level rise must be due to warming, that global warming is a result of burning coal producing carbon dioxide emissions into the atmosphere and hence all coal mining must be stopped. Such illiterate unbalanced folk are not aware that only 3% of annual emissions of carbon dioxide is from human emissions, that it has yet to be shown that human emissions of carbon dioxide drive global warming, that the human emissions of carbon dioxide are massively increasing due to the industrialisation of Asia concurrently with a plateau or decrease of global atmospheric temperature, that a very slight increase in atmospheric carbon dioxide has led to a greening of the planet and increased crop productivity, that the area of Pacific atolls is increasing over the last few decades when alleged global warming and a resultant sea level rise should have inundated these atolls, that coal has brought the West from grinding poverty, that burning coal has given Western activists the life that they now enjoy and that banning coal exports keeps Asian and Indian people in poverty.

During the peak of the last ice age 20,000 years ago, Scandinavia, Russia, Scotland, northern USA and Canada were covered by kilometres of ice. The weight of the ice sheets pushed down landmasses. Ice started to melt 14,400 years ago and the landmasses once covered by ice started to rise as their load had been lifted. This rise continues, there are beaches in Norway some 340 metres above sea level and the 12th Century castle at Turku (Finland), once built on an island, can now be reached by foot. The rate of land uplift can be calculated and it is surprisingly fast. As a result of land rise, other landmasses fall as a counterbalance and the Netherlands, northwestern Germany, Denmark and southeastern England are sinking. This sinking has been exacerbated by a post-glacial sea level rise of some 130 metres over the last 14,400 years.

Many substances are both brittle and plastic. If a rock or glass is hit with a hammer, it will break. However, if rock or glass is loaded for a long period of time, it will bend. A tour of tombstones in a cemetery will show that marble headstones that were originally planar are now bent and, from the date on the tombstone, the rate of bending can be calculated. Ice behaves in the same way. It can be broken with a hammer and it can flow slowly down a glacier under a gentle gravitational gradient. Flow is because ice is constantly recrystallising and the ice crystals become bigger from the head of the glacier to its foot.

Landmasses also rise and fall because of the pushing together and pulling apart of the tectonic plates. Mountains belts such as the Himalayas are rising with Mt Everest increasing in altitude by 2 centimetres per year. The Rift Valley of East Africa is sinking as are parts of inland Australia.

For more than 1,000 years the Dutch have been building dykes, pumping out water with wind mills and suffering from inundation when storms coincide with king tides. This will continue. The Romans noted that Londinium was sinking and built London on gravel terraces rather than next to the Thames River. Major engineering works such as the Thames Barrier have been built to deal with river flooding and storm surges resulting from the sinking of London due to geology, the extraction of ground water and traffic. The children's nursery rhyme *London Bridge is Falling Down* tells us that London is sinking. London will continue to sink.

Ancient cities like Lydia, the birthplace of coinage, are now metres below the water whereas other ancient port cities like Efesus, mentioned in the Bible (Acts 19: 1-7), have risen and are now inland. Subsidence can play some cruel tricks. For example, the tidal measuring station at Port Adelaide is sinking thereby recording a sea level rise! Bangkok, Mexico City, Denver and many other cities are sinking because of compaction after the extraction of groundwater. Oil and gas extraction has the same effect.

Sea level can also rise and fall. This is not only driven by cyclical global cooling and warming. Winds, tides, currents and low-pressure atmospheric systems can push seawater from one side of the ocean to another resulting in sea level change. The loading up of the sea floor with sediment or the adding of water to the oceans can result in the sinking of the plastic ocean floor. The gravitational pull of continents, especially with coastal mountain chains such as the Andes, can pull ocean water to a higher level. Submarine super volcanoes add huge amounts of lava to the sea floor and this results in a sea level rise.

There was a time once when the Straits of Gibraltar was closed and the Mediterranean evaporated. As a result of the northward drift of Africa, the Straits opened again and water poured into the Mediterranean basin to form the Mediterranean Sea and global sea level fell. Sea level also fell when the Bosphorus was gouged out and the Marmara Sea poured into a basin to form the Black Sea. Major tectonic processes are constantly changing the shape of the ocean floor with the formation of islands, ridges and trenches and these processes produce sea level change. To assume that sea level change is only due to climate is naïve.

During glacial times, water is locked in continental ice sheets resulting in a sea level drop. At times, there was so much water locked in ice sheets that there was no continental shelf. This suggests that natural sea level changes can be up to 600 metres. During glaciation and the associated sea level drop, there is stress and extinction of life. Coral reefs are exposed and die, shallow water habitats disappear, devegetation occurs, rivers dry up, soils change and the weather becomes colder, drier and windier.

During the peak of the last glaciation 20,000 years ago, there were copses of trees and grasslands in what is now the Amazonian jungle. Sea level was so low that one could walk from Papua New Guinea to Tasmania or France to England. After glaciation, ice sheets partially melted and water is added to the oceans. Sea level rises because of the added water and thermal expansion of the upper layer of water.

The West Antarctic Ice Sheet, once pinned to land, now has wet feet and is unstable as a result of post-glacial sea level rise. About two thirds of the ice sheet has collapsed into the oceans and if the last third collapses, sea level will be 6 metres higher. This is where it was 125,000 years ago. If the current interglacial warming goes to completion and all polar ice melts, sea level will be some 80 metres higher than now. This is where sea level was for much of time.

As a result of sea level changes, there are old beaches under water, beaches above water and kilometres inland and beaches denuded of sediment that later is redeposited. Beaches are constantly changing, again further evidence of an ever-changing planet. The most striking example of a coastal beach is a mineral sands mine in the desert at Pooncarie (NSW), some hundreds of kilometres from the current coast.

If humans live at sea level or at the margins of ocean basins, then they are living right at the edge. Why did the great civilisations evolve in inland valleys not in benign areas on the margins of ocean basins or have we already forgotten the 26th December 2004 catastrophic tsunami that killed at least 250,000 people? The south coast of NSW experiences a tsunami every 300 years when continental shelf sediments slide down the continental slope after a minor earth tremor in the Southern Highlands of NSW. If we live on the coast, we are exposed to known and massive risks.

Australia is, quite naturally, concerned about our neighbours living on atolls in the Pacific Ocean. If there were a sea level rise, we would expect every atoll in every ocean to be inundated. We don't see this. We would expect every harbour in the world to record a sea level rise. This is not recorded. Something is seriously wrong with the catastrophist dogma.

In 1830, Charles Lyell published the first of his three volume classic *Principles of Geology: Being an Attempt to Explain the Former Changes in the Earth's Surface by Reference to Causes now in Operation*. Charles Darwin received the first volume in 1830 which he took with him on HMS *Beagle*, the other two were sent to him *en route*. Darwin became fascinated with coral reefs and suggested that they form around the rim of ancient submarine volcanoes. Darwin's voyage allowed him to view many volcanic islands, coral reefs and atolls. In his 1842 book *The Structure and Distribution of Coral Reefs*, Darwin showed that volcanoes were at various heights above the sea floor. If sea level falls or a volcano rises from the sea floor, coral attaches itself to the volcano only to be killed upon later exposure to air. Places such as Vanuatu show coral reefs well above sea level on the sides of volcanoes due to the rise of a local volcano.

If sea level rises, volcanoes became inundated and coral attaches itself to the volcano and grows vertically and horizontally as sea level continues to rise. These produce coral atolls. The same occurs if a volcanic island starts to sink. Sea level rise produces coral atolls, it does not destroy them. Darwin showed this in 1842 and atolls were drilled to test Darwin's theory by Mawson's Antarctic compatriot Professor Sir T. W. Edgeworth David. The drilling was funded by the NSW Government who, at that time, was neither bankrupt nor corrupt. Darwin's coral atoll theory has now been validated by more than 150 years of independent interdisciplinary science. Darwin's theory was again validated by French and US drilling of atolls before detonation of nuclear bombs. Why has this been ignored by the climate catastrophists? Is it because it does not fit the mantra?

Coral atolls can also sink due to compaction of coralline sand, pumping of groundwater or sinking of the volcanic substrate. Again, this is a normal process that induces the rapid growth of coral to reform the atoll. This is what is happening in many Pacific Ocean atoll nations and this subsidence produces an apparent sea level rise. We naughty fossil fuel burners are not causing sea level to rise, some but not all of the Pacific Ocean atoll nations are sinking as part of a normal geological process.

When someone argues that we humans are causing sea level to rise, treat him or her as a fool. Because they are.

(2009)

The theology of climate change

Climate always changes. It always has and always will. For more than 80% of time the planet has been a warm wet greenhouse planet with no polar ice. Past temperate changes have been far greater and far more rapid than anything measured in modern times. We humans can live on ice sheets, in mountains, in the tropics, in deserts and at sea level. Past great climate changes have been driven by natural cyclical processes such as the position of our Solar System in the Universe, wobbles in the Earth's orbit, changes in the Sun, oscillations in the oceans and tidal changes. These processes have random inputs from sporadic events such as continental drift, volcanoes and asteroidal impacts.

The proposition that climate should not change is absurd and can only be promoted if all history, archaeology, geology, astronomy and solar physics is ignored. We do this at our peril. If an extraordinary claim is made, then extraordinary evidence must be given to support such a claim. Such evidence is yet to see the light of day.

Over the last 500 million years, there has been sequestering of carbon dioxide from the atmosphere into algal and coral reefs, shells, cements, sediments and precipitates. The atmospheric carbon dioxide content has been decreasing and, at times when vegetation thrived on Earth, both the atmospheric carbon dioxide and oxygen content of the atmosphere were far higher than at present. Over the history of time, the greatest biomass on Earth has been bacteria and the only life on Earth that has made great changes to the atmosphere have been bacteria and photosynthetic organisms. Since the first photosynthetic bacteria on Earth some 2,500 million years ago, there has been a sequestering of carbon dioxide by life. Carbon dioxide is plant food and to state in public that carbon dioxide is a pollutant is a public advertisement of a lack of basic school child science. Pollution kills, carbon dioxide leads to a thriving of life on Earth and increased biodiversity. Horticulturalists pump warm carbon dioxide into glasshouses to stimulate growth. This important gas is easy to demonise because it is colourless, odourless, tasteless and a small proportion derives from industry. It is easy to demonise something that is unseen such as carbon dioxide, radiation or bacteria. The main greenhouse gas is water vapour.

There has been global cooling for the last 50 million years. Because South America separated from Antarctica some 34 million years ago, the circum-polar current resulted in the isolated of Antarctica and the development of the Antarctic ice sheet. Despite numerous events when it was far warmer than at present for millions of years, the Antarctic ice sheet did not melt. It was only after two coincidental events 2.67 million years ago, the joining of South America to North America and a supernoval eruption that polar ice appeared in the Northern Hemisphere. Those who argue that human emissions of carbon dioxide change climate must demonstrate that changes observed today are not natural. This has not been done.

The polar ice sheets waxed and waned. The last great interglacial was between 128,000 and 116,000 years ago. Sea level was 7 metres higher than at present and atmospheric temperature was some 5°C warmer. The ice sheets did not completely melt and humans thrived. During the latest glaciation, the Toba supervolcano eruption 74,000 years ago led to increased cold and humans very nearly became extinct.

Ice core drilling shows very smoothed patterns for gases that were originally trapped in snow. The diffusion of trapped atmospheric gases through ice may increase the uncertainty of ice studies however numerous studies show that after a cyclical temperature change, the atmospheric carbon dioxide content increases some 800-1,500 years later. Again, there is a disconnect between warming and its alleged origin and it is quite possible that some of the 20th Century increase in atmospheric carbon dioxide derives from the Medieval Warming 800 years ago.

The zenith of the last glaciation was 20,000 years ago. Ice sheets were at latitudes of 38°, the latitude of Athens (Greece) and Melbourne (Australia). Ice melting led to a sea level rise of about 1 centimetre per year, a figure far higher than the most exaggerated catastrophist model for human-induced global warming. During the interglacial, there were a number of exceptionally cold snaps and temperature rose by as much as 20°C in 15 years after one of these periods. We humans did not suffer, we thrived. Some 6,000 years ago sea level was 1 to 3 metres higher than at present and it was at least 3°C warmer than now. Alternating cool and warm periods followed with desertification occurring in windy cool times. These cool dry times also led to the collapse of great civilisations.

The temperature and rate of temperature change in the Minoan, Roman and Medieval Warmings were greater than today. In the Roman Warming, olives were grown along the Rhine River and grapes were grown as far north in England as Hadrian's Wall. The Roman Warming came to a sudden end with a decrease in solar activity, the eruption of Krakatoa (535 AD) and Rabaul (536 AD). Atmospheric aerosols from these volcanoes and a cometary tail (November 536 AD) resulted in cooling, acid rain, crop failures, famine, and attacks on the weakened population by the plague, warfare, change of empires and depopulation. The Medieval Warming commenced with a very active Sun. Between 900 and 1300 AD, it was warmer, times were prosperous and generational wealth was used to build the great cathedrals, monasteries and universities of Europe.

The Vikings colonised Newfoundland and called it Vinland. No grapes could survive the cool climate of Newfoundland today. In the Medieval Warming, wheat, barley, sheep and cattle were grown in Greenland. Today there is no farming on Greenland because the climate is too cold. This shows that atmospheric temperatures were at least 5°C warmer than at present. A lazy Sun in 1280 AD led to the Little Ice Age. It took 23 years to change from the Medieval Warming to the Little Ice Age. There was crop failure, starvation and murderous food refugees roamed

Europe. The stressed population suffered the plague in 1347 AD, there was massive depopulation and it took Europe 250 years to again reach the population that existed in the Medieval Warming. It was especially cold in periods when the Sun was lazy and it was during these periods that there were revolutions, starvation, ice fairs on rivers, paintings of cold stormy weather, increased cloudiness and paintings of frosts, thick snow and bitterly cold landscapes.

The Little Ice Age ended about 1850. Since the end of the Little Ice Age, the world has warmed at the same rate from 1860 to 1880, 1910 to 1940 and 1975 to 1998. If humans had accelerated natural warming due to their carbon dioxide emissions, then the rate of warming over time would have increased. It did not. The four major climate centres in the world all show that atmospheric temperature has been decreasing in the 21st Century despite a measured increase in atmospheric carbon dioxide. The climate models show that temperature should have been increasing in the 21st Century. This disconnect shows that there is little relationship between carbon dioxide and temperature and that models of very complex chaotic natural systems should be viewed with great caution. There has been a decrease in global temperature in the 21st Century yet we are perpetually warned of dangerous global warming.

If such warmings took place in the historical past, why is a warming from 1976 to 1998 now due to human activity? These natural changes are far greater than any changes measured in the 20th and 21st Century yet modern natural climate changes are touted as "dangerous climate change".

Both the sea and the land rise and fall and it is extraordinarily difficult to measure current sea level changes and much easier to measure past changes. Scandinavia was covered by 5 kilometres of ice which started to melt 14,400 years ago. As a result, Scandinavia has rebounded and has risen by up to 340 metres. Surveyed coastal properties in Finland are now inland and one can now walk some 7 metres above the Gulf of Bothnia to the 12th Century Castle of Turku, constructed on an island. Scotland is also rising. The Roman Port of Efeses in now 15 kilometres inland and 7 metres above sea level and the ancient city of Lydia is now some 4 metres below sea level. Tuvulu is located where the floor of the Pacific Ocean is deepening and relative sea level at the Maldives has fallen 20 centimetres since the 1970s. The tidal measuring station at Port Adelaide shows a relative sea level rise of 2.3 centimetres per year as a result of sinking of the measuring station.

The planet's ice sheets are dynamic. If ice did not melt, then the planet would be covered in a permanent ice sheet. Ice on Greenland is increasing, as is Arctic sea ice whereas ice in East Antarctica is increasing and ice on West Antarctica is decreasing. Antarctic sea ice is increasing. Beneath the Antarctic ice sheet are active volcanoes with associated high temperature gas vents and hot springs. The last great eruptions were in Roman times. Records of mountain glaciers in Europe show multiple events of ice advance and retreat over the last 4,000 years and the retreat of the Fürtwangler Glacier on Mount Kilimanjaro probably results from changing land use and resultant decrease in humidity.

In the past, there have been six major ice ages. These have occurred when Earth was bombarded with cosmic radiation, two of these show that there was ice at sea level and at the equator and five of these ice ages occurred when the carbon dioxide content of the atmosphere was up to 1,000 times greater than now. The proposition that a high atmospheric carbon dioxide content creates global warming, "tipping points" and unstoppable global warming is incommensurate with the past.

The largest of these ice ages had kilometre-thick ice sheets at sea level at the equator, there was no continental shelf and sea level therefore must have fallen at least 600 metres. An interglacial sea level rise of at least 600 metres was associated with a sea surface temperature rise to at least 40°C. Bacterial life thrived and sequestered huge amounts of carbon dioxide into algal reefs, sediments and precipitates. The next great glaciation (and sea level fall) was followed by another great sea level rise, thriving of bacterial life and sequestration of carbon dioxide from the atmosphere. This ice age, the Cryogenic, was the greatest and most rapid climate change that has ever occurred on Earth. It is not understood and this should temper our views that we think we understand modern climate change. After two of these great climate changes, there was an explosion and diversification of life on Earth.

We have had attacks by a non-scientific media on the former Senator Fielding because he actually has the temerity to ask questions and did not believe the media spin on human-induced climate change. The ABC, especially Robyn Williams' *Science Show*, has taken it upon itself to be the protector of truth, promoter of government spin and has wheeled in a depleted army of alleged experts critical of an alternative valid scientific view based on published science yet does not allow the alternative view air time. Science is married to evidence and dissent yet the ABC *Science Show* now does the government's policy promotion. ABC journalists with no science training attempt to demolish scientific conclusions using ideology.

Our ABC has embraced irrational beliefs, it is not possible to reason someone out of a belief system that they entered without reasoning and the way to build a business, media or scientific career seems to be to join the human-induced global warming bandwagon. Journalists have become smitten with self-righteous trendy ideological causes and promote these causes by cut-and-paste journalism using no knowledge, analysis or criticism. ABC television such as The *7.30 Report* and *Lateline* give fawning interviews to the ideologues that suggest that there is dangerous climate change and, if any person with an alternative view is lucky enough to be given airtime, then there is an orchestrated character assassination, ambushing and loaded questions with constant interruptions thereby not allowing an answer. To suggest that the Emperor has no clothes or to remind people of King Canute is now a sin and there are many who fear questioning the popular paradigm.

Great institutions such as the ABC, CSIRO, universities, some professional societies and academies have become politicised.

Dispassionate independent fearless advice from government departments now no longer seems possible. I never thought I would see the day when the only balance on a matter of science derives from commercial radio. *The Australian* presents a diversity of opinions and all other major capital city newspapers appear to promote a doom-and-gloom scenario.

Criticism of my books has been savage because there are a large number of supporters of human-induced global warming who have carved out a career niche by frightening us witless about climate change and who would be unemployable outside taxpayer-funded climate institutes. Comments suggest that most of my critics have not read my books and obtain their information from blogs. The total politicisation of science, as demonstrated by the use of consensus and "the science is settled", has been easy because of the dumbing down of the education system, the fear of criticism and analysis and instant information.

In the mining industry, any public statement must be in accord with legal and scientific requirements (e.g. the JORC code) in order to protect investors. The signoff must be made by a senior professional accredited by a professional organisation and all material used must be transparent, available and have undergone the rigours of a due diligence. Economic decisions regarding emissions trading are many orders of magnitude higher yet there has been no transparent due diligence. There has been no scientific due diligence and the only source of information derives from a political body, the IPCC. If such decisions were made in the corporate arena, then ASIC would be very busy with prosecutions.

The global warming movement has not shown that emissions trading legislation will do anything to change the global climate and has opened up opportunity for unregulated opaque trading of thin air across political boundaries. Such trading requires huge bureaucracies and makes a fortune for bankers, brokers, economists and governments. These are the same folk who brought us toxic derivatives and now want to impose a guilt tax on thin air. This taxed substance in the atmosphere is what allows us to live on this planet.

The futility of environmental symbolism is breathtaking. About one billion people turned off their lights during Earth Hour in order to reduce carbon dioxide emissions into the atmosphere. It takes only 6 seconds of Chinese carbon dioxide emissions to cancel out the Earth Hour carbon dioxide emission reductions. Furthermore, the Earth Hour participants emitted carbon dioxide and toxins from their candles and still were able to have a hot meal, live in houses with air conditioning or heating and turn the lights on after their memorable hour. And why could they do that? Because the coal-fired power stations were not shut down as a spinning reserve was necessary. Those of us in the first world countries cannot stop five billion people burning cheap accessible carbon, if there is an 80% reduction in carbon dioxide emissions by the USA, about 1,000 new nuclear power stations need to be constructed before 2020 to replace the lost energy and, if the catastrophists are correct, such symbolism will only stop a global temperature increase of 0.07°C by 2050. Australia is even more exposed, as there is no large base load power alternative to coal-fired electricity generation and no neighbours to give us energy.

I argue that the global warming movement is a non-scientific urban religious fundamentalist movement detached from and damaging the environment. Adherents uncritically accept information from the web, Wikipedia and blog sites, they have lost contact with nature and have little knowledge of integrated interdisciplinary science. In science, I am in awe of Nature, religion inspires awe of God and worship through music, language and symbols. Religion allows us to cope with disappointment and failure. The new environmental religion is vacuous, in awe of nothing and has no intellectual foundation. There is a consensus of opinion, despite the fact that science does not operate using consensus and that no scientific breakthrough has ever been made by consensus. This consensus is reinforced by commercial interests, constant repetition of the mantra, research grants, subsidies, politicians looking for votes, international travel to vital Earth-changing conferences, proliferation of costly reports and investigations with predetermined conclusions, fame and fortune for journalists seeking headlines warning of an impending catastrophe, clamorous demonstrations and preaching of unchallenged gospel.

This movement has the elements of failed European socialism and Christianity, imposes guilt on the community, creates a fear of damnation, demands appeasement by selling indulgences to the faithful, ignores any contrary information, demonises dissenters, has its holy book (the IPCC Reports) which adherents have neither read nor have the knowledge to understand, breed gurus whose mantras cannot be challenged and insist on unqualified claims to bring happiness but only to true believers. The most dangerous aspect of this new fundamentalist religion is that it ignores history. Religious faith is so strong, blind and unreasoning that it allows adherents to just totally blissfully ignore all contrary information.

This new fundamentalist religion cannot answer simple questions. What is the environmentally ideal surface temperature for the Earth? What is the ideal carbon dioxide content of the atmosphere? How should enormous economic pain from emissions reduction be imposed? Why is carbon dioxide increasing yet temperature is decreasing? Why can't models be run backwards to replicate what we know? Why have major Earth processes been omitted from models? Who will be prevented from flying, driving or living a comfortable life? Who will be prevented from espousing an alternative view? What will we be allowed to think? Signs of these totalitarian elements are already appearing.

In English law (Nicholson v Grainger plc and others; ET2203367/08; 18th March 2009), a belief in human induced global warming is now legally no different from a religious belief.

It is indeed a dark day for religion.

(2009)

Ian Plimer with friend, the Venerable Dr Edwin Byford, Adelaide 2011.

Stop climate change

If we humans want to stop climate change, then we have a huge task ahead of us.

We need to stop continents moving, stop the shape of the sea floor changing, stop pulling apart the ocean floors, stop mountains forming, stop volcanoes belching out greenhouse gases and dust, stop hot flushes of gas rising from the Earth's interior, stop earthquakes, stop comets breaking up in the upper atmosphere, stop the changes in the Earth's orbit, stop the cycles of solar changes and stop radiation hitting Earth from deep space. Our generation did not discover climate change, the Earth's climate has always changed.

If we Australians stopped burning fossil fuels, this would make not one iota of difference to the global climate. The forces of Nature are far greater than the motor car and coal-fired power stations. The energy emitted by a tornado is that of a coal- or nuclear-fired power station whereas the energy emitted by a wind turbine is that of a horse. Previous climate changes have been cyclical and sudden. Previous changes have been in the order of decades and temperature changes have been far greater than recent temperature changes. Because of lags resulting from the large volume of seawater and ice, any sea level rise or changes in the ice sheets result from events that took place hundreds to thousands of years earlier.

Over time, humans have endured great climate changes. Periods of cold climate, especially combined with decreased sunspot activity, volcanicity and pandemics, have greatly depopulated the Earth. Humans and other organisms have thrived in times of warm climate. We humans live on ice sheets, on mountains, at the tropics, at sea level and in deserts. We are adaptable.

If we moved from Hobart to Darwin, the average temperature rise would be 18°C yet this warmth does not seem to be lethal for Darwinians. Both animals and plants constantly migrate and adapt to climate change.

The main greenhouse gas is water vapour. Without water vapour, planet Earth would enjoy an average temperature of a balmy -18°C. Other greenhouse gases are trace gases, including carbon dioxide. Only 0.117% of the carbon dioxide in the atmosphere is of human origin and carbon dioxide is not a pollutant. It is plant food. The addition of carbon dioxide to the atmosphere has been taking place for 4,567 million years. It is still taking place. Balancing the books on where carbon dioxide comes from and where it goes is hopelessly inadequate showing how little we know about the big natural systems operating on planet Earth.

The climate change cacophony demonstrates that the community knows little about how our dynamic evolving planet works. A little bit of basic geology would be a good start. An understanding of the processes of science would be another good start. Science is married to evidence that derives from observation, calculation, measurement and experiment. Scientists argue about the validity of this evidence and whether the evidence is in accord with everything else that has been validated. Science then tries to explain the evidence with a theory. Theories are refuted with new thinking and new evidence. Science is evolutionary, self-adjusting, anarchistic and bows to no authority. Science has no moral, political or religious view about anything.

The current President of the Royal Society told us that the science on human-induced global warming is settled. A previous President of the Royal Society also used his authority, this time to inform us that it is impossible for heavier than air machines to fly and that we know all that is to be known about physics! However, radioactivity was discovered a few years later and this has become a fundamental of physics. That was in the 1890s. Heavier than air machines were flying a few years later. So much for authority.

Science is not about consensus or belief, these words are those of politics and religion. Science is a celebration of uncertainty. Scepticism and criticism are valued and information from all different disciplines is integrated in an attempt to understand the world around us. Because the current theory on human-induced climate change is not in accord with validated geology and astronomy, then the theory must be rejected. However, the idea that wealthy Western humans change global climate is an attractive non-scientific idealistic political idea and this idea is currently promoted with great missionary zeal.

The tail has wagged the dog and squeaky wheels and a sensationalist media have forced both major political parties, against their better judgment, to make political comments about climate change. These comments have nothing to do with science. They are pragmatic political survival.

What is interesting is that the squeaky wheels are in affluent western countries that have lost the religious structure to society. Climate change has become the new dogmatic religion and woe betide heretics, sinners, workers and the wealthy. We are all now to pay papal carbon indulgences to the archbishops of climate change (on the condition that such payments only hurt the electorate a little). The problem is that these indulgences are now hurting too much as the cost of energy has skyrocketed, and in wealthy countries we now have energy poverty and unemployment as a result of the cost of energy.

My concerns are that the great gains made in the Renaissance and Reformation regarding logic, argument, challenges to authority, rationality, the use of evidence and an understanding of the world around us have been lost in the space of a decade or two. The risks and rewards encouraged in the Enlightenment are all but gone. This has been an incredible politically driven social change. The word sceptic is now a pejorative word and criticism, questioning and the integration of a broad spectrum of science is either dismissed or regarded as evil. There is no climate change debate, only dangerous dogma, the constriction of thinking processes and a negative view of the future.

Any future great environmental problems can only be solved by science and if the weapons of science are removed, then we place society at risk. Children now have a negative view of the future rather than equipping themselves with the tools to make the Earth a better place. We are now starting to reap the rewards of dumbing down science education. The real message from the politics of climate change is that science education in Australia is in a woeful state. Society is again in one of its great backward swings.

The only good news is that those who have only known the good times are reminded to be frugal with energy and resources and not to throw waste into our waterways and atmosphere. But we knew this anyway, didn't we.

(2011)

Human-induced climate change:
Why I am sceptical

I am sceptical because the empirical evidence from the history of planet Earth shows that natural climate changes have been rapid, large and unrelated to human activity. Any changes measured today are well within variability. Although humans may have a slight effect on the Earth's atmosphere, the Earth's atmosphere does not drive climate and human effects are swamped by the enormous natural changes on Earth.

Climate change

Planet Earth is dynamic. Climate has always changed. In the past, climate cycles are of galactic (143 million years), orbital (100,000, ~41,000 and ~21,000 years), solar (10,000, 1,500, 210, 87, 22 and 11 years), oceanic decadal (~30 years) and lunar tidal (~18.6 years) origin. Oceans have decadal oscillations (e.g. Pacific Decadal Oscillation [PDO]) and non-cyclical major events (e.g. El Niño-La Niña) where the surface temperature of ocean water changes. Amongst volcanologists, there is sneaking suspicion that El Niño-La Niña events may be related to periodic submarine volcanic events heating deep ocean waters. Climate change in the past has never been driven by carbon dioxide. Why should carbon dioxide drive climate change today?.

Because climate science is in its infancy, many of these events are starting to be documented and, until processes are fully understood and integrated with past climatic processes, there is no consensus in any area of climate science. Because of the heat capacity of water, it is not the temperature of the atmosphere that heats the ocean surface waters. It is the temperature of the ocean surface that heats the atmosphere. The 3,000 ARGO buoys are showing that the surface temperature of the ocean is decreasing yet the carbon dioxide content of the atmosphere is increasing. This is commensurate with the 21st Century cooling (derived from satellite and balloon measurements) during times of increasing carbon dioxide.

Galactic climate cycles derive from increased bombardment of the Solar System with cosmic rays. These cosmic rays induce the formation of low-level clouds that reflect heat. The Earth then cools. The six major ice ages that planet Earth has enjoyed were at times when Earth was in the Sagittarius-Carina (twice), Perseus, Norma, Scutum and Orion Arms. Each one of these six ice ages started when there was far more carbon dioxide in the atmosphere than now. Wobbles in the Earth's orbit produce cycles of warm and cold (Milankovich Cycles) resulting from changes in the distance between the Earth and the Sun. Despite a solar constant, the Sun is not constant and has a number of regular cycles and outbursts of energy. These influence climate because they result in changes in the solar magnetic field that, in turn, protects the Earth from cosmic ray bombardment. It may appear heretical to those advocating human-induced climate change, but the great ball of energy in the sky that we call the Sun actually drives surface energy systems and life on Earth.

Climate changes have sporadically occurred as a result of super volcanoes, supernoval eruptions, tectonism and possibly impacts. Large volcanic eruptions at tropical latitudes (e.g. Tambora, Indonesia 1815; Krakatoa, Indonesia 1883) eject aerosols into the stratosphere, these reflect light and heat and produce cooler stormy weather that lasts for a few years. Associated with eruptions are particulate and gaseous aerosols that change climate. Terrestrial super volcanoes (e.g. Yellowstone, USA; Taupo, NZ; Kamchatka, Russia) eject thousands of cubic kilometres of aerosols into the atmosphere and these can have a profound effect on cooling. Planet Earth started to cool 116,000 years ago at the beginning of the most recent glaciation. During this orbitally-driven cooling, Toba (Indonesia) erupted 74,000 years ago. It filled the atmosphere with aerosols and accelerated the rate of cooling. Humans very nearly became extinct. The same filling of the atmosphere with aerosols also occurs after an asteroid impact. The collision of India with Asia 50 million years ago resulted in the pushing up of mountains that have changed climate by affecting the jet stream. New mountains are stripped of soils, new soils form and extract carbon dioxide from the atmosphere, these soils are buried as sediment and bare rock in alpine areas creates monsoonal updrafts.

Planetary degassing and carbon dioxide

Since the formation of planet Earth, there has been degassing of water vapour, carbon dioxide, methane, sulphur-bearing gases and many other gases by plutonism, volcanism and metamorphism. Degassing occurs on other planets, as does climate change. Degassing of carbon dioxide occurs before, during and after volcanic eruptions from gas vents, hot springs and craters. Over a thousand terrestrial volcanoes are known and only two-dozen are accurately monitored.

Places such as the Hong Kong Geopark are wonderful examples of the power of volcanism and how one volcano can ruin your whole day because the ignimbrites on High Island formed from an explosion of an emulsion of gas, molten rock and solid fragments. The main gases were water vapour and carbon dioxide. Submarine degassing occurs from at least 3.47 million off axis submarine basaltic volcanoes and from the 65,000 kilometres strike length of mid ocean ridges. At mid ocean ridges, the oceanic crust of the Earth is pulled apart and gases from deep in the mantle leak to the surface. Each year some 10,000 cubic kilometres of seawater circulates through new mid ocean ridge basalt as a coolant. This heats the ocean. Experimental studies show that carbon dioxide is highly soluble in basalt and basalts collected from the sea floor, although containing carbon dioxide have vented most of the carbon dioxide before eruption.

In 1999, a slow spreading mid-ocean ridge (Gakkal Ridge, Arctic

Ocean) experienced an explosive submarine basaltic eruption. For basalt to explode at such a great water depth, at least 13.5% of the molten rock was carbon dioxide. The new volcanic rocks needed to be cooled by circulating seawater and the Arctic Ocean warmed for a short time. This warming was coincidental with a lunar tidal node that pushed warmer surface North Atlantic Ocean water into the Arctic. There is not one deep submarine measuring station hence the emissions of heat and carbon dioxide from submarine basaltic volcanism can only be deduced. In some places, liquid carbon dioxide has been found on the ocean floor and gas vents of carbon dioxide are very common. Furthermore, submarine carbon dioxide released from gas vents, hot springs and submarine basalt eruptions dissolves in cool high-pressure bottom waters for degassing to the atmosphere thousands of years later.

Degassing also occurs from rising bodies of molten rock that freeze kilometres from the surface (i.e. plutons). During ascent, they undergo constant degassing of steam, carbon dioxide and methane as do the intruded wet sediments and limey rocks. In places, these gases are used to drive geothermal power stations. Plutonic and volcanic rocks mainly occur where areas of the Earth's crust are pushed together, such as the collision of Africa with Europe. In this setting, mountains also form (e.g. European Alps) and, as rocks are compressed, gases such as steam, carbon dioxide and methane are released. These commonly form the spa waters typical of alpine areas.

Human emissions of carbon dioxide need to be placed in perspective. If annual emissions of carbon dioxide comprise 33 molecules, only one is from human emissions and the rest from natural processes. This one molecule of human-derived carbon dioxide is mixed with 85,000 other molecules in air. If human emissions of carbon dioxide drive climate change, then it has to be demonstrated that this terribly lonely single molecule in 85,000 drives climate change and that the 32 carbon dioxide molecules derived from natural processes do not. It has yet to be shown that human emission of carbon dioxide drive climate change. In fact, there is only evidence to the contrary.

For example, the Beer-Lambert Law shows that if the current atmospheric carbon dioxide content is doubled, global atmospheric temperature will increase by 0.2°C and if the carbon dioxide content is quadrupled, temperature will rise by a further 0.1°C. This assumes that no carbon dioxide is dissolved in oceans or used by life. In fact, if all of the world's fossil fuels were burned, the atmospheric carbon dioxide content would not even double. In the geological past, the atmosphere contained more than 10% carbon dioxide compared to the 0.04% today. Yet there was no runaway global warming. In fact, each of the six major ice ages was initiated at a time when the atmospheric carbon dioxide content was higher than at present, commensurate with the Beer-Lambert Law. As atmospheric carbon dioxide increases, more and more dissolves in the ocean waters (Henry's Law), a feature known by brewers for a thousand years. Ice core measurements show that with past interglacials, temperature rises some 800 to 1,500 years before the atmospheric carbon dioxide content rises.

In more modern times, planet Earth enjoyed the Roman and Medieval Warmings when there were 600 and 400 years respectively of times far warmer than now. These two warmings were separated by the cold Dark Ages when glaciers advanced, crops failed, famine was rife, the weakened population succumbed to the plague and there was massive depopulation. During the Roman and Medieval Warmings, sea level did not rise, glaciers retreated, there was no sudden ejection of carbon dioxide into the atmosphere from industrialisation and it was so warm that the Romans were able to grow crops at latitudes where such cultivation now would not be possible. The Vikings grew barley, wheat, sheep and cattle on Greenland in areas where farming would now be impossible. New evidence is showing that the Roman and Medieval Warmings and the Dark Ages and Little Ice Age were phenomena not restricted to the Northern Hemisphere and were global.

The Little Ice Age started in 1300 AD, the coldest periods were those of no sunspot activity (i.e. the solar magnetic field was small and allowed the ingress of more cosmic radiation). Temperatures fluctuated wildly, there were short warm periods interspersed with long cold periods, glaciers advanced and retreated slightly in warmer times, crops failed, people starved, the plague struck Europe in 1347 AD and there was massive depopulation. The coldest period, the Maunder Minimum, over 300 years ago. Since then, planet Earth has been warming and, if one is to claim that global warming is human-induced, then natural post-glacial warming needs to be differentiated from anthropogenic warming. This has not been done. Since thermometer measurements were recorded, temperature decreases (1880-1910, 1940-1976, 1998 to the present) and increases (1860-1880, 1910-1940, 1976-1998) show that there is no correlation of temperature with increasing atmospheric carbon dioxide. With no correlation between global warming and atmospheric carbon dioxide on geological, ice core and historical time scales, there can be no causation.

For claims to be made that one particular year is the warmest on record are misleading and deceptive, especially as these claims are made uncritically and use "corrected" data. In the last 10,500 years of the current interglacial, 9,099 were warmer than now. The planet has cooled since the time of Jesus, warmed since the Dark Ages, cooled since the Medieval Warming and warmed since the Little Ice Age. From 1910-1940, many parts of the Earth were warmer than now, the Northwest Passage was navigated in wooden boats and the polar sea ice decreased. Temperature has been increasing for the last 300 years since the zenith of the Little Ice Age hence it is no surprise that the highest temperatures are towards the end of this warming period. On a different time scale, Earth has been cooling for the last 50 million years during which there were spikes of warming and cooling.

Ice on Earth is rare, for more than 80% of time, planet Earth has been warmer and wetter than at present and, since about 2,500 million years ago, the atmospheric carbon dioxide content has decreased from ~20% to the present 0.04%. The decrease in carbon dioxide results from the long-term biota-assisted sequestration into carbonate rocks with less sequestration into altered rocks. In former times of high atmospheric carbon dioxide, oceans were not acid, there was no runaway greenhouse and the rate of change of temperature, sea level and ice waxing and waning was no different from the present. Ocean water has been alkaline for the history of time because the chemistry of seawater, addition of calcium via river systems, ocean floor sediments and new volcanic rocks on the sea floor buffer seawater to stop it becoming acid, even during times of carbon dioxide concentrations that were thousands of times the present value. When we run out of rocks on the sea floor, the oceans will become acid.

Because the atmosphere has >100 parts per million carbon dioxide, a doubling or quadrupling of human emissions of carbon dioxide will have very little effect on temperature unless atmospheric carbon dioxide residence times change to two orders of magnitude higher than past times. To argue that temperature and sea level are increasing depends on when measurements first started and depends on what is measured.

Coastal planning based on "global sea level rise" is asinine because local compaction, sedimentation, uplift and subsidence are ignored. Computer-modelled sea level projections by the IPCC and governments have already been shown to be hopelessly wrong. For example, areas covered with ice sheets during the last glaciation (116,000 to 14,400 years ago) sank. With the collapse of the ice sheets in the current interglacial, some lands are rising (e.g. Scandinavia, Scotland) and others are sinking (SE England, The Netherlands). Since the zenith of the last glaciation 20,000 years ago, sea level has risen 130 metres. History shows us that some port cities (e.g. Efeses, Turkey) are now inland whereas other cities (e.g. Lydia, Turkey) are submerged. In both the Maldives and eastern Australia, relative sea level has fallen. The Maldives is 70 centimetres higher now than in the 1970s and eastern Australia is 2 metres higher than 4,000 years ago. Without a detailed knowledge of local land rises and falls, subsidence and sedimentation, sea level predictions are only speculation.

Computer climate models throw no new light on climate processes and the science underpinning the hypothesis that humans drive global warming is not in accord with the past. Climate models tell more about the modellers than the climate as they produce pre-ordained conclusions, cannot be run backwards to show what has been validated and have been shown to be wrong by empirical measurements. Climate, atmospheric temperature and ocean temperature models have all been checked with empirical measurements and all models have been shown to be incorrect.

If one moves from Helsinki to Singapore, there is an average temperature increase of 22°C yet this does not appear fatal. Humans have adapted to live on ice, in mountains, in the desert, in the tropics and at sea level and can adapt to future changes. History shows that during interglacials, humans create wealth and population grows whereas glaciation is characterised by famine, starvation, disease, war and depopulation.

The story of planet Earth is a marvellous chronicle written in stone. Past climate changes have been very complicated in a chaotic non-linear system with sporadic randomness, these systems are poorly understood and it is only by looking at the past and integrating with what we know about the present that we can hope to understand major natural processes. That understanding is a long way away. For scientists to argue that traces of a trace gas emitted by humans into the atmosphere is the main driving force for climate changes on planet Earth is fraudulent. To argue that every change on a dynamic planet is due to human activity ignores the rich past that the chronicle of planet Earth gives us.

Although the history of planet Earth will always be incomplete, we have enough empirical evidence from the present, history, archaeology, glaciology and geology to show that past climate changes have never been driven by trace additions of carbon dioxide into the atmosphere hence there is no reason to conclude that present human emissions of carbon dioxide will be any different. Carbon dioxide is not a pollutant. It is plant food and used in photosynthesis. There can be no life on Earth without carbon dioxide.

Carbon dioxide is a minor greenhouse gas that has a very slight effect on atmospheric temperature. The main greenhouse gas that affects atmospheric temperature is water vapour and, as the ice sheets show, the thermal properties of water are why there has been no runaway global warming in the past. The air contains 0.04% carbon dioxide and we breathe out >4% carbon dioxide.

The corruption of the scientific method

This history of planet Earth has been ignored with the current popular catastrophist paradigm of human-induced climate change. If large bodies of evidence and history are ignored, then this provides a misleading and deceptive view of global climate. If scientists ignore integrated interdisciplinary empirical evidence, then they have politicised science to gain government favours and they are operating fraudulently. Using Popperian thinking, if just one iota of validated evidence is not in accord with the hypothesis that human emissions of carbon dioxide drive global warming, then the hypothesis must be rejected. Geology provides numerous examples that falsify the hypothesis of human-induced global warming.

Climategate, the adjustment of primary data to yield the required data for continuing the climate scare campaign, the corruption of the peer review process, the exclusion of contrary views from eminent scientists by the media, the lack of caution and reserve in making public statements about new scientific findings, the corruption of the temperature record, the non-correlation of carbon dioxide with temperature, the conversion of science and free independent inquiry into political advocacy, the corruption of the historical carbon dioxide record, the dampening or omission of the validated record of the Roman and Medieval Warmings, the creation of the "hockey stick" *ex nihilo*, the demonising of dissent, the denial that planet Earth changes by forces far larger than anything humans can create, the failure of models, the massive vested interests promoting the certainty of a human-induced catastrophe, the use of Orwellian language and the use of fundamentalist religious thinking processes all show that the gains made in the Renaissance, Reformation and Enlightenment have been lost in two short decades. Such behaviour is not that of scientists, these are the tactics of paid political thugs. Much of the political and media pressure comes from full-time climate advocates paid to misinform.

But what if I am wrong and a reduction of carbon dioxide emissions is necessary to "save the planet". If Australia stopped all carbon dioxide emissions today and the climate models are correct, global temperature would decrease by 0.0154°C by 2050 on the assumption that human emissions of carbon dioxide drive global warming. Such a temperature change is experienced by just standing up. Not only would Australia become bankrupt and could not feed itself, such voluntary acts of international environmental kindness would have absolutely no effect on the global climate.

Science has and will continue to self-correct over short periods of time. However, Western governments have uncritically and dogmatically embraced human-induced global warming as a mechanism of increasing taxation, redistributing wealth, eroding freedoms, maintaining power by doing deals with groups allegedly concerned about the environment, and constraining liberal thinking processes. These changes take only decades to enact and centuries to reverse following massive economic and human disruption.

We live on a dynamic planet. Nothing can be conserved. Nothing is permanent. Climate change is normal. Evolution is normal. What would spell the death of planet Earth is if climate did not change. We can be thankful that we exist because Earth is warm, wet, volcanic and dynamic. The Sun and the Moon are vital for life as is the Earth's magnetic field and radioactivity. Over time, there have been massive changes in sea levels, atmospheric composition and life. Life is integrated with the rocks, atmosphere and oceans.

Quick sound bites and bumper bar politics claiming that increasing carbon dioxide will somehow destroy Earth are advertisements of ignorance. The past is the key to the present and the past tells us that previous climate changes have resulted from supernovae, solar flaring, sunspot activity, meteorites, comets, orbital changes, drifting continents, mountain building, land level changes, volcanoes, sedimentation, gas outbursts from the ocean floor, ice armadas, breaching of melt water dams, ocean current changes, lunar tides and of course, life. To claim that one factor, increasing carbon dioxide in the atmosphere, changes climate is political policy but not science. Our real worries on planet Earth are not carbon dioxide but ignorance and poverty.

We frail humans commonly yield to fads, fashions, frauds and fools because we ignore the past. We ignore social, political, economic and geologic history at our peril. This is happening now.

(2012)

Drinking at the Post Office Hotel, Chillagoe, far north Queensland. A cattle and mining town.

Drinking at Chillagoe with my mate since 1964, John Nethery. There is a 2 week age difference and the whole light spectrum in the difference between hair colour.

How to make Australia efficient

The greens, environmental activists, social engineers and bureaucrat advocates all want to change our way of life. Well so do I. My proposal does not take away your freedoms as theirs would, it actually would make your life easier and would save zillions. My proposal uses induced reality by decentralisation in order to make Australia more efficient. My decentralisation suggestions will work because bureaucrats would become part of the community they serve and would have a first-hand understanding of the outcomes of their administration.

If my decentralisation ideas did not work, it would not matter anyway because the bureaucracy would have been greatly reduced. Because many Australians live in the towns chosen for decentralisation, I can't think of any reason why bureaucrats in Canberra would resign rather than relocate (unless, of course, they are very sensitive precious types who are more important than those who pay them). Thousands of private sector tax paying workers relocate each week so what's good for the goose is good for the gander. In order to make the administration more efficient and in contact with reality, I suggest that all the existing Federal government departments move out of Canberra. Decentralisation would provide infrastructure where it is needed.

The sterling folk from Agriculture, Fisheries and Forestry are concerned with eggs, fish, pigs, wine, cows, wool, grain, forests, horticulture, sugar, plant health and biosecurity. None of these activities occur close to Canberra. A suitable place might be Portland, Victoria. It is a fishing town, an aluminium smelting centre and agricultural export port (mainly live sheep). It is close to the prime agricultural areas of western Victoria and moderately close to the Coonawarra wineries and plantation forests in South Australia. It is only the sugar industries that are not proximal but they are not close to Canberra anyway. There are some wonderful scenic attractions in this part of Australia to be appreciated in time off. A weekend trip to the aluminium smelter would give a touch of reality about how the Australian economy needs large amounts of cheap energy to produce the taxation base for bureaucrats to put bread and wine on their tables. Maybe befriending an abalone fisherman would show how individuals lose jobs from decisions made by unknown bureaucratic faces out of contact with reality.

The most difficult placement is Attorney-General's portfolio. These folk administer the Federal police, administrative appeals, customs and border protection, native title, film classification and oodles of other really important things. Maybe a former penal colony like Norfolk Island is appropriate but for me the Tiwi Islands, NT is the pick place. This part of Australia is close to our northern neighbours hence they would be in the cauldron of borders, customs and native title. The port of entry into Australia could be the Tiwi Islands. This would solve congestion at southeastern Australian international airports. On those idle evening hours, maybe a few violent sexually explicit DVDs could be classified. Weekends could be spent watching the up and coming stars of the AFL, fishing, waiting for the next cyclone or just chilling out.

Broadband, Communication and the Digital Economy is ideal for a rural town like Wilcannia, NSW. In the 19th Century, the broadband superhighway for Wilcannia and the far west of NSW was the Darling River. Remnants of the port facilities still exist, phones and internet work most of the time, morning newspapers arrive in the afternoon and, if it were not for the repeater station, there would be no television or wireless. Each day, one bus goes east through town, another goes west. The pick-up point is late at night at the one and only service station and while waiting for a bus that's invariably late, bureaucrats could exercise on cold winter nights with martial arts training. All bureaucrats at Wilcannia need to be experts in martial arts. A message could be passed as a result of leading by example: rural areas will not miss out on the latest communications. Offices could have a panoramic view of the dry Darling River and long-term employees would be able see the floods every 30 years. Maybe jobs would be created for those in rural Australia who, out of hopelessness, have turned to methamphetamine and ice. Workers might care to use their time off pig shooting, fishing, yabbying, noodling at White Cliffs or seeing the sights of Cobar or Louth, both only a short drive away (in outback mileage). A quiet weekend away from all the stress of Wilcannia can always be had at Emmdale.

There are certainly some places in Australia that could do with a bit of global warming. One of these is Queenstown, Tasmania where I enjoyed a white Christmas in the 1960s. To site Climate Change and Energy Efficiency in Queenstown would remind workers that a bit of global warming can do no harm and that there are some places where the sun does not shine enough for solar energy. Workers could walk over the hill to work from Gormaston (as folk did in the past) as part of energy efficiency leadership and they might think twice about siting inefficient wind farms in their own back yard to exploit the roaring fourties. As part of leading by example, the Department of Climate Change and Energy Efficiency in Queenstown would have no heating. Tasmania's employment is dependent upon cheap long-term reliable base-load energy, something that solar and wind cannot provide. Weekend activities could rotate around *The Empire* and sightseeing at Zeehan and Strahan. The odd lobster or two from Granville Harbour with a Tasmanian Pinot to enlarge the bureaucratic bulge would be a fringe benefit. Tullah and Rosebery are suggestions for a quiet private weekend if the stress of incessant bureaucratic toil becomes too much.

The ideal place for Defence is Katherine, NT. Some 5% of Australians live in 50% of the country, the north. Huge wealth is generated from northern Australian mining, beef and agricultural industries yet the infrastructure is worse than in the Third World. Try using a mobile phone. Try getting television reception. Try to drive from A to B in the wet. Try getting health care when it is needed. The productive parts of northern Australia have little or no defence. If Defence fanned out from Katherine across the north, infrastructure would be improved, the wealth-generating assets of

Australia would be protected and any invasion from the north would be stopped before it reached Canberra. Why a hostile force would want to occupy Canberra is beyond me but can you imagine the blind confusion of a hostile force entering the gates of Canberra only to find that all government departments had been decentralised. Moscow memories. Weekends in a place where there are sporting speed limits must surely be an attraction for the boys as would a bit of barra fishing and camel riding. I understand unbranded cattle make great steaks for Grand Final BBQs. Gorge trips are a must when visitors come. For those in the military promoted to desk jobs, a bit of weekend croc shooting would keep their eye in.

Where does one site Education, Employment and Workplace Relations? For me, the ideal place would be Laverton, WA. Far too many here do not have the education and employment opportunities of other Australians and Laverton is proximal to mines, haulage roads, indigenous settlements and stations where safety and workplace relations are vital. First-hand experience for administering policy would be vital. It is only a hop, step and a jump to Kalgoorlie to see the School of Mines in action and work place relations operating at the Super Pit, mines and smelter. Although Laverton is not in northern Australia, maybe there could be discussions about how permanent centres with higher education could be established to service the north. Weekend activities are just too numerous to mention. Picnics at the Giles weather station, lost weekends in Kalgoorlie or a visit to the White House in Leonora come to mind. One can even step back in time to feel the ghost of an American president at the Sons of Gwalia. It doesn't get any better than that, does it?

Apologies to the rest of Australia but there is really no competition for Families, Housing, Community Services and Indigenous Affairs. It has to be Halls Creek, WA. What a unique opportunity to experience first-hand every single aspect of this portfolio in just one town. A one-stop shop is just too good to be missed. Halls Creek is closer than Canberra for administration of the Tiwi Land Council and it is a line ball whether Canberra or Halls Creek is closer for administration of the Torres Strait

Regional Authority. In order to fully understand administration details, there should be two shifts with the day shift at 6 am to 3 pm and the afternoon shift at 3 pm to midnight. The 9-hour shift is a compromise between the 12-hour shift that most in reality land work and a Canberra working day. A quiet lonely walk home at midnight after work would sharpen up afternoon shift thinking on indigenous policy. Spare time could be spent in the beautiful Kimberleys, tourists pay huge amounts to visit such attractions and the opportunity to live in the middle of paradise I am sure just could not be resisted by bureaucrats. Bungle Bungles here we come.

Considering that Australia is kept alive by mining and agriculture and that some 4,950 permits, approvals and agreements were necessary to start the new employment- and wealth-generating Roy Hill mine, there is huge competition for the siting of Finance and Deregulation. Luina, Tas., Tennant Creek, NT, Roxby Downs, SA, Kalgoorlie, WA, Parabadoo, WA, Telfer, WA, Mount Isa, Qld, Alpha, Qld and Weipa, Qld all received a certificate of commendation. It was only by a short margin that Gladstone, Qld was chosen. Around Gladstone, new proposed mining and gas projects are bound up for years by red, black and green tape, the coal mines are proximal, sugar farming is on the coast with beef cattle inland and the aluminium refinery and coal loader are right at the back door. Gladstone is a huge exporter of LNG. Each minute these activities are stopped by regulation costs the country and trainees would be required to get work experience at the mines, smelter and loader before entering the bureaucracy. Gladstone's activities help to keep the bureaucracy financed and this can only be appreciated first-hand. There are endless weekend activities on the water, visits to coal-fired power stations and weekends in Mount Morgan for those wanting quiet time away from the bustle.

Asia needs to be close for Foreign Affairs and Trade. We need to continually shake hands and kiss babies with our near neighbours and if it were not for daily ship loads of iron ore, coal, concentrate, refined metals and LNG to Asia, then we could not afford to buy our mobile 'phones, iPods, iPads and Toyotas. The ideal place is Port Hedland, WA. It is only a 3-hour flight to Singapore, one can view trains unloading and ships loading while thinking how towns like Port Hedland contribute to the GDP. Maybe in a quiet reflective moment, a bureaucrat might look across the Indian Ocean, think of West Africa and deduce that all could be very quickly lost in northern Australia because of bureaucratic impediments. Restful weekends can be spent fishing, viewing petroglyphs, train spotting or just chilling out at Karratha, Roebourne or Dampier. A few hours every weekend is needed to clean the dust that penetrates everything in Port Hedland. A step back in time at the ghost town of Cossack would be a great weekend. Other weekend trips to Mount Tom Price, Parabadoo or Mount Newman may even be part of work duties and, if wangled right, could be paid for by the taxpayer. For entrepreneurs, there are some great real estate investment opportunities in Port Hedland if the WA government ever decides to release land.

The Commonwealth Parliament definitely should not be in Canberra. It must be held all over the country in town halls, CWA meeting rooms, mechanics' institutes and public libraries with the occasional sitting on river banks, clay pans, salt lakes and sand dunes. A sitting in a large open pit such as Mt Whaleback would be classy. Cabinet may even do what the Maldives did for a publicity stunt and hold a meeting underwater. The air supply would guarantee a short meeting. Prime Ministers would not have to be stabbed in the back, tampering with the air tanks would easily do the job. Local pubs are often the places for outback public meetings and a little bit of lunatic soup imbibed before question time would make it even more entertaining, especially if Bob Katter was elected speaker. This would allow politicians to meet the taxpayer in the ultimate public gallery. Politicians would not be required to have an expensive Canberra office where they could hide when parliament sits. It is a turpitude that the unproductive place called Canberra has the highest average salary and house prices yet produces nothing. Canberra produces red, black and green tape that makes it even harder for the productive industries to survive and pay their taxes which keep Canberra alive. The great benefit of a feral Federal parliament is that the media circus would have to spend a large amount of time in inland Australia and this may then broaden their life experiences, balance their reporting and give them some perspective as to how a dollar is actually generated. Struggling local businesses would thrive. If the media did not chase parliament all over rural and outback Australia to get their stories, then that would also be a plus. A feral Federal parliament is clearly a win-win-win scenario.

Fair Work Australia, the Federal Court, the Family Court and the High Court are all administered by Courts. Why build an ugly above ground building in Canberra when one can be excavated for a profit? My recommendation therefore is Coober Pedy, SA. Courts would be proximal to areas such as Woomera where there are Commonwealth-State considerations. Litigation with the UK regarding cleaning up atomic bomb sites requires a short drive to the bomb sites, the town is close to aboriginal lands for land claims issues, close to uranium mines for environmental litigation and in the heart of an area where many folk disappear with no trace, don't pay child maintenance, escape arrest warrants or have a dodgy past. Imagine the tourist attraction of having the High Court of Australia in a dugout. During long boring hearings, judges could pick out a bit of colour from the walls of the court house. One presumes that the folk from Courts are civilised and play golf. The golf course at Coober Pedy has a "Keep off the grass" sign even though there is no grass. Now, how civilised is that? Other civilised weekend activities could be at William Creek, Marree and Lyndhurst. A visit to Farina is a must, it shows how quickly climate has changed naturally and how decisions made on short-term thinking have been economically disastrous.

With Health and Ageing, I go to my sentimental favourite. It is Broken Hill, NSW. It is no different from many rural towns with an ageing and decreasing population, increased strains on the health system, a lack of health care investment, a lack of employment and training, moving out of young people to cities for employment, moving in of welfare recipients capitalising on cheap housing and the impossibility of finding work thereby guaranteeing continuing welfare and an ice epidemic. Rural populations do not have the health care and longevity of city populations and the challenge would be to reverse this situation starting with a soft target. Bureaucrats could run a book as to whether their child would be born in Broken Hill, born mid-air in a RFDS plane or born after airlifting to Adelaide. This all depends upon whether an obstetrician is in town or not. The RFDS base allows workers to see rural health first hand. Maybe a summer time trip with the RFDS landings and takeoffs at 10 stations and hamlets in a day would sharpen up decision-making. What a place for time off. One could go up the river for fishing and yabbying, there are many places to see if aboriginal culture is in your blood and, for the sensitive artistic types, Broken Hill now has more art galleries than pubs. Sunsets over the Mundi Mundi are so emotionally taxing that revival at Silverton is necessary. I am told that the St Patrick's Day and Silver City Cup race meetings are pretty good but I can't remember.

Human Services handle Centrelink, child support and Medicare. Of course, the western suburbs of Sydney and Melbourne come to mind as do the northern suburbs of Adelaide but the real problems lie in complex rural societies. Coen, Qld is the outstanding choice. The great attraction is that it has tropical foods, endless protein from the land and sea and a climate that would make bureaucrats wonder why they suffered Canberra winters for so many years. Most of the community on the Cape would be clients of Human Services and there is every reason for the bureaucrats to know their clients personally rather than deal with pieces of paper, endless spreadsheets and mind-numbing meetings. And what a place for recreation with the wild rivers, pristine wilderness and proximity to numerous tropical paradises. If an overseas weekend trip is contemplated, then I recommend Thursday Island.

There are some good possibilities for Immigration and Citizenship. Christmas Island was short-listed. Another possibility was using the deserted Baxter Camp at Woomera for headquarters but the odds on favourite drew the barrier. We should never have scuttled HMAS *Adelaide*. It could have been moored off Ashmore Reef as a one-stop shop to meet and greet illegals. This would allow rapid on-site processing thereby avoiding illegals hanging around detention centres for years and then burning them down. Of course, the large guns would have to be dismantled as they would frighten off illegals coming to Ashmore Reef. With the HMAS *Adelaide* moored at Ashmore Reef, naval patrols could do what naval patrols should be doing rather than answering mobile 'phone calls from illegal boats once they are in territorial waters. This would streamline processing and, if the illegals' 'phone batteries were dead, HMAS *Adelaide* would be visible from miles away. Public servants could do what a very large number of other people do, fly-in fly-out and live in a dry camp. There are daily helicopter FIFO trips to the rigs from Learmonth, bolting on a few extra fuel tanks may get the choppers to Ashmore Reef. FIFO requires long shifts for many days in a row with no relaxation time but I am sure that public servants could unwind by dropping a line over the stern and watching the brilliant sunsets. Now that is reality.

Infrastructure and Transport should really be sited where there is no infrastructure and transport. The problem with such a siting is that this happens to be most of inland Australia so the choices are endless. Administration could be managed with conference calls and Skype, except in the wet season, dust storms and times when the lines are down. This is almost always. This mobile-free zone would enable bureaucrats to concentrate on work and minimise social 'phone calls during work hours. Why should meetings be held in a sterile room in Canberra when they could equally as well held at Rabbit Flat, NT? I know of one large building there that could be used as a conference venue. This portfolio administers rail, air and marine activities and associated safety. Landing at Rabbit Flat has a Sir Hubert Wilkins-type heroic aspect to it so every landing would be a first-hand experience of air safety. The north-south rail line is not too far away and it is only a short trip to visit where the infrastructure hubs should be in northern Australia. As for weekends.... well, where do I start? The choices are infinite. What about an intimate weekend at Fitzroy Crossing?

There are a couple of towns in Australia that have really punched above their weight with Innovation, Industry, Science and Research. Although differential froth flotation was invented in Broken Hill, Mount Isa, Qld certainly takes the cake with the invention of new smelting, grinding and flotation processes. Innovation, science and research are certainly absolutely vital for deep high temperature mining, ventilation, smelting, underground safety and communications, the successful release of wealth from fine-grained ores and novel transport systems. With new projects on the horizon in the Mount Isa-Cloncurry area, all the firepower needed should be close at hand. The choices of weekend activities are daunting. Fishing up the Gulf and in the rivers, horse riding, water sports, supporting the impoverished Irish Club and the annual world famous rodeo. Weekend trips to Dajarra, Mary Kathleen, Cloncurry and Tennant Creek could offer a private get away from all the stress of bureaucratic life in Mount Isa.

The office of the Prime Minister and Cabinet must remain in Canberra, ACT as a memorial to our stupidity. We need to have memorials surrounded by reality. We converted a perfectly good productive sheep paddock into the national capital. Sheep paddocks produce wealth, Canberra consumes wealth as shown by the fact that the economic growth of Canberra is higher than the primary producing state of Western Australia. *Quelle scandal!* To have this office in Canberra is commensurate with its administration of all sorts of trusts, museums, galleries and libraries. Maybe bureaucrats could work in a glass office so tourists could stand outside and view first-hand the frenetic pace of administration of our museums. And as for public service recreational activities in Canberra, I am at a loss to think of something. Maybe they could visit their own galleries, libraries and museums as part of self-assessment.

Where are Resources, Energy and Tourism all rather close to each other? No contest. It is Chillagoe, Qld. There are active and old metal mines, active and old marble quarries and old smelters in and around town. Perhaps there will be new mines. Coastal tourists have now discovered Chillagoe. Geoscience Australia has already left its footprint in the

Featherbed Ranges and would feel at home in a town where there is already a vibrant geological community. Direct Perth-Cairns flights go overhead and would remind public servants that they must administer offshore petroleum safety with occasional hands on visits to the West. They could even use the Immigration and Citizenship choppers for hopping from one offshore rig to another. Chillagoe is the pick spot for public service recreation. The Walsh offers swimming and fishing without worrying about salties (although the Johnson River crocs can give you a bit of a heart start). During the wet when the roads are closed, town activities rotate around the caves, The Hub, John and Donna Burton's *Post Office*, the old smelters, the old Red Dome mine and the defunct railway station. The Big Weekend rodeo and races is the social event of the year. No point in leaving Chillagoe at weekends, everything is there.

Sustainability, Environment, Water, Population and Communities is a bit of a mouthful. They deal with Antarctica, botanic gardens, Bureau of Meteorology, water and the Great Barrier Reef. There is just no place proximal to all these responsibilities. Heard Island was pipped at the post by Walhalla, East Gippsland, Victoria because it has Antarctic-like winters, there are pristine cool temperate forests that are essentially God's botanic gardens, there are numerous large rivers where water is unused and flows to the sea and it was only a few hundred million years ago that there were Great Barrier Reefs in East Gippsland. It was only 100 million years ago that Gippsland was joined to Antarctica, which then was covered by temperate rainforests. Who says climate does not change naturally? As for the Bureau of Meteorology, we get weather everywhere so it matters not whether they are in Walhalla, Warburton or Woop Woop. Much of the water from Gippsland is for cooling of thermal coal power stations in Yallourn, without this water the lights would be off in Victoria and there would be no drinking water for Melbourne. Recreational activities vary from wood chopping to fly fishing and fossicking to bushwalking (although one has to be a bit careful as stumbling onto a forest cash crop can create difficulties). The summer forest fires provide wonderful sunsets. Twin town holidays could be taken in Regensburg, the home of the mythical Walhalla in Germany.

The name Marble Bar conjures up a romantic image of a marble-lined bank with underground gold ingot-filled chambers, serenity and wealth. The *Ironclad* at Marble Bar also suggests that there is a Fort Knox equivalent at Marble Bar. And that is certainly the case. Many have entered the *Ironclad* and have never been known to leave. This romantic infrastructure should be exploited. Marble Bar, WA is clearly the perfect place for Treasury. The Australian Taxation Office would be well suited for Marble Bar, the high tonnage of duplicate records could be stored securely in old underground mines and the Australian Mint could make coins from local gold. A large amount of Australia's wealth is collected in the Pilbara so the taxation office would be close to its core business. Recreation could be intertwined with formal visits to Karratha, Mount Newman, Hope Downs, Mt Tom Price, Parabadoo, Roy Hill, Port Hedland and Argyle. If one wanted a very private dirty weekend away, then I recommend Nullagine (although you have to book well in advance).

Rural, outback and northern Australia is doing its bit to make Australia efficient, prosperous and habitable. Now it's Canberra's turn to show some leadership, reduce waste, reduce costs, get out of the Canberra bubble and get real.

(2012)

Renewable energy targets

A simple evaluation of ideological electricity shows that it is unsustainable. The answer is certainly not blowing in the wind. The amount of energy embedded in steel pylons, concrete footings, blades, wiring, magnets, land clearing and roads is more than a wind pylon would ever generate in its working life. Wind industrial complexes cannot generate electricity in a gentle zephyr or a gale, cannot operate continuously and optimistically operate at 20% of nameplate capacity. These wind industrial complexes are not wind farms because farms have to economically produce something useful for humans.

Wind industrial complexes have the life of a parasite because they freeload themselves onto existing grids paid by conventional efficient energy, need subsidies and drain electricity from the grid when it is too cold. Wind turbines don't run on wind, they run on subsidies. From the taxpaying consumer. Without subsidies, we would save huge amounts of money and would have guaranteed tried-and-proven reliable base load power from conventional sources that have served us well for a century.

Government policies on renewable energy targets have resulted in massive never-ending subsidies (paid by the consumer) that have been scooped up by opportunistic businesses signing long-term take-or-pay contracts. Because governments cannot abandon a renewable energy target policy that appeases a few percent of the electorate, consumers are left with expensive unreliable electricity, a chaotic distribution scheme unable to handle surging and no energy security. The cost of electricity is so high that businesses are closing and people are losing their jobs. It will all end in tears. The only way governments will change policy is when people die as a result of blackouts. Watch this space.

A single 1,000-megawatt wind industrial complex produces at least 7 million tonnes of carbon dioxide in component construction and concrete. Thousands of diesel-driven truckloads of concrete are required just for the footings. Maintenance by diesel-powered vehicles only adds to emissions. Wind industrial complexes need 24/7 backup from carbon dioxide emitting coal-fired power stations. Wind industrial complexes actually increase human emissions of carbon dioxide yet the story touted is that wind industrial complexes save carbon dioxide emissions.

A wind industrial complex using 660-kilowatt generators requires 7,600 generators at 20% efficiency to produce 1,000 megawatts. At $2,000 per kilowatt installation, this would cost $10 billion. This is ten times the cost of a 1,000-megawatt reliable clean coal-fired generator and more than twice the cost of a reliable nuclear 1,000-megawatt generator.

The environmental damage from wind industrial complexes is devastating. They are an ugly blot on the landscape. Construction of wind farms in rural areas results in a decline in residents' mental and physical health, decreased property values and community disharmony. A recent study showed hearing loss for people experiencing low frequency noise. Some companies, such as AGL, try to signal their environmental credentials when they want to destroy the environment by constructing a new wind industrial complex and concurrently generate electricity from old poorly maintained brown coal generators.

In the UK renewable energy costs, principally from wind, create fuel poverty for 2.4 million folk. In the 2012-2013 UK winter, there were an additional 35,000 deaths. This translates as 6 sick, elderly or vulnerable people killed every year for each installed wind turbine.

At 20% efficiency, 1,000 megawatts of delivered electricity requires about 800 square kilometres of cleared land. Bugger the wildlife. A nuclear or coal-fired 1,000-megawatt power station requires up to 60 hectares of cleared land. Habitats are destroyed by land clearing to reduce turbulence, generator fires are common and the resultant grass and bushfires that cannot be water bombed as wind pylons are a flight hazard.

In Spain, at least 18 million birds are slaughtered annually by wind turbine blades. Bird deaths in Germany are more than 300 per turbine and in Sweden almost 900 per turbine. German turbines kill more than 200,000 bats per year and in the US turbines kill some 2.8 million bats. Not to worry. Greens feel morally superior because they think that wind industrial complexes emit less carbon dioxide into the atmosphere and hence are saving the planet. They are certainly saving the planet from birds and bats yet climate will continue to do what it always does: change. If a nuclear- or coal-fired electricity generator damaged the environment as much as wind farms, there would be an outcry yet there is no outcry from environmentalists about the environmental damage by wind industrial complexes. Why not? Is it that environmentalists have no interest in the environment and just want to take control of everyone's life without the bother of having to face an electorate?

Wind industrial complexes are meant to be a contribution to prevent human-induced global warming resulting from carbon dioxide emissions. However, patient people have been waiting for three decades for the evidence showing human emissions of carbon dioxide drive climate change. The evidence is still missing in action.

The same calculations can be made for solar power. The amount of embedded energy in the metal, concrete, glass and roads is far greater than can ever be produced in a solar industrial complex's life. Construction of solar panels leaves toxic chemicals in someone else's backyard. The amount of carbon dioxide released in manufacture and maintenance is greater than the saving and coal-fired generators need to be on standby all the time because solar power is not continuous. Solar power has an efficiency of about 10% and, until the laws of physics are changed, this cannot be improved.

Biofuels make even a larger dent on the environment. Increased land clearing, food shortages and food costs and carbon dioxide emissions are the norm for alcohol production. It seems such a waste to burn alcohol in a car rather than the human body. Greens must be very pleased that the 4,000-megawatt Drax power station in Yorkshire has changed from coal to wood burning. Some 70,000 tonnes of wood is burned each day. Clear felling of forests in North Carolina, rail transport, pelletising, ship loading, 5,000 kilometres of ship transport, unloading and train transport does not sound very environmentally friendly and results in huge carbon dioxide emissions from diesel and bunker fuels. The EU has deemed that carbon dioxide emitted from wood burning is recycled by plants yet carbon dioxide emitted from fossil fuel burning is dangerous. Go figure!

Why are the Greens silent about the environmental damage of wind, solar and biofuel electricity generation? Wind power is unreliable, uneconomic and environmentally damaging. No wind industrial complex could provide mains power without generous subsidies, increased electricity charges and horrendous damage to the environment. It is the poor who suffer for increased electricity costs and the Greens just don't care about their fellow man. Few jurisdictions have plans for disassembling a wind industrial complex after its useful life. Mining companies are compelled to plan for mine closure and, in order to force the issue, are required to lodge a bond of tens of millions of dollars in case they go bankrupt. A few defunct wind pylons should remain on the skyline as a reminder to future generations of our environmental ecocide and as a memorial to stupidity resulting from caving into irrational green pressure.

Fund managers have invested in wind energy to make money, not to save the environment. Their due diligence would have shown that wind industrial complexes are a costly unreliable subsidised high-risk method of ruining the environment and that a Renewable Energy Target was unobtainable. Rather than plead to the government for even more money, fund managers should be sacked. It is not the role of government to bail out high risk investors who follow fads, fashions and frauds and spend more money on advertisements in newspapers rather than on due diligence.

Australia is well blessed with huge amounts coal, gas and uranium that could generate electricity for many hundreds of years. Base load electricity in Australia is from coal, gas and hydro and only a very small proportion of power can be added to the grid from solar or wind. Because of the abundance of coal in eastern Australia, advances in clean coal technology and the low cost of power generation, there is every reason to continue to have the bulk of our electricity generation from coal. Advances in clean coal technology invented in Australia may have huge markets in India and China.

To expand the hydro systems on the planet's driest habitated continent without massive mountain ranges is not feasible and gas power generation is more expensive than coal. Australia is exceptionally rich in gas but not in common sense and one jurisdiction has banned the exploration and exploitation of onshore gas. Hot dry rock geothermal energy is still in the experimental stage as are other technologies. Tidal power just does not have the head and energy density of hydroelectricity and is misty-eyed green ideology with a history of failure elsewhere.

If there is really community objection to cheap safe clean coal-fired electricity, then there are few choices left. As demands for base load power increase concurrent with the lack of construction of new coal-fired power stations, the nuclear option must be explored. The only tried-and-proven technology to generate large amounts of cheap electricity is nuclear. We have one small 20 megawatt nuclear reactor at Lucas Heights for creation of medical isotopes and scientific research, this needs to be near Kingsford Smith Airport as medical isotopes have a short half-life and delivery to hospitals on the other side of the continent takes time hence the isotope may decay to uselessness if the reactor was in a remote area of Australia.

There are three nuclear debates. The first is a cradle to grave nuclear industry wherein Australian yellowcake is beneficiated into fuel for leasing and Australia is paid to store waste generated from the leased fuel rods. This would a massive long-lived economic advantage for Australia. The second debate is whether base load electricity and even desalinated water is produced in southeastern Australia from nuclear reactors. The third is an economic debate about energy, including the nuclear option. The major economic cost to nuclear energy is environmental lawfare. These debates must be had as scores of other countries benefit from cheap safe nuclear power. However, it is easy to run scare campaigns on the invisible such as radiation, GM crops, bacteria and greenhouse gases.

However, as with all green scare campaigns, one expects negativity, bad science, misinformation and dark ages thinking and, quite frankly, I am sick to the back teeth of negativity and misinformation from the greens. When they are hunter gatherers and preach to me from their caves, I may deem to listen.

If Australia was really serious about maintaining its standard of living and quality of life, it would add employment-creating nuclear-powered electricity to the grid, use small portable modular nuclear power stations to run remote mines and towns, and establish a nuclear reprocessing industry to beneficiate spend fuel from other countries. Maybe Australia could launch itself into the 1950s and purchase nuclear-powered submarines. However, Australia has contracted to purchase nuclear submarines from which the nuclear power unit is removed and replaced with a diesel power unit.

In Sweden, a country considered to be an environmentally conscious democracy, Oskarshamm has three nuclear reactors and an interim spent fuel storage facility and Oesthammar has three reactors. The Swedish Nuclear Fuel and Waste Management Company undertook feasibility studies in eight municipalities for a deep waste repository. A poll showed that 79% of Oskarshammar and 75% Oesthammer residents supported a deep waste repository in their own towns. By contrast, Australia has 40% of the world's uranium reserves, exports yellowcake yet piously declines to add value by creating well needed jobs and infrastructure in embattled rural areas geologically suitable for waste disposal. Furthermore, Australia exports yellowcake knowing full well that waste products will be generated. The geologically stable ancient rocks of Sweden are no different from those of Australia.

Australia has closed university departments that teach nuclear science and engineering and hence the scientists and engineers who will be needed for the inevitable future nuclear power stations will have to be trained abroad. Ironically, they will probably be trained in nuclear power stations that derive their yellowcake from Australia. In similar displays of great foresight, there have been closures of numerous university geology, metallurgy and mining engineering departments despite the economic prosperity reaped from the minerals industry that provides some 44% of export earnings.

We are in a new dark age when scare campaigns promoted by Marxist dark greens with missionary zeal impute that it is sinful to have air conditioning, heating, cars, houses and a high standard living. Of course, sin has draconian consequences and doomsday garbage-in garbage-out modellers try to frighten us with projected temperature increases of 2 to 4°C and a projected sea level rise of 50 centimetres in 100 years. Dark greens want materialist Western countries to feel guilt about unproven global warming.

Do we really know that before the Industrial Revolution in the Medieval Climate Optimum (900-1300 AD), the temperature was at least 5°C warmer than now and there were crops and livestock in Greenland? No such farming exists on Greenland now. Rather than catastrophic depopulation, disease and sea level rise, there was great prosperity, less war and less disease. If one moves from Hobart to Darwin, then there is an average warming of 18°C but refugees from colder climates don't seem to drop like flies.

Since the zenith of the last glaciation, there has been a 130-metre sea level rise in 14,400 years resulting from natural climate change. This sea level rise is almost twice that predicted by the dark age doomsdayers and is normal in an interglacial. Throughout historical, archaeological and geological times, sea levels have been rising and falling, as has temperature.

To paraphrase a founder of Greenpeace, Dr Patrick Moore, the green movements have been taken over by neo-Marxists promoting anti-trade, anti-globalisation, anti-freedom and anti-civilisation. There has been no debate about the effects of anthropogenic greenhouse gases, only dark ages dogma with the result that the community has been politically and scientifically misled and deceived.

In order to avoid misinformation, I suggest that the green lobbyists be required to fulfil the same provisions of the law as company directors. Sections 180(2), 1317S and 1318 of the Corporations Law and the former Section 52 of the Trades Practices Act come to mind. These would require the greens to have done appropriate validated due diligence, to act in good faith and for proper purpose and to tell the truth. Directors of energy companies are required to fulfil the provisions of the Corporations Act, why can't the anti-coal and anti-nuclear lobbyists have the same ethical standards? It is only when the scientific misinformation ceases that Australia can have a knowledge-based economy and public debates based on validated information.

Maybe a long hot summer with power failures will stimulate the community to consider the nuclear option. As a resident of South Australia, my solution was simple. I purchased a fossil fuel-driven generator for my house.

(2013)

Australia's impact on global climate

The 24 million people in Australia generate 1.5% of annual global human-induced CO_2 emissions. Australia has 0.33% of the global population. USA emits 14 times and China emits 26 times more CO_2 than Australia.

Our high standard of living, a landmass of 7,692,024 square kilometres with a sparse inland population and greenhouse gas-emitting livestock combined with the transport of livestock, food and mined products long distances to cities and ports and the export of ores, coal, metals and food for 80 million people results in high *per capita* CO_2 emissions. Australia's exports of coal, iron ore and gas contributes to increasing the standard of living, longevity and health of billions of people in Asia.

If Australia emits 1.5% of global annual CO_2 emissions, 3% of the total annual emissions are anthropogenic and the atmosphere contains 400 parts per million by volume of CO_2, then one molecule in 6.6 million molecules in the atmosphere is CO_2 emitted from humans in Australia. This molecule has an atmospheric life of about 7 years before it is removed from the atmosphere and naturally sequestered. If Australia reduces human emissions of CO_2 by 5%, 50% or 100%, then this will make absolutely no difference whatsoever to the global atmospheric CO_2 content. An annual reduction in Australia's emissions by say 5% is surpassed by China's increase in emissions in a blink of the eyelid. It is totally pointless to reduce CO_2 emissions, especially as CO_2 is plant food and no one has yet shown that the human emissions of CO_2 drive global warming.

Australia has far greater economic priorities than to change a whole economy, increase energy costs, decrease employment and decrease international competiveness because of one poor lonely molecule of plant food in 6.6 million other atmospheric molecules. It is a very long bow to argue that this one molecule of plant food in 6.6 million other atmospheric molecules derived from Australia has any measurable effect whatsoever on global climate.

Australia exports a significant share of the global refined aluminium, zinc, lead, copper and gold and hence takes a hit for countries that import and use Australia's metals because smelting and refining in Australia results in CO_2 emissions. Neither smelting nor refining of the metals for other countries could take place without burning fossil fuels.

Annual Australian *per capita* CO_2 emissions are in the order of 20 tonnes per person. There are 30 hectares of forest and 74 hectares of grassland for every Australian and each hectare annually sequesters about 1 tonne of CO_2 because CO_2 is plant food. On the continental Australian landmass, Australians are removing by natural sequestration many times the amount of CO_2 they emit. Crops remove even more CO_2 from the atmosphere. Australia's net contribution to atmospheric CO_2 is negative and this is confirmed by the net CO_2 flux estimates from the IBUKI satellite CO_2 data set.

Australia's continental shelf is 2,500,000 square kilometres in area. Carbon dioxide dissolves in ocean water and the cooler the water, the more CO_2 dissolves in water. Living organisms extract dissolved CO_2 and calcium from seawater to build corals and shells. This natural marine sequestration locks away even more Australian emissions of CO_2 and adds to the negative contribution of atmospheric CO_2 made by Australia. Using the thinking of the IPCC, UN and activist green groups, Australia should be very generously financially rewarded with money from populous, desert and landlocked countries for removing from the atmosphere its own emitted CO_2 plus the CO_2 emissions from many other nations.

Satellite measurements show that there has been a greening of the planet over the last few decades, thanks to a slight increase in traces of plant food in the atmosphere. Without CO_2, there would be no plants and without plants, there would be no animals. Geology shows that atmospheric CO_2 has not driven global warming since planet Earth formed. Why should it now? Dangerous global warming did not occur in the past when the atmospheric CO_2 content was hundreds of times higher than now. Each of the major ice ages was initiated at a time when there was more CO_2 in the atmosphere than now.

The planet has not warmed for two decades despite a massive increase in CO_2 emissions during the industrialisation of Asia. Computer models predicted a steady temperature increase over this time and over 30 million weather balloons have not detected a modelled hot spot over the equator. All models have failed and are not in accord with measurements.

Australia has wasted billions on the assumption that reduction of human emissions of CO_2 will have some effect on the climate and that human emissions of CO_2 drive global warming. Reliable base load power systems are being closed and destroyed in the forlorn hope that solar and wind energy will provide anything from 20 to 50% of Australia's energy. The end result will be expensive electricity, power outages and collapse of a transmission system due to surging.

We continue to waste billions yet we have a national debt of hundreds of billions.

(2014)

Along the road between Blinman and Arkaroola lies the solitary grave of
Peter Fagan, who passed away in January 1871.

Green view from the red dirt

I argue that the green movement is a city-based fundamentalist religious movement divorced from science and active in politics. I write from the Arkaroola Wilderness Resort in the far north Flinders Ranges of South Australia where I undertake geological field work in this mountainous unforgiving wilderness. This is indeed a privilege. Fieldwork is an attempt to understand nature and this intimacy with nature stimulates questioning.

There are some pilgrimages that one should make. The Kimberleys, the Great Barrier Reef and Arkaroola are my top three. At Arkaroola, the outstanding arid mountainous scenery with endemic plants, animals and minerals shows us how great processes have changed the planet, that we humans might not be very important at all and how little we really understand. Huge pressures and heat melted sediments such as sands, silts and muds some 1580 million years ago. The sediments were cooked up to a great variety of schists, some of which contain sapphire, and the molten rocks sucked up most of the uranium, thorium and potassium from the sediments. These melts cooled and solidified as a uranium-rich granite some 12 kilometres beneath a mountain range that was later flattened by weathering and erosion. The giant supercontinent, Rodinia, started to break up 830 million years ago. Continental breakup was associated with the spewing out of basalt lava, the opening of a large shallow basin (Adelaidean Sea), the deposition of shallow marine sediments and evaporation of parts of this sea to form large salt deposits. Only bacterial fossils were present then as multicellular life had not yet appeared on planet Earth.

A remarkable event took place. Ice sheets many kilometres thick formed at the equator at sea level some 700 million years ago. This was the greatest climate change that our planet had ever enjoyed and yet we don't know exactly why this ice age started and why it ended after tens of millions of years. This was the time of snowball Earth. A huge amount of glacial debris was left behind at Arkaroola by the retreating ice. Soon after this ice age ended, there was an experiment with multicellular life during the interglacial (Arkaroola Reef) when the global temperature had risen just slightly from about -40°C to +40°C and the oceans had been filled with nutrients as melt waters washed very fine particles of rock flour into the oceans. These nutrients stimulated experiments with life. Environmental activists are worried about a 0.7°C temperature rise over a century (which may be natural anyway) and don't seem to know that at temperature rise of 0.7°C takes place by standing up or walking into another room.

The Arkaroola Reef formed at about 650 million years ago and fossils of multicellular sponge-like organisms unlike any later life on Earth are preserved. The reef was killed off by another ice age about 600 million years ago. Again, we do not know exactly why we had an ice age and why the ice age conditions changed to warmer conditions. The Arkaroola Reef is one of the few known well-preserved failed experiments with multicellular life on Earth. After more than two billion years when only bacterial life occurred on the planet, multicellular life made an appearance but it was just a cameo appearance.

After the second major glaciation, the Earth became warmer and again, there was another experiment with multicellular life. This was the Ediacaran fauna, discovered by the founder of Arkaroola Dr Reg Sprigg AO in 1946, which existed from about 583 to 542 million years ago. The soft-bodied jellyfish-like Ediacaran fauna are the key to understanding how animal life evolved on planet Earth. Predation led to the end of the Ediacaran fauna that ate algal mats, the new predators grew protective scales, shells and skeletons and the soft-bodied Ediacarans were no match. Sea floor sediments older than 542 million years in age are finely banded whereas anything younger has bioturbation and burrows demonstrating that since the Cambrian explosion of life there was a meal in eating the bacteria in mud as well as soft-bodied critters. Today the greatest biomass on Earth is still bacteria, with most life living in rocks down to 4 kilometres depth.

The 1580 million year old granites had a thick cover of sedimentary rocks and had cooked up perhaps 7 kilometres of overlying sedimentary rocks and glacial material deposited after the rifting and breakup of Rodinia 830 million years ago. The granites were rich in uranium, thorium and potassium; these elements break down by radioactive decay to give out heat, subatomic particles and form new chemicals. Around 500 million years ago, the whole sequence in the Flinders Ranges was compressed into folds and cooked up to about 300°C. In the Arkaroola area, the 1580 million year old granites were already at about 600°C, had cooked up the overlying insulating blanket of sedimentary rocks and had remelted the 1580 million year old granites. These remelted granites were even richer in uranium, thorium and potassium and solidified 441 million years ago. Arkaroola is the only place in the world where rocks have been cooked up and melted by radioactive heat. There has been some recent exploration in the Arkaroola area to use these hot granites to generate hot dry rock geothermal energy.

Rocks between 830 and 542 million years in age were also thrust onto the 1580-million-year-old granites 500 million years ago and ground waters penetrated the fractured rocks. These ground waters were heated by the 1580 and 441 million year old granites and eventually became so pressurised and hot that there was a massive gas volcano explosion (Mt Painter) at about 510°C. Gas streamed through the crater floor, precipitated minerals from waters and gas, hardened the crater floor and the softer rocks of the crater wall were later weathered and eroded. Mt Painter is now actually a crater floor with the crater walls removed by weathering and erosion, one of the rare cases of reverse topography.

Multiple gas explosions resulted in the precipitation of iron and uranium minerals, the multiple breaking up of rocks and the filling of the spaces with new haematite (iron oxide) and quartz. At Arkaroola, I have measured nine separate events of rocks breaking from gas explosions that took place from about 360 to 300 million years ago. The vented gases formed geysers and boiling mud pools at Mt Gee with a number of sinter terraces (Mt Painter) that were draped over the old landscape like in the volcanic fields of New Zealand or Yellowstone (USA). The Arkaroola area has the only known volcanic and geothermal system driven by radioactive heat. It is unique. What is more interesting is that bacterial life lived in these ancient hot radioactive springs and these hot spring sites are actively studied by NASA to measure a suitable landing spot on Mars to search for ancient and modern life.

By that time, Australia had drifted to the South Pole, glaciation was taking place and some fractures blasted out by gas explosions contain materials left behind by retreating glaciers about 260 million years ago. The area had been cleaned off by moving ice during this glaciation, heat was no longer trapped at depth and the uranium-, thorium- and potassium-rich granites were then able to radiate heat to the atmosphere and the heat was not trapped deep down in the rocks.

To the east and west, the area was covered by a giant inland sea and the sediments of the Great Artesian Basin were deposited. Arkaroola may have been covered by these sediments or may have been exposed to the elements. I suspect the latter because we still have an old land surface about 120 million years old preserved at Arkaroola, the Mawson Plateau and Freeling Heights. This was when Arkaroola was at the South Pole enjoying a temperate climate. There is also evidence of ice sheets at Arkaroola at this time. These warm times finished about 6 million years ago, glaciation gave alternating periods of orbitally-driven cold and warm. It was warm for a few thousand years about 6,000 years ago in the peak of the current interglacial. Some of the vegetation surviving in the arid Arkaroola area in hidden valleys is actually tropical vegetation, a remnant from these past warm wet times.

What we do know and can measure is that the north Flinders Ranges has been rising, probably for the last 100 million years but at least for the last 30 million years. It is still rising as shown by the regular earthquakes in the area at present mainly centred on Copley. On a sunny cloudless day I have heard the earthquakes, they sound like distant thunder and then it feels like someone has hit the soles of the feet with a hammer. This earthquake activity is because Australia had the good sense to move northwards away from Antarctica in the breakup of the giant supercontinent Gondwana about 100 million years ago. We moved northwards at up to 7 centimetres a year, got rid of New Zealand (and a good thing too) by rifting the Tasman Sea and creating Tasman Sea volcanoes (e.g. Balls Pyramid, Lord Howe Island, Norfolk Island). Parts of continental Australia were under stress and rose (e.g. Great Dividing Range, Barrier Ranges, Flinders Ranges) and other parts were stretched and sank (e.g. Lake Frome, Lake Eyre). This process is still taking place as Australia continues to move northwards.

The rise of the far north Flinders Ranges is along faults (i.e. areas where rocks have been broken rather than bent). These faults are currently active and move every now and then. Each event of movement breaks rocks and produces an earthquake. At the Paralana Hot Springs, water at 57°C has been heated by radioactively decaying uranium, thorium and potassium, the water is only a few days old, derives from the Mawson Plateau and bubbles of the radioactive gas radon (as well as carbon dioxide, methane and rotten egg gas) rise through the warm water. The hot springs are one of the few examples of hot springs in the world where the heat is from radioactivity and not volcanoes. But that's not the interesting bit.

On the floor of the hot springs is an algal mat that clearly survives in conditions that are hot, bathed in sunlight and radioactive. This is a window into how ancient life on Earth would have lived billions of years ago. In the hot radioactive water are scores of different species of bacteria and are the very same bacteria that exist in the cooling waters of nuclear power stations. The Paralana Hot Springs are full of extremophiles, the type of life we could expect on Mars, in deep fractures in the Earth or on ancient Earth.

What a great story the Earth history at Arkaroola gives us. This is the history of great uplift and sinking, melting of rocks, bending of rocks double, evolution of complex life, gas explosions, radioactivity, climate change and major planetary processes that are still taking place today. This scientific story is not the final story. The Arkaroola Reef was only found a decade ago, many more interesting discoveries are to be made and there is great argument in scientific circles about the Cryogenian glaciations and the appearance of complex life on Earth. Arkaroola is a place that shows us that science is not settled on any issue.

Science is based on dominant paradigms that are open to change at any time. Our understanding of nature requires a depth and breadth of knowledge, a healthy uncertainty, a willingness to change and a measure of awe provoked by the complexity of nature. Nature changes very rapidly and continues to surprise. Climate, sea level, atmospheric composition, life, landscapes and temperature all change very rapidly by many mechanisms for a great diversity of reasons. For millions of years hominids and other organisms have survived, adapted and become extinct as a result of these changes. Nature is not mysterious, it is quantifiable. Science is married to evidence and divorced from value judgment.

We scientists argue about the data, which may be from measurement, observation or experiment. The explanation of data, a theory, is the neatest way of explaining such data and this too provokes healthy argument. New data or a re-evaluation of old data commonly results in the abandonment of a treasured popular paradigm. This is the methodology of science.

Herein lies the problem with city-based greens and other religious fundamentalists such as the creationists. The idol for worship is a dogmatic ideology enshrined in value judgments that allows no change despite scientific data to the contrary. Nature is made the mystery by greens in isolation from integrated interdisciplinary scientific knowledge, somewhat contrary to traditional Christian views where the mystery is the supernatural. It is for this reason that I argue that environmental groups are a modern urban religion, albeit terribly flawed. From theologian Paul

Tillich's perspective, the change from the dominant paradigm to dogma is a shift from preliminary to ultimate concerns resulting in evil.

Creationists have not evolved from the science and inexact literalist contradictory theology of the mid 17th Century when the popular scientific paradigm was that the planet was 6,000 years old and a mythical great flood shaped the planet's surface, deposited fossiliferous sediments and killed sinners.

The greens cannot accept that the good old days were not good old days, that natural changes are far greater than even their worst case human-induced doomsday scenario and that we now live in a society blessed with saviours such as science, technology and industry. Our greens bathe in the benefits of an industrial society yet, for reasons of nefarious politics, hypocrisy and ignorance, decide to be both within and without our industrial society. They have a black and white view of the world. Their opinionated dogmatic restricted city-based view of the world (good) is in contrast to the testable and changing conclusions of interdisciplinary interdependent international science (bad).

Many city folk have lost contact with nature and when exposed to nature this can be deeply disturbing. Such disconnection produces a romantic yearning for that which never existed, a yearning to be at one with nature despite a lack of understanding of nature and a yearning to do something, whatever something might be. This disconnection produces irrationality, contradictions and the creation of green fundamentalism as the new religion of urban environmentalists. Disconnection of city people from nature has only added to the frustration of depoliticised rural people thereby creating political instability.

In the cities, this disconnection is exacerbated by the lack of connection between seasons and seasonal foods or killing for meat protein and an uncompromising dogma about those outside cities who take risks to produce the energy, water, food and mineral resources we so voraciously consume.

We watch asinine concocted survival programs unaware that there are twenty film support crew out just of shot. Such programs appeal to our primitive instincts yet show how disconnected from nature we really have become. We plant gardens comprising water-hungry European vegetation, consume more and more water, don't build new dams and don't collect roof rainwater. City folk purchase a 4WD, drive on sealed highways out of the cities as part of a big adventure and, as soon as they meet a perfectly good dirt road, they stop. A big family discussion takes place, the vehicle turns around and continues to drive on the sealed road. I have seen this pathetic disconnect from reality many times.

We feel good to see large green areas on maps called national parks and then promptly forget about these areas. My recent bush walks in national parks from Benambra (Vic.) to Tharwa (ACT) shows such community assets are appallingly maintained by governments and the privately owned wilderness areas, such as Arkaroola, are far better maintained. A few weeks at Arkaroola might actually show city-based green fundamentalists that the world is exciting, evolving, not black and white and everything they claim to be concerned about fades into insignificance.

The ancient monastics were correct. An extended time in a desert wilderness allows the discarding of trivialities, an interaction and connection with nature and an understanding of our place in the world. And it is not really a very important place after all.

(2015)

Human emissions of hot air

Climate change has taken place for thousands of millions of years. The extraordinary claim that humans cause climate change must be supported by extraordinary evidence.

It has not been shown that any measured modern climate change is different from past climate changes. In the past, climate has changed due to numerous processes and these are still driving climate change. Why should physics and chemistry change because we are alive?

Past global warmings have not been driven by an increase in atmospheric carbon dioxide (CO_2) and, during the time that humans have been in Earth, there has been no correlation between temperature change and human emissions of carbon dioxide. Without correlation there can be no causation.

The underpinning assumption is that human emissions of CO_2 drive global warming and, in order to arrest the warming trend, human emissions of CO_2 must be reduced.

Emissions of CO_2 from human activities such as production of energy, metals and cement; land, air and sea transport; and heating and cooling account for about 3% of total annual emissions. Despite very generous research funding from the public purse, it has yet to be shown that the human emissions of CO_2 actually drive global warming.

If it could be shown that the human emissions of CO_2 drive global warming, then it would also have to be shown that the natural emissions of CO_2, 97% of total annual emissions, do not drive global warming. This has not been done.

Natural emissions are mainly from oceanic degassing and mantle degassing via millions of submarine volcanoes, mid ocean ridge volcanicity and ocean floor fractures with less voluminous emissions from mantle degassing via terrestrial volcanoes, mountain degassing, fractures and earthquakes and respiration.

In past times when the Earth's atmosphere had hundreds of times the current CO_2 level, there was no runaway greenhouse, no irreversible warming and no climate catastrophe. In fact, there were ice ages.

The erroneous assumption that the dominant driving force for global warming is the emission of CO_2 by humans has been made in the absence of considering the effects of the Sun, tectonics, the Earth's orbital oscillations, oceanic oscillations and extra-terrestrial radiation.

The oceans remove most of the CO_2 from the atmosphere. What is rarely considered is that CO_2 is plant food, it is rapidly removed from the atmosphere and it has an atmospheric life of about 7 years. Soils and rock weathering also quickly remove CO_2 from the atmosphere. There is an underlying assumption that once humans emit a CO_2 molecule, it stays in the atmosphere for a very long time or even forever. Any CO_2 emitted by humans is part of the carbon cycle that involves recycling of CO_2 through the atmosphere, life, water and rocks.

The human-induced global warming ideology is underpinned by the perception that the planet is static and that dynamic change only occurred once humans started to emit CO_2. Nothing could be further from the truth.

The Industrial Revolution in the UK, Europe and the USA triggered a great increase in human emissions of CO_2 from the use of fossil fuels. This led to increased prosperity, health, longevity and the rise of the middle class, many of whom now object to the use of coal.

The planet has been warming over the last 300 years since the Maunder Minimum and it has not been shown that any part of this general warming trend is of human origin. Furthermore, during this general warming trend, there have been both cooling and warming events.

Another Industrial Revolution is taking place in Asia, fossil fuels are bringing people out of poverty and the rate of emissions of CO_2 from burning fossil fuels has accelerated. However, there is no correlation between the emissions of CO_2 by humans and temperature. In fact, the increased content of CO_2 in the Earth's atmosphere has led to the greening of the planet and increased agricultural productivity.

If only human emissions of CO_2 drive global warming, then there should have been no warming and cooling events before the Industrial Revolution. However, pre-Industrial Revolution climate changes were fast and numerous events of cooling led to depopulation.

The arguments to support human emissions of CO_2 drive global warming are based on models whereby the principal variable is CO_2. Measurements and observations do not support this hypothesis. Past natural warmings have had a delayed effect on increasing atmospheric CO_2. This is the exact opposite of the populist catastrophist mantra. If climate models are run backwards, past events of cooling and warming are not seen.

We have now had more than two decades of climate models and these models have not predicted what was measured. Without correlation of CO_2 with temperature over time, there can be no causation hence there is only one conclusion: Human emissions of CO_2 do not drive global warming. This shows that complicated models in a multi-component chaotic dynamic system are unreliable and naïve attempt to understand Nature.

Models, research and energy policy are underpinned by the fallacious assumption that human emissions of CO_2 drive global warming. Such ideology thrives in a dumbed-down educational environment where there is little knowledge of history and geology.

Because it has not been demonstrated that there is a relationship between human emissions of CO_2 and global warming, then climate policy, renewable energy targets, carbon capture, global warming research and "renewable" energy are unnecessary, delusional and a waste of money. New financial instruments have been created by an army of spongers to steal money from electricity consumers.

Coal-fired Australian electricity used to be the cheapest in the world, especially in Victoria. Because of the unsubstantiated belief that human emissions of CO_2 drive global warming, Australian electricity is now among the most expensive in the world. Electricity in developing nations such as Ethiopia and Ecuador costs 10% that of South Australia which has intentionally placed itself into sub-Third World reliability and costs. Victoria has now joined the suicidal race to the bottom.

Green ideology and frightened politicians detached from reality have led to expensive and unreliable wind energy that is devastating for birds, bats, koalas, landscapes and human health. This is not environmentalism.

Green ideology is based on false assumptions and unvalidated science and has led to unreliable expensive electricity and environmental devastation.

Maybe environmentalism is about total control of people and deindustrialisation rather than the environment.

(2017)

Global warming, meet creationism

Any system that allows a questioning of beliefs is an enlightened system. The truth can only be determined by fearlessly having vibrant critical and analytical discussion, by embracing rather than fearing uncertainty and by not suppressing evidence contrary to one's beliefs. This does not happen with the populist climate movement. Human-induced global warming is an unproven scientific hypothesis that has become an article of faith.

The peer review and grant processes are controlled by the secular equivalent of the *Collegium Romanum* and leave faith unchallenged. In schools today, scientific 'facts' are taught in the same way as theological 'facts' were taught centuries ago. Contrary scientific facts are now casually dismissed as 'alternative facts', primary data measurements are 'homogenised' and the alleged real world is now defined by computer models, not measurements.

Creationists also ignore or amend validated scientific measurements to try to show that the planet was created 6,000 years ago, that the planet suffered a great flood 4,000 years ago and that there was no biological evolution of life. The logical consequences are that the continents started to fragment 4,000 years ago, for the continents to drift to where they are now would have created a 100-metre high bow wave, that there would have been catastrophic volcanic eruptions every few minutes with associated devastating earthquakes and tsunamis. No one seemed to notice or record such events over the last 4,000 years. Maybe it was just not possible to write history in billowing volcanic dust and reorganise notes every few minutes when they were shuffled around by tsunamis. To accommodate their unfounded scientific beliefs, creationists even attempted to change the speed of light and tried to reduce the number of species on Earth to stop the horrendous traffic jam as millions of species sprinted up the gangplank of Noah's Ark. Similarly, global warmists ignore the cyclical events of a warming and cooling planet over 4,500 million years.

Creationists cannot answer simple questions. How did the blind marsupial mole get from where the Ark beached on Mt Ararat across oceans and land masses to Australia? Environmental fundamentalists have never been able to answer why measured changes in modern climate are within variability of past changes or why there were no tipping points or runaway global warming in former times when atmospheric CO_2 was hundreds of times higher than now and have never shown that the human emissions of CO_2 drive global warming. Creationists and global warmers have a problem with time. Their solution is simple. Ignore or change history and geology. This thread of dishonesty unites these fundamentalist religions.

Today's Westerners have enjoyed the greatest wealth, health, diet, food abundance, safety, equality, freedoms and longevity that humans have ever experienced on Earth. Pestilence, famine, death and war, the Four Horsemen of the Apocalypse, are now in retreat thanks to the liberating forces of capitalism, democracy, science and technology. Previous events of global warming such as the Minoan, Roman and Medieval were times of great prosperity and population increase whereas Jack Frost has been the deadly killer in times such as the Dark Ages and the Little Ice Age. Science, engineering and architecture will protect most Westerners against the inevitable future cycles of cooling and warming. Humans have burned and eaten everything that nature offered since Adam was a boy and we are the first generation to try to act otherwise. We are also the first generation to fear warmth.

Established religion in the West has declined yet many yearn for a spiritual life and want something to believe in. People will believe almost anything to fill a yawning spiritual vacuum. Extreme environmentalism incorporates many of the characteristics of Christianity and communism such as sin, guilt, sacrifice (as long as it is done by others), payment of indulgences, repentance, redemption, dogma and blind submission to authoritarianism. Judgement Day in the form of extinction, sea-level change and global heating is close. For the new religion, the planet is static and any change must be because of human activity. The romantic environmentalist's lost Eden never existed. It was a world of disease, dung and death – now rebadged as sustainability.

The new religion is urban, atheistic and disconnected from nature, rural life and the realities of food, fibre, water, energy and mineral production necessary for survival. All necessities come from shops, followers are blameless as they enjoy the fruits of an affluent consumer life and real life occurs on a screen. Followers are terrified of doubt, scepticism and uncertainty. Dogma, suppression of alternative ideas and reliance on authority are typical of fundamentalist religions. The secular urban environmentalist religion claims to be underpinned by science yet ignores history, geology and logic and has no need for accurate reproducible data and the scientific method. Just as the Roman Empire discovered, once the masses have embraced a new religion, the state must follow. Like many fundamentalist religions, it attracts believers by announcing apocalyptic calamities unless we change our ways. Fear is bankable, fear is politically exploited and there is a never-ending sequence of disasters promoted by the media – now due to climate change resulting from Westerners sinfully emitting CO_2. The far higher emissions by the Chinese and Indians apparently don't create natural disasters. In the past natural disasters were punishment from God for our sin. Natural disasters now kill on average 60,000 people a year. What is not stated is that hundreds of years ago the figure was millions of people a year despite the smaller population. As always, disasters affect those in poverty most heavily.

A new class of high priest and vacuous follower deem that one element in the periodic table represents original sin. They try to re-mystify the world and seek miracles and magic from element number six. This element forms the backbone of all life on earth. Fundamentalist religions foster a sense of moral superiority and guilt and no need to tell the truth.

In science, we are in awe of nature; in religion, in awe of God. The new environmental religion is spiritually vacuous, in awe of nothing and loathes humans. The only climate change catastrophe is that we inflict upon ourselves a huge intellectual, moral, spiritual and economic cost because we ignore the past. We see a dumbed-down education system, social media vulgarity and violence, water and electricity shortages and massive fuel loads in unmanaged forests. Geology showed centuries ago that creationism was rubbish. It also shows that the new climate religion is total nonsense.

(2020)

Cash levels rising

Samoan Brianna Fruen, 23, was turned into a climate activist by her school teacher and 350.org when she was 11. She gave a first person account to world leaders at Glasgow's COP26 about what it feels like when her home and free and easy way of life is threatened by rising sea level. A 30-second search on a smart phone would have shown that atoll nations are growing in area. Her teacher and 350.org had fed her lies. Bumbling Boris followed showing that he too needs a basic education in critical thinking, logic and science.

In 1830, Sir Charles Lyell published the first of his three-volume classic *Principles of Geology: Being an Attempt to Explain the Former Changes in the Earth's Surface by Reference to Causes now in Operation*. Charles Darwin received the first volume in 1830 which he took with him on HMS *Beagle*, the others he received during his voyage. Lyell suggested that coral atolls formed around the rims of ancient submarine volcanoes.

Darwin's voyage allowed him to inspect many volcanic islands, coral reefs and atolls. In his 1842 book *The Structure and Distribution of Coral Reefs*, Darwin showed that volcanoes were at various heights above the sea floor. If sea level falls or a volcano rises from the sea floor, coral attached to the volcano is killed upon exposure to air. If sea level rises, coral attaches itself to a volcano and grows vertically and horizontally as sea level rises. Even very rapid sea level rises enlarge coral atolls and do not destroy them. Darwin drew a cross-section of a coral atoll on a sunken volcanic substrate showing the effects of a relative sea level rise by the sinking of a volcano.

In 1897, three holes into the Tuvalu's main atoll were drilled by Professor

Sir T.W. Edgeworth David to test Darwin's theory. More than 300 metres of coral was intersected showing that coral kept growing as the substrate sank. Deep drilling through coral at Mururoa Atoll in French Polynesia in the 1960s intersected volcanic rocks at depth. The theories of Lyell and Darwin were validated.

An analysis of more than 600 coral reef islands in the Pacific and Indian Oceans showed that some remained stable (40 per cent) or increased in area (40 per cent). Only 20 per cent decreased in area yet it is widely promoted in green activist circles that coral islands, atolls and reefs are disappearing with sea level rise. Some islands grew as much as 5.6 hectares in a decade. Tuvalu's main atoll, Funafuti, comprising 33 islands around the rim of a lagoon, gained 32 hectares during the last 115 years.

Over the period from 14,400 to 6,000 years ago during the 130-metre post-glacial sea level rise, coral reefs kept up with sea level rise. The coral sand atoll islands were actually produced by the destruction of reef material during the two-metre sea level fall over the last 4,000 years which led to the emergence and death of coral.

Tuvalu is the symbol of a drowning Pacific island nation yet the total land area of Tuvalu has increased by 2.9 per cent over the last four decades. At the 2019 South Pacific Forum in Tuvalu, Australia was berated for refusing to commit economic suicide and close its coal industry despite handing out $500 million for climate change to the region. There was no mention of China. This shows the essence of the politics of climate change. It is a cash grab that knowingly ignores validated science.

Time magazine on June 2019 had a cover article entitled *Our sinking planet* featuring a photograph of UN chief António Guterres thigh-deep in water at Tuvalu. He claimed that Tuvalu was one of the world's countries most vulnerable to global warming and that human emissions of carbon dioxide drive global warming resulting in polar ice cap melting, sea water expansion, sea level rise and inundation of Pacific island nations.

Every single aspect of this narrative is scientifically wrong. It has never been shown that human emissions of carbon dioxide drive global warming. Ice cores show warming is followed by a rise in carbon dioxide. Ice melts for a diversity of reasons and the Pacific atoll nations have grown in size.

Guterres flew to Tuvalu in a carbon dioxide emitting jet made out of aluminium, a metal that requires huge emissions of carbon dioxide during mining, transport, processing, smelting and refining. I guess it's acceptable to be a hypocrite and fraudulent for a cover photograph on *Time*, a magazine that had a cover article of 1977 entitled *How to survive the coming ice age* and a 2007 article *The global warming survival guide*. No point in changing magazines, *Newsweek* warned us of the forthcoming ice age in 1975 and later warned we would fry-and-die.

In South Tarawa, Kiribati's 15-square-kilometre island capital, crowded with some 50,000 people, coral blocks are used for seawalls, causeways between islands and creating new land. This has led to greater storm erosion, changes in sedimentation patterns and more common inundation during storm surges. The real danger to atolls is a sea-level fall and human activity such as removal of coral sand for cement, building of roads and airstrips together with ground water extraction, blasting of reefs for shipping lanes and use of reef blocks or coral sand in concrete for sea walls.

It was predicted in 1988 that some of the 1,196 islands of the Maldives would be under water by 2018 and that drinking water would run out for the 200,000 inhabitants. Thirty years have been and gone since this dire prediction. The Maldives is thriving, has potable water, the population has doubled and there has been a building boom of waterside tourist facilities.

A global scale analysis of 221 islands in the tropical Pacific and Indian Oceans reveals *a predominantly stable or accretionary trend in an area of atoll islands worldwide* throughout the 21st century. Land area for the 221 studied islands had increased by six per cent between 2000 and 2017. The Maldives alone expanded 37.5 square kilometres from 2000-2017.

This is in accord with a 2019 global scale analysis of 709 islands in the Pacific and Indian Oceans that revealed 89 per cent were either stable or growing in size and only a few small islands had slightly decreased in size.

Climate activism by the IPCC and COP is littered with lies, false claims, fraud and cooked data. Young women like Brianna Fruen and Greta Thunberg are paraded to deliver an emotional fact-free message and yet claim to follow the science. The COP26 doomsday scenario for Pacific atoll nations has nothing to do with climate, the environment or the welfare of islanders. These are UN-sponsored meetings to use their sticky fingers to extract money from Western countries that do not protect their economy, freedoms and sovereignty.

(2021)

Švejk sedition

Some time ago I attacked creationists for their scientific fraud, a charge I now lay against climate activists and the Greens party. Taxpayer-funded media networks incorrectly assumed that because of my attacks on fundamentalist protestant creationists, then I must be an atheist. They were wrong. Christianity is the lynchpin of Western civilisation and our society.

In a TV program on Australian atheists, I was asked to describe my own funeral. I suggested that my coffin would be made out of dead galvanised iron and a deep grave dug in an outback saltpan thereby facilitating my rapid decomposition. Family and friends, some of whom are men of the cloth, would celebrate my life at a bush BBQ accompanied by copious quantities of fermented fluids with the environmentally sensitive disposal of bottles, cans, bottle tops, chop bones, cigarette butts and other refuse into the grave before covering the future archeological treasures with the coffin. Eulogies from hypocrites were to be jeered and mourners would later pass out in the surrounding sand dunes to face the warm rays of the sun at dawn. Construction of a future archaeological midden was deemed politically incorrect and cut from the broadcast.

One of the unexplained scientific mysteries of the universe is that I may have spent a millisecond or two in outback pubs. The publican of the Post Office Hotel in Chillagoe in Far North Queensland watched the interview and asked my best mate, a Chillagoe resident, when next their mining and cattle town would be graced by my presence. Chillagoe has a rich mining history and spawned the Labor crook Red Ted Theodore.

Upon entry a few months later into the Post Office Hotel, I was confronted with a sea of furiously imbibing anorexic and obese locals with their warts, torn singlets, missing digits, hairy backs, sweat, dress thongs, tats and scars. Fashion clothes were yet to appear in this neck of the woods. I knew quite a few of the local miners and eccentrics at the front bar. Freddy, a very thirsty local, preferred liquid bread to solid food and was so skinny that he couldn't go outside on windy days. When he was seriously ill in hospital down the coast on a glucose drip, he actually put on weight! One lady with a bandy-legged ringer consort commented that I looked far better on TV than in person. The pub was warming up for a big Friday night.

The publican made an announcement. There was to be a wake. I wondered who had died as most of the likely candidates were well into the grip of Bacchus and were valiantly stopping the front bar from falling over. A rusty hessian-lined corrugated iron coffin appeared with the letters painted in gaudy pink on the lid RIP I.R.P., my initials. I was instructed to lie in the coffin, beer in hand, the lid was pulled up and I had to listen to character-assassinating speeches full of mature tadpole droppings. The dead can't sue so I had to suffer the libel.

There was a great discussion about the coffin, which was a tad short. Would my head be cut off and tucked under an arm, a task to be undertaken before *rigor mortis* set in, or would they chainsaw off my feet? It appears that I am known as a talker and it was unanimous that my head was to be cut off just to make sure I'd never talk again. I had been abstemious for a few months before but one could not abstain at a wake. That would be totally improper and disrespectful, especially at one's own wake which few have the privilege of attending.

Just when the wake speeches and wailing were at fever pitch, a couple of German tourists came into the pub. They took one look, realised that this was a tired and emotional wake and bolted into the bush rather than stay in town. A band from Cairns had been hired, there was singing, dancing and goodness knows what else until the wee hours. It appears that at the bewitching hour I was dancing with my coffin which now resides in a private museum in Chillagoe.

The privilege of enjoying one's own wake.

Outback folk are the real Australians, make their own fun, are politically incorrect and are divorced from precious city people. They know that there are two sexes, don't worry about mythical genders and pronouns and know how food, fibre, energy, building materials and metals are made and find their ways to cities. They use a handshake rather than a written contract and the jungle drums soon tell everyone who is a rotten egg.

Bushies know how to live life and often are off the bureaucratic radar. They are free. For example, there are more members of the Lightning Ridge District Bowling Club than inhabitants recorded in the Census for the whole Lightning Ridge district. In such places, people only are known by their nicknames, look after each other, earn their own way, solve their own problems, can fix any piece of broken machinery, drive unregistered vehicles on station and mine tracks, use cash and don't exist on the electoral roll. They have no bank, Medicare and ATO records. Only the unwise will ask such people about their past. This country-city divide is now an impossible gulf so how do city people survive the loss of freedoms imposed by unelected bureaucrats in the WuHuFlu epidemic?

A hundred years ago, Jaroslav Hašek gave us the answer in *The Good Soldier Švejk*. The Selver translation removed the naughty bits and painted Josef Švejk, a Czech soldier in the Austro-Hungarian army in the first world war, as a bit of a drongo who bumbled along avoiding going to the front. During my visits to communist Czechoslovakia in the 1970s and 1980s, I realised that this translation missed the point and that Czechs subjugated by the Soviet Union modelled their interactions with Russians on Švejk who offered passive resistance by feigned idiocy, incompetence, dumb insolence and stupidity. Švejk followed instructions to the letter, exploited bureaucratic ambiguities, exposed incompetent bureaucrats with his anti-war, anti-authority, anti-establishment and anti-religious exploits and was a survivor because he allowed nothing to upset or stress him and just didn't care about anything. The more bawdy recent Perrott translation painted Švejk in this light.

For us to survive in these times of creeping socialism, loss of freedoms and control of every aspect of our lives by unelected inexperienced incompetent bureaucrats, we need to follow the tried-and-proven Švejk solution.

(2021)

Talking Tonga

For decades I have avoided listening to, watching or being interviewed by the ABC preferring the *Wilcannia Weekly* and the *Andamooka Argus*. Can you imagine my shock when a geological colleague informed me that the ABC were actually scientifically correct regarding gas emissions from the January 2022 explosive volcanic eruption of Hunga-Tonga?

The Tongan eruption is not unprecedented yet it was given celebrity billing because of the footage captured by satellites and on the ground in a news-free silly season. The small number of fatalities from tsunamis in Tonga and Peru is commensurate with Hunga-Tonga being a modest-sized submarine explosive eruption.

Before, during, and after eruptions there are earthquakes as rising lighter molten rocks push aside solid rocks. As with all explosive eruptions, the sonic boom does a few laps of the planet, as will the high-altitude Hunga-Tonga ash cloud. There was a lightning storm in the ascending ash plume and there were associated tsunamis because the explosion was in shallow water.

Ash and sulphur dioxide 20 km up in the Southern Hemisphere atmosphere will reflect light and heat producing slight cooling over the next few years. This is normal and is unrelated to the current lower output of energy by the Sun.

Explosive eruptions derive from water dissolved in molten rocks at depth which, upon buoyant ascent, flashes to a monstrous volume of steam thereby creating an explosion, especially if fractures from earthquakes allow an ingress of seawater. Sulphate from seawater is converted to sulphur dioxide, a common and toxic volcanic gas that was measured at Hunga-Tonga.

Volcanic explosions suddenly cool molten rock into glass which is explosively fragmented into minute razor-sharp spicules that can petrify lungs of breathing animals, inundate reefs and landscapes with ash thereby killing life and cause drowning in blood from myriads of cuts to lung tissue. It is well known that such ash can remelt on the turbines of jet aeroplanes causing engine failure.

The most common volcanic rock on Earth, basalt, occupies about 75 per cent of the surface of the continents and ocean floor. Partial melting of the mantle occurs most commonly when rocks held at high pressure and temperature in the presence of a flux such as carbon dioxide or water are depressurised. Molten basalt can contain up to 13.5 weight per cent dissolved carbon dioxide. Molten basalt from depressurisation erupts on the ocean floor at mid ocean ridges, off-axis fractures, oceanic hot spots such as Hawaii, above continental hot spots such as western Victoria, along continental rifts and at asteroid impact sites. These processes have been replicated experimentally.

More than 95 per cent of the world's basalts occur on the sea floor. Sea floor basalt volcanoes at 1,200°C release huge amounts of heat and carbon dioxide into cool basal ocean waters. Most basalt eruptions are not explosive although some sea floor basalt eruptions with at least 10 per cent dissolved carbon dioxide can be explosive, even if there are kilometres of water weighting down on the volcano minimising explosivity. We know there are at least 3.5 million sea floor basalt volcanoes and at least 65,000 km of mid ocean ridges that add carbon dioxide and heat to the oceans.

By contrast, there are only 1,711 active volcanoes at, near or above sea level. One of these, Hunga-Tonga on the Tonga-Kermadec Arc, is where sea floor basalt with a thin skin of wet sediment on the Pacific Plate is being pushed westwards under the Australian Plate. When wet sea floor basalt is remelted at depth in volcanic arcs, it produces andesite with a large amount of dissolved water that operated as a flux. Andesite is molten at 700°C and experiments show that very little carbon dioxide can dissolve in molten andesite. As the hot molten buoyant andesite rises, it boils off dissolved water and, when the weight of the overlying rocks close to the surface is less than the gas pressure, there is a volcanic explosion such as at Hunga-Tonga. The steam cloud from Hunga-Tonga reached nearly 60km in the atmosphere, some twice the height of terrestrial volcanoes, and created rain bombs around the world for a few years.

Many of those who question human-induced climate change asked me about the carbon dioxide emissions during the Tonga eruption. The answer is SFA. The unseen and unmeasured basaltic sea floor volcanoes are a major contributor of heat and carbon dioxide to the oceans yet are never considered by climate modellers. Why not? They also have never shown that human emissions of carbon dioxide drive global warming.

Stay sceptical of everything that's not published in the *Andamooka Argus*.

(2022)

At the Umberumberka mine, approximately 25km WNW of Broken Hill, 2009.

Snot

Snot catches some of the 50 million particles inhaled with every breath. These particles are one hundredth the size of a human hair and comprise mineral dust, industrial and traffic dust, microorganisms and extraterrestrial particles. Some 40,000 tonnes of extraterrestrial dust falls to Earth each year and, if you are really lucky, your snot may contain a particle that came from the asteroid belt between Jupiter and Mars. Check it out in the privacy of your home and give snot the scientific respect it deserves.

Every now and then, our planet passes through a cometary cloud (e.g. 730-740 AD) which produces cold times because dust reflects light and heat and hundreds of years of cold times follow if this coincides with a weak sun and explosive volcanism (735-737 AD). This happened in the Dark Ages (400-900 AD).

Most desertification occurs during periods of glaciation when winds are stronger, rainfall is lower and vegetation is sparse. There is a good geological record of sand dunes, salt lakes and dust storms during long periods of aridity. A mate of mine who used to live in my Broken Hill house opened all doors and windows when billowing clouds of fine red dust approached on the assumption that the dust would blow right through the house. It didn't. My place never passed the white glove test but at least it was clean dust from inland Australia. The normal rain after a dust storm covered cars in a desert-red patina.

Red bed copper deposits formed in mid-latitude glacial wind-blown sand dune sediments because of changes in groundwater chemistry, sea level and sedimentation. The major deposits formed in snowball earth times 650 million years ago (e.g. Copperbelt of Central Africa), when

Gondwana drifted over the South Pole (e.g. Kupferschiefer of Europe) and the modern ice age (e.g. salt pans in Texas and Saudi). If we want electric cars, then ironically an understanding of ancient climate is one of the tools used to find the copper needed for the cars.

Explosive volcanic eruptions add huge amounts of dust to the atmosphere. Most of these volcanoes are in the circum-Pacific and Mediterranean-trans Asiatic belts. The dust, incorrectly called ash, comprises minute sharp needles of glass from lava supercooled by the instantaneous release of expanding gas when supercritical water flashes to steam. Breathing volcanic dust near an explosive eruption cuts lung tissue, reduces lung capacity and lungs can be lithified. Humans drown in their own blood which fills the cut lungs.

Volcanic dust rises 25 to 60 km into the atmosphere, does a few laps high in the atmosphere as it falls to earth and creates lightning storms, spectacular sunsets and heavy rain by nucleating droplets. Combined with La Niña, this was the reason for heavy rains in eastern Australia after the Hunga Tonga eruption of 15th January 2022. Notwithstanding, the normal suspects brayed that the heavy rain and flooding were due to climate change and how it was all the Prime Minister's fault.

Hunga Tonga was a small submarine eruption. Previous past large terrestrial eruptions such as Tambora in 1815 led to years of cooling and 1816 was a year without a summer. The 1783-1784 eruption of Iceland's Laki covered Europe with dust and choking toxic sulphurous fumes – thousands died from respiratory problems, torrential rainfall and cooling destroyed crops and famine followed. Empire-changing eruptions such as the Minoan eruption of Santorini about 1600 BC are recorded in ice drill cores. The Indonesian supervolcano Toba erupted some 74,000 years ago covering much of the planet with thick volcanic dust which is still preserved in India and Alaska. The tropics were devegetated and soils were removed by torrential rainfall, the surviving population migrated north and south, the orbital-driven cooling cycle of the planet accelerated and sea level rapidly dropped.

Airborne dust is precipitated in restricted lakes where there is neither turbulence nor a massive input of sediments, in deep ocean sediments where there are no strong currents and in polar ice. Dust shows us that there are cycles of climate unrelated to human activity. At times the atmosphere has a higher dust content due to impacting, dusty comet tails, desertification, drought, overgrazing, industry and volcanism. Pollen, spores and charred fragments in dust layers show the history of forest fires and evolution of plants. The chemistry of dust and acid layers in polar ice can be used to show when and where an explosive volcano occurred. Iron-rich dust from deserts stimulates carbon dioxide-consuming algal blooms in oceans.

Closed-minded climate activists claim that every natural event is due to climate change and that human emissions of carbon dioxide are to blame. The joy of integrated interdisciplinary science with all of its exciting uncertainties and detective work should be used to stimulate young people rather than trying to fill their minds with guilt, fear, hopelessness, depression and ignorance.

(2022)

Eat beef, save the planet, outback 1999

Eat beef, save the planet

Yet again, farmers are under attack. This time, it is the beef industry because, apparently, cattle burp and fart out methane and we'll all fry-and-die because of the accelerated global warming produced by this methane. Is this fact or fiction? In my field of science, we often do mass balance calculations because material is added, exchanged, and lost during natural processes. Let's do the same with the beef industry.

Grass grows by using carbon dioxide from the air as plant food. Why do climate activists want to reduce the amount of plant food in the atmosphere? Cattle eat grass, some grass remains as roots and stubble, and hence not all carbon atoms in grass end up in cattle. The carbon from grass is stored in meat, milk, intestines, bones, and skin and the amount of stored carbon increases with growth. Semi-solid waste materials from cattle fertilise grass for further recycling of carbon.

Humans are omnivores with teeth for cutting plants and animal flesh and then masticating to create a large surface area to assist digestion. We have the gut enzyme trypsin specifically for breaking down meat. Not all plant material can be broken down into nutrients which is why there is little nutritional value in us eating grass, stems, wood, or bark. Unlike cattle, humans cannot digest cellulose in grass. Bacterial and enzyme reactions in ruminant's stomachs release the gas methane as burps and farts during digestion. This methane, a carbon-hydrogen compound, very quickly oxidises in the atmosphere to carbon dioxide and the most abundant greenhouse gas in the atmosphere, water vapour.

For me, there is nothing like medium rare beef with a matching red-coloured fluid derived from releasing carbon dioxide into the atmosphere by grape fermentation. The beef is digested in my body because of trypsin which breaks down meat into amino acids for circulation in my bloodstream. Meat fat ends up as brain food. Vegetarians and vegans ignore the benefits of human evolution and waste trypsin by not eating meat. In evolutionary terms, meat-eating has allowed the human brain to grow over time. In a past life when I took university student geological field trips, I noticed that the meat eaters were the first to the tops of mountains, vegetarians were struggling way behind and vegans were still trying to work out how to get out of the vehicle!

Some of the carbon in beef I eat is used and stored by my body, the rest is oxidised and exhaled. I breathe in air with 0.04 per cent carbon dioxide and exhale air with more than 4 per cent carbon dioxide. The gaseous waste product from cattle digestion is methane, and the gaseous waste product from human digestion is carbon dioxide. Some of the milk or cream I use in coffee and on morning porridge is stored in my flesh and bones as is the butter used in cooking.

When I've snapped my hobbles and decompose in a grave, most of my body carbon, including that from eating beef, will be released as methane and the rest will end up sequestered in soils. Blood and bone from cattle is used as a fertiliser and is sequestered in soil. Cattle skins are used to make leather which is sequestered into footwear and other leather goods. The whole process of going from grass to grave involves a carbon cycle and short-term sequestration of carbon atoms.

The number of carbon atoms returned to the atmosphere from beef farming is less than that removed by grass growth. Therefore, cattle farming and eating beef is a carbon sequestration process. If the popular mantra is used, we are saving the planet by eating beef.

If we do not eat meat, then grass decomposes anyway and releases methane into the atmosphere for oxidation to carbon dioxide and water vapour. If the grass is burned, carbon dioxide is returned to the atmosphere. The cycle of atmospheric carbon dioxide via meat production and digestion removes carbon dioxide from the atmosphere and then later releases this carbon dioxide back to its source. What's the problem? Whether grass is used to grow meat, decomposed, or burned, no new carbon atoms are created in this carbon cycle and, by growing beef, some carbon atoms are removed from the cycle for short-term sequestration.

It is absolute nonsense to claim that beef farming accelerates hypothetical global warming. Carbon atoms are just being recycled. We are being conned with a scare campaign by unelected climate activists who want to control every aspect of our lives, including the source of our animal protein.

If beef is replaced by insects is on the menu, then I'll pass. I will get all my nutrients from 47 pints of Guinness, 2 glasses of milk, and one of orange juice each day.

(2022)

Underground in Broken Hill, 2008, with Derek Wyness, artist, teacher, actor, film set manager and former owner of a BSA Gold Flash, (died in 2020).

Rain, rain, go away

The Copernicus Sentinel-5P satellite showed that the greatest methane emissions are from the tundra in Canada and Russia, and the tropics – especially the Amazonian, Central African and Indonesian wetlands. Smaller emissions were from tropical South America, north-western America, China, west Africa, Antarctica, and Cape York.

No significant emissions were detected from the large coalfields of Europe, Canada, America, Botswana, South Africa, and Australia. Nor were major emissions detected from the beef-growing areas of South America, South Africa, America, and Australia.

Termite-infested areas of northern Australia and our farmlands, rice-growing areas, major dams, and oil and gas fields were not pinpointed. The 2020 measurements were at a time of reduced industrial activity yet showed the largest increase in methane emissions since the 1980s.

What's going on?

Heavy rains in central Africa in 2020, especially in South Sudan and Uganda, may be one of the smoking guns. Water releases from Lake Victoria increased flow into the White Nile which feeds the Ugandan and South Sudan wetlands. The Sudd wetlands contributed over 25 per cent of the growth in global methane emissions. There were also significant increases in natural methane emissions from eastern Canada in 2020 where there are a large number of lakes and wetlands.

In the tundra, soils comprise glacial debris overlain by peat bogs. The bacterially-assisted decomposition of vegetation into carbonaceous debris and peat releases methane which commonly self-ignites, as recorded by Shakespeare. Caliban's reference to the scary will-o'-the-wisp in bogs, swamps, and marshes in *The Tempest* was a reference to the spontaneous ignition of methane-air mixtures.

Most landmasses are draped with sedimentary rocks that contain entrapped methane which leaks into the atmosphere, especially from carbon-rich organic sedimentary rocks. Methane is trapped in coal and is released by natural fracking, up drill holes that tap coal seam gas, and by rock depressurising during mining. Good underground ventilation, smoking bans underground, and a ban on using machinery that could produce sparks is normal procedure in Western coal mines.

If air contains 5-15 per cent methane, it is highly explosive and can self-ignite, especially if mixed with coal dust and carbon monoxide. Since the 1880s, more than 400 men have died underground from explosions in Australian coal mines. The largest was at Bulli (NSW) in 1887 (81 men). At Mt Mulligan (Qld) in 1921, the loss of 75 miners in an underground explosion killed three generations of men resulting in the permanent closure of the town and mine. Every family at Mt Mulligan lost a breadwinner.

The combination of the Indian Ocean Dipole, La Niña, and volcanic ash high in the atmosphere probably were the major contributors to heavy rain in much of Australia in 2022. This rain also increased natural methane emissions due to accelerated plant debris decomposition. The past shows us that after heavy rains in eastern Australia, the undergrowth in eucalypt forests grows rapidly. When followed by hot dry windy weather, forests become incendiary bombs. This is known by arsonists who ignite some 75 per cent of all grass and forest fires.

Recently I was in Leura in the Blue Mountains of New South Wales. Huge rains in 1955-1956 built up the forest fuel load and were followed by massive bushfires in 1957. Vacant blocks, lonely chimneys, and burnt-out relics remain today in Leura to remind us of these catastrophic bushfires. Massive bushfires will be repeated after the 2022 heavy rains because of the inability to learn from history. Of course, the next inevitable catastrophic fires in eastern Australia will be claimed as unprecedented and blamed on Climate Change rather than on ideological neglectful forest maintenance.

It was the same 1955-1956 rains that flooded towns on the flood plains along the Murray, Darling, Murrumbidgee, Hunter, Manning, Hastings, Clarence, Richmond, Wilson, and Brisbane Rivers. Flood plains have fertile sediment that has accumulated from thousands of large floods over millions of years and, for millennia, were the perfect place for agriculture and settlement. Maybe, before climate change is blamed for floods in 2022, the history of flooding of the great rivers such as the Nile and Ganges where humans have lived and recorded flood history over thousands of years should be studied. Sometimes there is too much rain, other times there is not enough. Modern floods, droughts, and bushfires are certainly not unprecedented.

Humans have grazed cattle on flood plains since the first domestication of docile animals during an exceptionally cold period 12,900-11,700 years ago. Cattle emit methane and, if a carbon balance calculation is performed, cattle are already at Net Zero. The increasing attacks on the farming industry are yet another attempt by the Greens to stop productive industry. Bacteria comprise the largest biomass on Earth and emit more methane than any other life form hence the Greens should focus on reducing bacterial methane emissions. Don't wait up.

The first time it rained on planet Earth was unprecedented.

Running surface waters 3.8 billion years ago at Isua (Greenland) left the oldest preserved gravels in the world which, when dissolved in acid, yield a carbon-rich residue with the chemical fingerprint of bacterial life that lived in a world without oxygen gas. At that time, the Earth's atmosphere was rich in methane, carbon dioxide, and ammonia. On Earth since that time, water and life have always been hand-in-hand. Mars had water before Earth and lost most its water and atmosphere with the loss of the Martian magnetic field. Water-bearing minerals and water-worn structures are on Mars and it is only a matter of time before fossil and even modern bacteria are discovered in its rusted rocks.

Climate change cannot be understood using computer models that attempt to predict the future with incomplete information and invalid assumptions. The past is the key to the present and destruction of history, archaeology, and geology in the climate wars can only lead to hardship.

(2022)

The joys of drinking

As I sit in my study at the end of the day listening to the heavy rain and wondering when I should open a bottle of red fluid that contains 85.5 per cent water, my mind strayed to that weird molecule we all take for granted. Water.

As soon as liquid water was on the planet's surface some 4 billion years ago, life appeared. I suspect the same happened on Mars. Water dissolves more substances and in greater quantity than any other liquid. This allows cells to function. Water's high light transparency allows photosynthetic life to live in deeper water.

Except for ammonia, water has the highest heat capacity of all solids and liquids. This prevents extreme ranges in temperature on Earth and allows a heat transfer in the oceans from the equator to the poles thereby giving us zoned climates. Heat transfer from the oceans to the atmosphere drives climate. If water did not have atoms held together by hydrogen bonding, it would boil at -30 degrees C and ice would be denser than liquid water. If ice was denser than water, oceans would freeze from the bottom up during ice ages and there would be no warm water currents. This would produce ice oceans that would reflect radiation producing a permanent iceball.

If ice is at 0 degrees C, it needs a lot of heat to convert it to water at 0 degrees C. If your choice of drink is whiskey, which contains 60 per cent water, when ice blocks are added the whiskey cools down by giving up heat to melt the ice. It's far better to drink quality whiskey with no ice and two drops of that weird molecule to draw out the flavour. Evaporation and precipitation of water provide an upper limit to air temperature. It is evaporation and precipitation that buffer temperature on Earth because both involve an exchange of heat. It is the properties of weird water that stop a runaway greenhouse or permanent freezing of the Earth because the atmosphere operates like an evaporative air conditioner.

Townsville and Mount Isa are almost at the same latitude, the air in both places has the same carbon dioxide content and yet The Isa is far colder in winter and far hotter in summer than Townsville. This is because the air in the humid tropics at Townsville contains up to 4 per cent dissolved water in contrast to the drier air of Mount Isa. Forget carbon dioxide, water vapour accounts for at least 80 per cent of the planet's greenhouse warming. Water vapour is the third-most abundant gas in the atmosphere whereas carbon dioxide is a trace gas with unremarkable properties.

The Earth's climate system attempts to attain equilibrium but it is never exactly at equilibrium. The Earth's surface has two turbulent fluids, the oceans and the atmosphere, interacting with each other on a rotating planet that is unevenly heated by the Sun and adsorbs solar radiation unevenly. This uneven heating drives atmospheric and oceanic circulation with heat in ocean waters transported from the equator to the poles. The atmosphere interacts with the irregular land surface distorting the airflow and heat-carrying ocean currents are diverted by the topography of the sea floor and the irregular shape of land masses.

Water as solid, liquid and gas changes from one state to another and this affects the heat balance. Each state of water affects incoming and outgoing radiation differently on time scales from seconds to thousands of years. If water was not weird, there would be no heat held in the atmosphere and oceans and the air temperature would be a balmy -18 degrees C. If the water cycle did not have positive feedback involving water vapour, clouds and precipitation, then there would have been no dynamic equilibrium of the Earth's climate for billions of years.

The atmospheric carbon dioxide content has varied from 0.02 per cent to over 20 per cent yet all six ice ages over billions of years commenced when the atmosphere contained far more carbon dioxide than at present. Carbon dioxide had nothing to do with past climate changes and there is no reason to think that because we are alive today, then the physics and chemistry of carbon dioxide has changed.

Climate activists ignore the past, the states of water, clouds and heat transfer and claim that a trace gas emitted by Western industrialised countries controls global climate and that humans can change climate and the amount of this trace gas with taxation.

The only weird thing about carbon dioxide is that it has an inverse solubility in water. Cold water dissolves more carbon dioxide than warm water. Polar ice drill cores show that when past polar air temperature increased, some 600 to 1,500 years later the atmospheric carbon dioxide content increased. This is in accord with a law of chemistry and opposite to the popular belief that an increase in atmospheric carbon dioxide drives in an increase in atmospheric temperature. An increase in atmospheric carbon dioxide does not lead to global warming. It is the inverse.

Pour a champagne or beer and watch the carbon dioxide bubbles continue to rise as the drink warms up. This is exactly what happens in the oceans.

One needs to be a drinker to fully understand climate.

(2022)

Ian Plimer with Prof. Oskar Thalhammer, Senior Consultant and former Professor of Mineralogy and Petrology at Cafe Charlie, Göss, Austria. (1984)

Cancel Mozart

Why should we stop at cancelling the world's greatest explorer, Captain James Cook, and the greatest playwright, William Shakespeare? Why not the world's greatest composer: Wolfgang Amadeus Mozart? In his operas, his acceptance of slavery, racism, white privilege, authority, misogyny, anti-Islam, wife-bashing, man-woman marriage, and marital fidelity make him a prime candidate for cancellation. Weighted against this is Mozart's casting of a girl dressed up as a boy which today's Woke generation would support. Don't blame Mozart's various librettists, guilt by association makes Mozart also guilty. Just ask Moira Deeming. He also wrote church music. Why should we allow people to be spiritually uplifted by beautiful music glorifying God? And don't even think of Mozart's piano music where he uses both black and white keys!

Burn Mozart's operatic scores and rewrite his piano scores so that only black notes are used, dismantle the talented white privilege male-dominated orchestras that are the epitome of Western Civilisation, excellence and hard work, and have opera singers retrained to perform negro folk songs of repression. In Hitler's time, Jewish musicians lost their jobs in orchestras and Jewish composers were not performed so there is already a precedent for cancelling Mozart. We should put the culturally inappropriate Mozart back in his miserable little 18th century Austrian box.

Let's start with *Don Giovanni*. The Don's diet is sexual gluttony. He's arrogant, misogynistic, abuses everyone, and resorts to racial derision. He is a murderer but it's hard to tell whether murder is acceptable or not to the Woke generation because the Don's victim Il Commendatore was high class, white, privileged, and defending his daughter's honour. Through Woke eyes, he probably deserved his fate. The Don's sidekick Leporello keeps a scorebook (*Madamina, il catalogo é questo*) and description of the Don's sexual conquests who were blonde, brunette, short, tall, fat, skinny, young, and old. No freckled redheads. No blacks. No men or boys. Only women. Why? Although the Don's conquests were 640 in Italy, 231 in Germany, 100 in France, 91 in Turkey, and 1003 in Spain, there was not a single first nations sexual conquest. Why not? Surely this is discrimination of some sort or other. During short-lived droughts, the Don ravished old women just to keep the scorebook ticking over.

Those who define themselves with various letters of the alphabet were not mentioned in Leporello's catalogue aria which is reason enough to pull down Mozart's statues in Salzburg. Don Giovanni seduces the peasant girl Zerlina on her wedding day (*La á darem la mano*) and she pleads to her beau Masetto to beat her for her sins (*Batti, batti, o bel Masetto*). It's hard to know whether today's anti-women demonstrators would support or abhor Zerlina's plea. To make matters worse, *Don Giovanni* was the first opera ever to use a trombone. Surely someone somewhere must find that sonically offensive and discriminatory? Get rid of this opera from the repertoire and make the world a better place.

Mozart's best-known opera, *Le nozze di Figaro*, is riddled with sexual innuendo. That's acceptable if half-naked trannies are cavorting in front of impressionable kindergarten children in today's Woke world but, in the opera, these are heterosexual references. Surely this is the ticket for cancellation? The play which gave inspiration to the opera's libretto had been banned in pre-revolutionary France because it promoted the wrong political ideas. This is another reason to ban the opera more than two centuries later. The only saving grace in today's Woke world is that the page boy Cherubino is sung by a female soprano dressed as a boy. Woke music scholars are still arguing about whether Cherubino identifies as a boy or is a girl in the wrong body.

In *Cosi fan tutte*, Mozart needed some over-sexed bad guys and Albanians won this honour some 200 years before modern Albanian gangs created their evil European people-smuggling business. The libretto of *Cosi fan tutte* must be changed to make the Albanians innocent under-privileged refugees so that the opera can be performed to today's Woke audiences. Misogyny and marital fidelity are highlighted and the aria *Una donna a quindici anni* shows that sex with a 15-year girl (called a woman in the opera) is quite acceptable.

In *Die Entführung aus dem Serail,* Turkish harems, fidelity and racism raise their ugly heads again. In order to signify that the Ottoman Turks Selim and Osmin are evil, they are given bass parts rather than tenor parts, normally reserved for the heroic good guys. *Die Zauberflöte* highlights racism, sexism, and class differences. The Ottoman Turk Monostatos is considering rape of the white sleeping beauty Pamina and he describes himself as black, ugly, and unable to enjoy the pleasures of the flesh with a white woman. He is painted as a despicable coward whereas the Queen of the Night is evil because, as a woman, she refuses to submit to male authority. Mozart punished her with only two arias in the opera, both of which are extraordinarily difficult. Class differences between two heterosexual couples, the low-class Papageno/Papagena and high-ranking Tamino/Pamina, show prejudice and discrimination. The unfinished obscure work *Zaide* stars a Sultan's female European slave and is anti-Islam and sexual assault raises its ugly head in *Idomeneo.*

The Woke world would not see the context of Mozart's operatic characters with the librettos based on old stories, all with moral overtones. Times in Europe in the late 1700s were very different from today. The world was in its normal state with no democratically elected governments. There was universal poverty and food shortages in a Little Ice Age world with massive class differences and despotic leaders ruled from their cathedrals, palaces, and farm estates. Human rights did not exist, Europe was Christian, state censorship was universal and peasants were owned and treated as beasts of burden. Death was everywhere and was a release from grinding earthly hardship with rewards in Heaven.

There had been a 300-year struggle by Christian Europeans against the invading Islamic Ottomans which ended in the Siege of Vienna a hundred years before Mozart's operas were written. The operas were written for the common man who knew of this long conflict because they were drafted as cannon fodder to do the dirty work. It's no wonder Ottomans were portrayed as exotic and evil.

When you are in a reflective state of bliss listening to the second movement of the concerto for flute, harp, and orchestra (K299), remember that the world's greatest composer could undergo cultural revisionism overnight because nothing is sacred to the left who willingly destroy the best of Western Civilisation and replace it with a totalitarian vacuum.

(2023)

The Earth is already at Net Zero

The greenhouse gas in the air that has the greatest effect on atmospheric temperature is water vapour. Why have governments tried to ban carbon dioxide, methane and nitrous oxide emissions and not water vapour?

Carbon dioxide is plant food. This is the first science that children should learn at school. Plants use carbon dioxide from the atmosphere with water and nutrients from the soil to grow plant tissue.

The Earth's first atmosphere contained hydrogen, helium, ammonia, carbon monoxide, rotten egg gas and methane. It derived from planetary degassing and didn't last long.

The second atmosphere lasted for billions of years and contained up to 20 per cent carbon dioxide, again from planetary degassing. Much of the carbon dioxide from the second atmosphere dissolved in ocean water, was precipitated as the rock dolomite in warm shallow marine conditions and there it remains naturally sequestered.

During the times of very high carbon dioxide in the atmosphere, the planet enjoyed a number very intense ice ages when kilometres of ice formed at sea level at the equator. We are told by climate activists that a few parts per million increase in atmospheric carbon dioxide resulting from human activities will lead to unstoppable global warming and a climate crisis. The past shows this is false.

The current oxygen-rich atmosphere formed some 550 million years ago. The oxygen came from life which is why there is a search for oxygen and ozone on exoplanets to determine if there is life somewhere out there. The planet does not degas oxygen gas. All oxygen in the atmosphere derives from photosynthesis. At times, the atmospheric oxygen content rose to 35 per cent and there were massive global forest fires. At other times during mass extinction events, the oxygen content fell to less than 5 per cent.

We hear that the Amazonian rainforests are the lungs of the Earth. This tree-hugging ideology is wrong. The lungs of the Earth are the floating phytoplankton in the oceans that have been around for billions of years and use carbon dioxide as plant food and excrete oxygen as a waste product. It's very hard to get emotional about green slime being the lungs of the Earth.

For the last 550 million years there has been a decrease in atmospheric carbon dioxide from 0.8 per cent to 0.04 per cent. Because of an explosion of animal predation, carbon dioxide was used to make protective shells, most of which are locked away as fossils in ancient rocks. If oceans were acid during past times of high atmospheric carbon dioxide shells would have dissolved and would not be preserved as fossils. Shells removed dissolved carbon dioxide from seawater. Limestone reefs, limey muds and black carbon-rich muds removed even more carbon dioxide from seawater. Ancient carbon dioxide is now locked up in rocks.

Land plants appeared 470 million years ago and removed massive amounts of carbon dioxide from the atmosphere. They still do. Massive accumulations of plants in cool climate wetlands led to huge volumes of plant material that were later compressed to thick coal seams. There were no plant-decomposing bacteria then and plant material accumulated into very thick piles. The carbon in coal came from the atmosphere. By burning coal, this carbon as carbon dioxide is put back into the atmosphere where it originally came from.

In a forest-rich large underpopulated country like Canada, there are 318 billion trees that use 7.6 billion tons of carbon dioxide as food each year. Canadians release 545 million tons of carbon dioxide each year from fossil-fuel burning, smelting and cement manufacture. Canada is already at net zero. Canadians pay tax for the carbon dioxide they release.

In the USA, there are 228 billion trees that each year photosynthesise 5.47 billion tons of carbon dioxide as plant food. Americans release 5 billion tons of carbon dioxide from fossil-fuel burning, smelting and cement manufacture each year. This is 14 per cent of global emissions. The US is already at net zero.

In Australia, the grasslands, rangelands, forests, crop lands and continental shelf waters each year photosynthesise ten times the amount of carbon dioxide that is released by Australian industry and individuals. Australia is already at net zero and releases only 1.2 per cent of global emissions. Australians pay tax for the carbon dioxide they emit for plants to use as food.

On planet Earth, there are 3 trillion trees that suck up 72 billion tons of carbon dioxide as plant food each year. Humans emit 37 billion tons of carbon dioxide each year. The planet is already at net zero, despite China's massive emissions. Why even bother about net zero? Unless, of course, there is a quid to be made with energy used as a weapon for unelected elites to take away freedoms and control people.

And here is the problem. If the whole world is at net zero, where does the extra carbon dioxide come from? Obviously, it's natural and it comes from a slight warming of the oceans. Some 97 per cent of annual emissions are from ocean degassing with minor amounts from volcanoes and animals. Carbon dioxide has an inverse solubility in water, as all beer and champagne drinkers know. The lower the temperature of water, the more carbon dioxide can dissolve in water.

Analysis of the chemical fingerprints in ice cores drilled in Greenland and Antarctica show that whenever there has been a natural warming event, the atmospheric carbon dioxide content rises hundreds to thousands of years later. If the oceans warm, they release carbon dioxide. Maybe the rise in atmospheric carbon dioxide is due to solar-driven warming of oceans after the 1300 to 1850 AD Little Ice Age?

The conventional view is that the oceans warm up by increased solar radiation because Earth is closer to the Sun or because the Sun releases more energy. What has never been considered is that the planet has been releasing heat for 4,567 million years and still is. At present, 70 per cent of the heat released by the planet ends up in the oceans. There are thousands of submarine eruptions each year with basalt melts at 1100°C solidifying by transferring heat to 2°C ocean bottom waters. Submarine basalt melts contain up to 13.5% by weight of dissolved carbon dioxide, most of which is released into the oceans as the melt rises towards the ocean floor.

Although there is a paucity of data, there are hints that the El Niño-La Niña cycle may be related to submarine volcanic activity. There is stronger evidence that plate tectonics is a major driver of climate change. This has never been considered in climate models.

Maybe the rise in oceanic temperature resulting in the increased emissions of carbon dioxide from the oceans is due to planetary cooling expressed as increased submarine volcanicity? These are fundamental scientific questions but, because they do not fit the government ideology, such research will never be funded because 97% of scientists funded by the government agree with those who fund them.

The natural world is far more exciting than a demon-haunted woke world that frightens folk with a dogma claiming that small amounts of a trace gas drive a major planetary process. We've been fed a pup. It will cost us dearly.

(2023)

Bring back blackbirding

Tuvalu was first settled by Samoans, Tongans, and other Pacific islanders about 700 years ago. The Spanish were the first Europeans to sight Tuvalu in the 16th Century and in the 19th Century, European whalers, traders, and missionaries settled Tuvalu. Blackbirders made sporadic visits. The British colonised the Gilbert and Ellice Islands in 1892 which were split into independent Polynesian nations in the mid-1970s comprising Kiribati (Gilbert Islands) and Tuvalu (Ellice Islands).

Pacific islanders are great rugby players and play in top teams all over the world. If Tuvalu is now concerned about inundation by rising sea levels resulting from global warming, Australia should restart the blackbirding trade, kidnap young athletic Tuvalu teenagers and educate them on Rugby Australia scholarships in the rugby-specialising private schools of Queensland and New South Wales.

Tuvalu is a deeply Christian country and blackbirded teenagers would continue to receive a Christian education, immigration would again have a Christian focus and the woefully poor feedstock for the Super Rugby and Wallabies would be improved. Australia might even regain its position as one of the top rugby nations of the world.

This scheme would start to depopulate Tuvalu well before it is inundated by a hypothetical sea level rise, successful Super Rugby and Wallabies players from Tuvalu would send money back to their families and the Australian taxpayer would be spared from providing hundreds of millions of dollars to assist Tuvalu with a hypothetical sea level rise.

If blackbirded Tuvalu teenagers received a Wokeless Australian education, they could bring back knowledge to their homeland and make Tuvalu a better place. They would learn from Charles Lyell's 1830-1833 *Principles of Geology* that their atoll nation has been the centre of scientific interest for nigh on 200 years. Lyell's three volumes showed that the planet changed over time and that we can use the past to understand the present. Lyell argued that Pacific island atolls were perched on top of volcanoes that were subsiding. As a volcano subsided, the capping coral atoll kept growing upwards and outwards. This is the same as a sea level rise.

Charles Darwin was greatly influenced by Lyell's book during his 1832-1836 voyage of the *Beagle* and was fascinated by Lyell's concept on the origin of atolls. Lyell was the key thinker who inspired Darwin to cement his ideas about evolution. Darwin studied Pacific Ocean atolls, especially Tuvalu, confirmed Lyell's theory and in 1842 published his book, *The structure and distribution of coral reefs*.

In 1896-1898, Professor Sir Edgeworth David drilled Funafuti atoll in Tuvalu. Drilling stopped after intersecting 928 feet of coral but no volcanic basement. David showed that Lyell's theory of coral atolls validated by Darwin was correct. Since the end of the last glaciation 14,400 years ago, sea level had risen 425 feet and the volcanic basement at Funafuti had sunk at least 500 feet. The rate of past coral growth far exceeds the projected rates of sea level rise so Tuvaluans can sleep safely with no fear of getting a wet big toe.

Climate catastrophists have predicted a sea level rise of 2 metres by about 2100. During the peak of our current interglacial 7,000-4,000 years ago, sea level was 2 metres higher than at present hence any speculated rise in sea level rise would equal the past measured sea level rise. As a result of this sea level fall, many coral atolls were left high and dry and died.

In the late 1940s in the Marshall Islands, there were 21 shallow and 3 deep drill holes on the Bikini Island and Eniwetok Island atolls. These were drilled by the Atomic Energy Commission and Los Alamos Laboratories in preparation for underground nuclear bomb tests. Two drill holes reached depths of 1,346 and 2,556 feet yet did not reach volcanic rocks. They intersected fossilised coral atolls separated by layers of beach rock. Deep holes intersected basalt volcanic rocks older than

34 million years at 4,610 feet depth (hole F1) and 4,158 feet (hole E1). All this can be checked in a US Geological Survey Report of 1960. The theories of Lyell, Darwin, and Edgeworth David were again validated.

On the Marshall Islands, a basalt volcano had been sinking for more than 34 million years while a coral atoll cap had been growing upwards and outwards in what was a relative sea level rise. During this 34-million-year period, there had been over 300 glaciations when sea level dropped by 130 metres, coral reefs died and beach rock formed. Other atolls kept growing while both the sea level fell and the substrate sank. During this 34-million-year period, there were more than 300 interglacials when sea level rose about 130 metres and island atolls grew.

Studies using 40 years of satellite imagery of more than 1,100 coral atolls in the Indian and Pacific Oceans have shown that most coral atolls have been growing in area, especially large atolls such as at Tuvalu. A few were static and some smaller atolls decreased in size. Some atolls had decreased in size because of compaction, extraction of coral for roads, airports, buildings and cement manufacture and groundwater extraction. Again, these satellite measurements confirm earlier theories that coral atolls grow when there is a relative sea level rise.

There is absolutely no science whatsoever to support the view that Tuvalu, or any other island nation, will be inundated by a speculated sea level rise. Only the contrary. The past shows that a relative sea level rise results in a growth of atolls. This has been known for nearly 200 years. The cash grab by the island atoll nations' unctuous politicians and the UN should be called out for what it is. Maybe younger folk educated on Rugby Australia scholarships and with a Christian ethical foundation could change political thinking in the Pacific island atoll nations upon return to their homelands.

Come on Australia. Break away from your woke chains. Rather than hand out shedloads of cash to Pacific island nations for some silly hypothetical future catastrophe, bring back blackbirding for the sake of the Pacific island atoll nations and Australia. This is a win-win. You know it's common sense.

(2023)

Chuck Wilkenson, 1960s singer Pat Boone (with a copy of *Not For Greens* in hand) with Ian Plimer, Los Angeles, 2014.

Let's be Cretans, not cretins

I recently returned from Crete. Apart from eating fresh local foods, drinking soft Cretan reds, swimming in the Mediterranean, and chatting with friends, the geological and human history captured my interest.

Crete contains 20-million-year-old muds, silts, limestones, and bits of the 140-million year-old ocean floor that have been cooked, broken and bent. On a clear day, the volcanic island of Santorini is visible and, at times, Crete was blanketed with volcanic ash. Sporadic large earthquakes emanate from great depths due to the northward movement of Africa. Rotation of bits of plates produces regular shallow earth tremors from movement along faults. These faults move blocks eastwards and downwards a couple of centimetres each year.

There has been continuous settlement of Crete for up to 700,000 years. Numerous glaciations on 100,000-year cycles allowed people to walk from the mainland when the sea level was low. Palaeolithic people on Crete and the Cyclades islands hunted macrofauna such as deer and dwarf elephants to extinction. Fossil evidence for this exists on nearby Milos where I worked for a decade.

Australian macrofauna was also hunted to extinction. The original people in Australia came from the north during the last glaciation when the sea level was 130 metres lower than now. The most likely time for the first wave of immigrants was immediately after the Toba (Indonesia) supervolcano eruption 74,000 years ago when tropical vegetation was destroyed and humans were stressed almost to the point of extinction. It was a case of migrate or die. Low sea levels between 116,000 and 14,400 years ago during glaciation, and proximity to northern islands allowed many waves of immigrants to enter Australia.

In Mesolithic times (9000-7000 BC) on Crete, tools became more refined and in Neolithic times (7000-3500 BC) stone houses were built, ceramics pots were used to carry wine and olives, farming and animal husbandry were practised, beads and jewellery were worn, and there was trade with the mainland and other islands. This did not occur in ancient Australia. People were nomadic, migration on the land was driven by the weather, and there were hundreds of small clans at war with neighbouring clans. Violence and death were everywhere.

In the Bronze Age, the Minoans settled Crete (3500-1460 BC) and were part of an empire that covered the Aegean, western Turkey, southern Greece and northern Egypt. The largest Minoan city on Crete, Knossos, had up to 100,000 inhabitants. Minoans built grand palaces and, in almost 100 cities, built separate commercial, religious, administrative and residential buildings in urban centres. Minoans had ships and used the wheel. No such population centres existed in Australia in pre-European settlement times.

The Minoans conducted trade with what is now Turkey, Egypt, and Greece, wrote indecipherable texts on stone and clay tablets that evolved from one style to another, carved figurines, made pottery which evolved with changes in technology and culture, used bronze and copper tools, made gold-peridot jewellery using materials derived from outside Crete and, it appears, that there were two parallel civilisations living together.

The Minoan empire was destroyed by the eruption of Santorini about 1600 BC and the weakened Crete was then dominated by Mycenaean warriors from the north who blended cultures after much plundering and killing (1450-1100 BC). Nomadic Australian aboriginals stayed Palaeolithic without writing, pottery, ceramics, long-distance ships, wheels, bronze or gold-gem jewellery.

The Dorians from northern Greece displaced the Mycenaeans and ruled from 1100-900 BC. They spoke Greek and had blonde hair and blue eyes, a characteristic that some Cretans still retain. They had metal javelins and ornate pottery and enslaved the locals. Some Cretans escaped to the nearly inaccessible forested mountains. In a later Greek period from 900-650 BC, the Phoenician alphabet was used and there were city states with more sophisticated pottery. In the classical Greek period, Crete did not fight the Persians but there were long and intense wars off and on for hundreds of years between Cretan cities. The island was deforested for buildings and ships and pockets of the original forests remain in isolated mountainous regions. Australian aboriginal deforestation by fire was to facilitate hunting.

A massive earthquake in 368 BC destroyed 80 of the 100 cities on Crete. There were various unhealthy alliances between cities and empires. At one time there was an alliance between Cretan cities and the King of Macedonia, Phillip V. There was war with Rhodes and later the Romans which ended with Roman occupation of Crete from 67 BC until 350 AD. After the death of Constantine the Great, Crete became part of the Byzantium Empire. The island was later overrun by Arabs who arrived in 40 ships. Some Cretans have Arabic features. The second Byzantine Period (961-1204 AD) started with retribution for Arab barbarism and some 40,000 Arab soldiers were killed in battle with 160,000 Arab soldiers and citizens beheaded later.

In 1204 AD, the Byzantine prince Alexios gave Crete to the Fourth Crusade leader Boniface Monferatico who then sold Crete to the Doge of Venice for 5,000 gold ducats. A Cretan aristocracy developed in parallel to a Venetian aristocracy, the island became prosperous through trade but a large earthquake in 1508 AD again weakened Crete.

The Venetians were attacked many times by the Turks and finally succumbed. The Turks imposed heavy taxes on the locals and repelled attacks from the Venetians and Greeks. Internal revolutions plagued Crete which became Greek again in 1898 AD. After bitter costly battles, Crete was captured by the Germans in the Second World War. There are more than 2,000 Commonwealth war graves on Crete, many containing

Australians. After the war, Crete again became Greek.

The story of Crete is one of multiple invasions, interbreeding, genocide, violence and survival over thousands of years, as in Australia. In Europe, there were tens of thousands of years of clans and tribes constantly at war before consolidation into nations over the last millennium. This did not happen in Australia. If sometime in the last 500 years Australia had been colonised by the Chinese or Portuguese, the aboriginal population would have been almost totally destroyed as was the local Cretan population in Dorian and Arabic times.

Humans migrated many times from the Rift Valley of East Africa to all parts of the globe over the last 1.75 million years. The only endemic humans with a continuous occupation are those still living in the Rift Valley. All others were immigrants sometime in the past. In many parts of Europe, Africa and Asia, there has been continuous migration and occupation by humans for far longer than there has been occupation of Australia which only occurred during the latest glaciation. Human occupation of the Americas from Russia took place towards the end of the last glaciation around 15,000 years ago.

Who is a Cretan? Is it someone with Palaeolithic, Minoan, Roman, Venetian, Byzantine, Turkish or Greek blood? Is it a Greek speaker who lives on Crete? Should those Cretans with Dorian features have more rights than those with Arabic features?

About 70 per cent of Australians are indigenous. What is an Australian aboriginal? Will aboriginals ever be legally defined quantitively using DNA? How many generations can we go back before a culture is totally diluted? Cretans don't care about their race, colour or genetic lineage. They are all equal, proud to be Cretan and just get on with life. We must be smart and learn from the Cretans that unity rather than division enriches and strengthens a culture.

(2024)

History in remote hills

For almost a century, geochemists have been making minerals and rocks in high-pressure high-temperature laboratory experiments. Water fluxes melting rocks and increases melt viscosity. By changing the water content, measuring geothermal gradients and melting rocks at different temperatures and pressures, we get a pretty good idea of what happens deep down in the Earth and way back in time.

In the late 18th Century, Abraham Werner (1750-1817 AD) of the Bergakademie, Freiberg (Saxony) proposed that granite was originally an oceanic sediment. European scientists agreed and the science was settled. The founder of modern geology, Scottish naturalist James Hutton (1726-1797 AD), argued that granite was once a molten rock that solidified at great depth. In Britain, Hutton's ideas were the settled science. Consensus has never existed in science.

At Siccar Point in Scotland, Hutton observed sequences of sandstones that demonstrated deep time with long periods of no sedimentation. He concluded that modern processes are the same as past processes and that the planet is dynamic. Hutton was forced to abandon his belief in young Earth creationism because of his own scientific evidence.

With the ability to observe granite at different erosional levels all over the world and to make granite in the laboratory, our knowledge of granite has increased. Granite melts are an emulsion of liquid rock, gas and solids. They are buoyant mainly because of dissolved gases, principally water vapour. The solids are crystals, fragments of wall rocks ripped off as the molten rock ascended and fragments of the parental rocks that were partially melted to produce a granite melt.

Granite forms at depth from the partial melting of older sedimentary rocks, partial melting of igneous rocks or is the last melt fraction from the cooling of a large body of molten rock. The minerals of a granite can be used to calculate the depth of solidification and, by using granite radioactivity, the time of solidification of a granite can be calculated.

At *Poolamacca* Station on Campbells Creek 50 km north of Broken Hill, a two-mica granite solidified 1,590 million years ago at a depth of at least 20 kilometres. Draped over the granite outcrop is lithified ancient glacial debris called tillite. Magnetic minerals in the tillite show that debris left behind by glaciers was at the equator and magnetic studies of similar tillites all over the world show that at that time globe-covering ice sheets were kilometres thick at sea level.

The tillite at *Poolamacca* contains rounded fragments of the underlying two-mica granite showing that the granite must have been exposed to the surface 700 million years ago during glaciation to enable moving ice to pluck and round granite boulders from the substrate and dump these boulders at the surface as ice sheets retreated.

Experimental mineralogy shows that dolomite can only form as a shallow marine mud when there is an exceptionally high atmospheric carbon dioxide content. Because dolomite was a universal rock type at that time and common at *Poolamacca*, it is concluded that the atmosphere contained at least 20 per cent carbon dioxide during glaciation yet our climate activists claim that a very slight increase from the current 0.04 per cent atmospheric carbon dioxide will create a global warming climate catastrophe.

The chemistry of the granite at *Poolamacca* shows it formed from the compression and heating 1,590 million years ago of 1,660-million-year-old muddy rocks formed in a temperate to tropical climate. A Himalayan-type mountain range formed along the eastern boundary of the continent of Australia 1,590 million years ago. The mountain range has since been flattened by the removal of at least 20 kilometres of overlying rocks over a 900-million-year period and only the mountain range root remains. The mountain range rose after removal of material during erosion.

The same is happening today in the Himalayas. In my life, Mount Everest has risen 60 centimetres and one day it will not be the highest mountain on Earth. Others are rising faster. Gravity, erosion and weathering keep removing material from the mountains as they are rising. If you are ever asked in a quiz show *How high is Mount Everest?*, the only correct answer is *When?*

The land level goes up and down, as does sea level. It's not possible to talk of sea-level change without discussing land-level change in the same breath. It's not possible to observe a rock outcrop without seeing evidence of past climate change.

The East India Company undertook the Great Trigonometrical Survey of India between 1802 and 1832 to provide accurate maps of India. The survey covered 165,342 square miles. Surveyors found that close to the Himalayas, the plumb bob was not vertical and a correction for the gravitational pull of the mountains was applied. This correction created slightly greater accuracy. It was then concluded that mountains must have roots with a gravitational influence. When the gravitational pull of the roots of the Himalayas was also used in calculations, the survey then had a very high degree of accuracy.

The collision of the Eurasian and Indian plates 50 million years ago led to the rise of the Tibetan Plateau which created frequent massive earthquakes. Sedimentary rocks 200 million years old deep under the Plateau melted under high pressure and high temperature to form granites. They did not rise to the surface to erupt as volcanoes because the high dissolved water content. The same happened at *Poolamacca* aeons ago.

There is a theory that the weathering of the freshly-exposed rocks of the Tibetan Plateau withdrew carbon dioxide from the atmosphere which led to the present glaciation. This theory is rejected because atmospheric carbon dioxide has been declining since the appearance of complex life on Earth 520 million years ago and glaciation is cyclical with no relationship to mountain building.

In the 1860s, *Poolamacca* was one of the early sheep stations in the rough hilly Barrier Ranges. There was a false gold rush in the area in the 1860s, a tin rush at nearby Euriowie in the 1880s and Tarrawingee, a town of 400, was established in 1890 to provide limestone flux that was transported to the Broken Hill smelters along a tramway. Tarrawingee now has neither residents nor buildings. The tramlines were cut up for fence posts from 1932 for a regeneration area encircling Broken Hill. The regeneration area greened Broken Hill and reduced temperature extremes and dust storms. This first revegetation program in Australia was paid for and undertaken by the mining companies. There was not a greenie in sight.

I first stayed at *Poolamacca* in 1968. It was one of the grandest historical stations in far-western NSW. Previously it was in the heart of the Kidman empire. Since acquisition using taxpayer's money by the Wilyakali Aboriginal Corporation in 2002, the historical fences, shearing shed, shearing quarters and homestead have gone to rack and ruin and are full of garbage. There has been no maintenance and *Poolamacca* will soon just be a pile of rubble like so many other outback stations.

Why do Aboriginal corporations want Aboriginal history preserved and yet allow settlement history to be destroyed?

(2024)

Cop this!

You could have knocked me over with a feather when I learned I had been appointed to organise the Australian climate change wingding known as COP 31. After everything I have said about Mr Bowen in public, I can only conclude that he oozes Christian kindness and forgiveness and, in a show of uncharacteristic leadership, he sacrificed a few Muslim votes. My brief is simple. Organise a low cost, unforgettable conference with a genuine Aussie flavour.

Our capital city airports are already overcrowded with unreliable flight schedules and our regional centres could benefit from an influx of wealthy foreign visitors. So here's my plan: the conference will be on a claypan near Mount Isa in the last week of January, 2027. There are no conference facilities in the Isa for the expected 30,000 hypocrites. Travel to Mount Isa by fossil fuel-powered private jet will not be possible as the tarmac parking area is limited. Delegates will travel by bus from proximal airports at Cairns, Townsville, Broken Hill, Roma, Cunnamulla, Longreach, Tennant Creek and Alice Springs.

In the interests of the environment, buses will have no window glass and no air conditioning. Some hard left socialist greens will walk or travel by bicycle which would guarantee the Guterres gut reaches net zero.

The welcome feast will be camel horse's doovers on bark plates with acacia seed biscuits. There are thousands of acres of spinifex surrounding the venue for vegans to forage. Beef is off limits for ethical environmental climate reasons and, at comfort stops, bus passengers will collect roadkill for their conference meals.

Production of alcoholic beverages releases carbon dioxide so food will be washed down with bore water which hopefully will be only muddy and not full of green slime or magnesium as Epsom salts. The zillions of flies and other insects plus roadkill of the day will be the delegates' protein source. Organic food fanatics can experience my patented bush diet of sardines rolled in Milo followed by a raw onion and then washed down with warm XXXX.

Delegates will sit on swags out in the open in circles around a stage of planks supported by 44-gallon drums. After a gruelling day devising schemes to rob taxpayers and destroy the planet, satisfied delegates will retire to their swags with ablutions in a nearby sandy dry watercourse

A ringer in moleskins, check shirt, Rossi boots and a Kidman hat will belt the drums with a shovel to announce proceedings and use his stock whip to quieten idle chatterers or sunstroked groaners during unctuous self-serving monologues.

The welcome to country will be given by Senator Susan McDonald. She will welcome people to her country in her capacity as a former station girl from nearby Cloncurry. She will explain that the locals who lived in this area before her had a social structure whereby infanticide, perpetual tribal warfare, revenge killing, kidnapping of women from other tribes, mass rapes of children, genital mutilation of young girls, violence against women, starvation, cannibalism and senicide now almost no longer exist due to the Western legal system, democracy, education, hospitals, schools, food, clothing, medicines, reticulated water, sewerage systems, roads, electricity, employment and use of fossil fuels. Stock whips will guarantee that the three hearty cheers after Senator McDonald's welcome will be boisterous.

The local federal member, the inimitable Bob Katter, will open the conference but I will not tell delegates that he is likely to speak for 7 hours in an interpreter-challenging address about crocodiles eating people in his electorate. He will give the flesh-ripping details while laughing. Bob will also talk about the necessity for UN recognition of a new state of Far North Queensland, feral animals such as donkeys, camels, goats, brumbies, cats, pigs and wild dogs and the pros and cons of using .44

Henry, 56-56 Spencer or 5 mm Remington Rimfire Magnum cartridges to rid the world of these ferals. Bob's discussion about ammunition for effective killing should interest the numerous dictators who attend COP money-grabs and I'll arrange a private meeting at the gun club between the Taleban and Bob so they can extract some of the finer details.

The cultural event will be a rodeo. Delegates will mingle with locals to learn first-hand about environmentalism, the mythical climate catastrophe, the future of the planet and how net zero really works. The rodeo highlight will be the chase and capture of a greasy piglet by local children, our future nation rebuilders.

The net zero field trip will be mandatory. A bus field trip to Innamincka will show delegates what net zero really looks like in an area where it only rains once a decade. In this part of Australia there is no grid electricity, no reticulated water, no mobile reception, no internet or TV, no supermarkets, no schools, no hospitals, few airstrips for the dying flockter, no sealed roads and no infrastructure. Just perpetual drought, red dust, corrugated roads, gibbers, heat, flies and mateship. Sensitive city delegates will experience flies going up their nose and flying heavily laden out their mouth. EV activists will travel separately for hundreds of kilometres on these lonely roads until their batteries die and, because no one wants to upset their virtuous moral stance, they will be left in net zero land. If a dam or artesian borefield is passed, delegates could enjoy their first wash of the conference. If it rains, delegates will be immobilised in knee-deep mud for weeks to enjoy Third World net zero conditions.

Another field trip will visit what were rainforests in eastern Queensland, now totally destroyed by wind industrial complexes. From the fragmented blades dumped on the ground, delegates will see the balsa wood for turbine blades harvested from Amazon rainforests impregnated with toxic epoxy chemicals banned in most countries in the world. Global food experts will admire transmission lines criss-crossing lands, destroying family farms and reducing the amount of food produced. Delegates will be presented with fossil fuel-produced slightly toxic Chinese-made plastic souvenir koalas, eagles and bats, all of which were once common in the area before the arrival of the planet-saving renewables. Renewables activists will be left on site with picks and shovels to clean up the mess.

The most popular field trip for Asian delegates will be to the coalfields of central Queensland. Delegates will be able to appreciate the sacrifice our miners make to keep their lights on, feed their industries with cheap energy and out-compete Australia with their manufactured goods. An overnight stay in swags underground will give delegates an appreciation of the hot, humid, dark, wet, dangerous 12-hour shift conditions that Australians work under to feed Asia.

At the Great Barrier Reef, delegates will realise that there is no climate crisis, that the Reef is not threatened, that hinterland farming has no effect on the Reef, that over the last few million years the Reef has come and gone dozens of times and that the greatest threat to the Reef is sea level fall during glaciation.

In the final session of the Australian COP, the few surviving delegates will unanimously agree that there will be no more COP money-grabbing fraud festivals. Some murderous dictators will remain in Australia with like-minded recent immigrants because coups took place during their absence.

President Trump will land at Mount Isa, give a robust closing address and give away Maga trinkets to any of the few remaining delegates who pledge to leave the Paris Accord.

(2024)

The carbon crisis

We have a carbon dioxide crisis in Australia. There is not enough of the gas produced locally. We import carbon dioxide from China, Malaysia, Singapore, New Zealand and Italy yet we bury carbon dioxide in old hydrocarbon wells. Food grade carbon dioxide with more than 99.9 per cent carbon dioxide is used for carbonated drinks and food preservation and normally is a by-product from ammonia manufactured for fertilisers and explosives. Industrial grades of carbon dioxide are used to create an inert blanket for grain storage, welding and metal working, fire extinguishers, life jackets, foaming rubber and plastics, water treatment, and immobilising animals before slaughter. Carbon dioxide is used to decaffeinate coffee: solid carbon dioxide ('dry ice') is used as a coolant.

There are some vital facts that drinkers need to know. Fermentation of sugars releases carbon dioxide into the atmosphere and drinks such as beer, champagne and cider have added food-grade carbon dioxide. Carbon dioxide has an inverse solubility. The colder your carbonated drink, the more carbon dioxide is dissolved. As your carbonated alcoholic drink warms, which in my world is a heinous sin, it exsolves carbon dioxide and keeps bubbling well after its drink by time. The gas to push keg beer along the lines is carbon dioxide but Guinness uses nitrogen thereby creating a creamy texture and the surge and settle effect by bubbles one hundredth the size of carbon dioxide bubbles. Try telling a drinker in the embrace of Bacchus that they should lead a net zero life and see how far you get.

Food and industrial grade carbon dioxide in Australia is produced from wells in the Otway Basin. Carbon dioxide from old oil wells needs compression, purification, dehydration and cooling to make easily transportable liquid carbon dioxide. Caroline-1 well near Mount

Gambier was an abandoned oil well that produced 811,000 tonnes of liquefied carbon dioxide from 1967 until 2017. It has been replaced by Boggy Creek-1 in Victoria drilled as a wildcat oil well in 1992. The Langwarrin-1 well in South Australia was drilled in 2019, is not in production and could produce 100 tonnes per day of liquefied carbon dioxide. Water and carbon dioxide are extracted from coal-seam gas and conventional gas from oilfields. The Longford gas plant in Gippsland produces about 60,000 tonnes per annum of liquefied carbon dioxide for the Australian and New Zealand beverage industry. Liquid carbon dioxide is pumped down old wells to push out the last remaining oil and gas and it is also sequestered underground in abandoned oil and gas fields to 'save the planet'.

Worldwide every day 1.7 billion cans of Coca-Cola are consumed. Each can contains about 6.5 grams per litre of carbon dioxide. Mineral water contains 6.1 grams per litre and beer contains 2.3 to 2.8 grams per litre. Guinness contains only 1.2 grams per litre of carbon dioxide and, if you think carbon dioxide creates climate chaos, it is your moral duty to drink Guinness to save the planet.

Water vapour is more than 100 times more abundant in the atmosphere than carbon dioxide and is the main atmospheric greenhouse gas. We should demand net zero for water vapour, devapourise the planet, sell water vapour emission certificates and reclassify water vapour as a pollutant. However, carbon dioxide has been demonised as the greenhouse gas villain. Restrictions on carbon dioxide emissions are a mechanism of deindustrialising Western society.

All plants use carbon dioxide as food. Compared to the past, the atmosphere currently doesn't contain enough carbon dioxide for plant life to flourish as it did in the past. Horticulturalists burn hydrocarbon gas to release the warm carbon dioxide and water vapour exhaust gas into glasshouses. The atmosphere contains 0.04 per cent carbon dioxide whereas the exhaust gas contains over 0.1 per cent carbon dioxide. With increased carbon dioxide, the breathing holes in leaves close and reduce in number, plant growth is accelerated and water loss is reduced. Satellite imagery shows that over the last 40 years, the planet has greened due to a slight increase in atmospheric carbon dioxide. Crop yields have increased due to increased atmospheric carbon dioxide, better farming practices and synthetic fertilisers. This has resulted in no increase in cultivated land, a longer growing season and more drought resistance. If you are frightened by a colourless, odourless, tasteless, non-poisonous plant food mainly released from ocean degassing, you should stop your personal carbon dioxide emissions in an attempt to reach net zero by not eating plants or plant-derived meat, not eating bread, not drinking soft drinks or alcoholic beverages, not exhaling 100 times the carbon dioxide content that is inhaled and not using any of the 6,000 daily products made from fossil fuels.

We had global warming in Minoan, Roman, medieval and modern times but, according to the mantra, it is only the modern warming that has resulted from human emissions of carbon dioxide. During these past warm times, people had more food and lived longer, populations increased, economies boomed, great empires arose and there were fewer wars. The current warming has not reached the temperatures of previous warmings.

Over the last 300 years of warming, 169 glaciers shortened before humans started to release carbon dioxide from the burning of fossil fuels. Sea level has been rising since the end of the last glaciation 14,400 years ago and has no relationship to changes in atmospheric carbon dioxide. Extreme weather has always been with us, there is no increase in flooding and wildfires however there has been an increase in hysterical reporting of natural variability in the occurrence of floods and wildfires. Polar bear populations have increased over the last seven decades, mainly from less hunting.

There is a new ascientific religion that claims that carbon dioxide caused by humans burning fossil fuels is a deadly sin; that we humans can absolve our sinful behaviour by buying indulgences called carbon credits or burying carbon dioxide which could have fed plants; apocalyptic scenarios are promoted by the high priests in the UN and IPCC; heretics are pilloried as deniers and metaphorically burnt at the stake; the truth is held by the ennobled cardinals who are the climate 'scientists' who feed off our taxes and are blindly supported by the modern-day preachers called journalists; bureaucrats have reclassified the gas of life as a pollutant; the Bible has been renamed Wikipedia which names and shames deniers and promotes the IPCC narrative; and we can obtain salvation with net zero, decarbonisation and renewable energy.

Politicians tell us that we can change the global climate by spending money taken from taxpayers and electricity consumers and, without reference to emissions from China, emitters of carbon dioxide in Australia can change a major planetary process. The effect on Australia of this new religion is that good money is thrown after bad, debt increases to a crippling level, energy becomes unreliable and expensive, education has changed from scholarship to propaganda and Australia loses competitiveness and sovereignty.

There is neither a carbon crisis nor a climate catastrophe. There is a crisis in common sense, basic knowledge and education.

(2025)

Shag on a rock

Australia is now no longer self-sufficient with oil. We import more than 80 per cent of our refined petroleum products across disputed seaways that could be closed at any minute. Proximate Chinese warships should be the wake-up call.

Refineries in South Korea, Singapore, Japan, Malaysia, Taiwan and China blend Middle Eastern, Asian and African crudes for production of imported Australian petroleum products. If one tanker is stopped by a hostile force, insurance is voided and carriers would not risk transporting liquid fuels to Australia.

The Bass Strait oil and gas field is in its last days. A small amount of crude oil is produced from the mature Cooper, Surat, Perth, Canning and Amadeus Basin wells and some crude oil is produced as condensate from gas. Australia has about three years of known oil in the ground. Oil exploration is challenging, mainly due to the Gimme Munni tribe's lawfare, approvals and lack of infrastructure. We would need decades of high-risk exploration with no guarantee of success to become a self-sufficient producer.

Despite the successful fracking of 1.6 million wells globally over the last 70 years and Australian hydrocarbon basins containing large volumes of rocks with a high organic carbon content, only the Northern Territory government has approved fracking. Most states have a moratorium on fracking. Victoria has gone a step further.

The Gippsland and Otway Basins of Victoria have been significant producers of oil and gas with large volumes of oil and gas that could be extracted by fracking. The massive volume of Victorian brown coals also contain oil which is not extracted. From 2012 to 2021, it was illegal to explore or produce onshore gas in Victoria despite known drilled gas fields in the Gippsland Basin. Victoria changed its constitution in 2021 to permanently ban fracking and coal seam gas exploration in an act of self-harm. To change the Victorian constitution requires support from three-fifths of both houses which makes the local supply of fracked oil and gas a distant dream. Royalties from Bass Strait oil and gas were a bonanza for Victoria for 60 years. These times are finished yet bankrupt Victoria refuses to replace its petroleum production with new reserves and continuing royalties.

Australia exports significant amounts of light sweet crude oil and condensate from the North-West Shelf. This needs to be blended with heavier crudes to make a product suitable for refining into petrol, avgas, diesel and other products. Australia had eight small high-cost refineries in 2000. Refining local and imported crude oil is now at the two remaining refineries in Geelong and Brisbane. These are subsidised by the taxpayer to keep them operating. Australian governments have always had their fingers in petroleum with subsidies, royalties, fuel excise, levies and regulation.

For most of Australia's history, there was no local crude oil. During the late-19th century and especially during the first world war, oil shales were mined and retorted to produce wax, grease, oil, diesel, kerosene, petrol and gas from the southern, western and northwestern parts of the Sydney Basin, the northern part of the Bowen Basin and central Tasmania. Operations stopped after the second world war when oil shale products could not compete with imported petroleum products. Taxpayers subsidised oil exploration until the discovery of the Bass Strait field in the 1960s. Consumers then paid a levy on locally-produced fuel because imported Middle Eastern crude was cheaper than that from Bass Strait.

Australia is obliged as an International Energy Agency member to hold the equivalent of 90 days of oil imports. In the last year, Australia has run down its liquid fuel reserves from 54 to 22 days and has a just-in-time liquid fuel policy. Some fuel is stored in the US which is a very long way from bowsers in Australia. We are now running on empty. Without diesel, no ploughing, seeding, weeding, harvesting and transport of food to the cities occurs. Without diesel, many towns would have no electricity and there would be no back-up for the regular failures of renewables. Without liquid fuels, there could be no road, train, air or ship transport. Without diesel, Australia could not generate revenue from mining, agriculture and fishing. With no food delivered to the cities by truck, train, ship or air, civil unrest and anarchy would occur within a fortnight.

What could we do if Australia did not receive refined petroleum products from abroad during a period of conflagration? Queensland has massive resources of oil shales in Gladstone, Mackay and Julia Creek which could produce oil at the current crude oil price or in a time of war. This would take time, capital and a lack of legal eco-terrorism.

In the second world war, German sea routes were closed and liquid fuels were locally produced for their massive war effort by converting coal to liquid fuel using the Bergius and Fischer-Tropsch processes. Since the 1950s, South Africa operated their SASOL process using coal-fired electricity, gas and coal to make liquid fuels and petrochemicals. Why can't we do the same? The Bergius Process uses coal-fired electricity to make hydrogen from steam and hydrogen is reacted with coal to make liquid fuel. We have massive quantities of coals which would be ideal for making petroleum from coal. The annual oil equivalent of our exported coals is about 50 per cent of the annual oil exports from Saudi Arabia. Why not use our uranium to generate cheap reliable electricity and preserve our coals to make diesel and steel? This would be our insurance policy against blockaded liquid fuel supplies.

Eight projects attempting to make hydrogen from cripplingly expensive 'renewable' energy for burning to make electricity have unsurprisingly been cancelled. Natural hydrogen is very rare. Reactions between circulating seawater and seafloor rocks produce hydrogen, methane and rotten egg gas which are released into seawater, mainly by hot springs. Most of the hydrogen escapes into space. Other chemical reactions between circulating waters and granite on the Yorke Peninsula have produced hydrogen-dominated gas trapped in rocks awaiting production at 20 per cent the cost of manufactured hydrogen. Rather than burning this hydrogen to make electricity, it could be used to make liquid fuels.

We have fallen for the carbon dioxide skam. Australia could fall to a hostile force that would risk neither assets nor personnel if liquid fuels were blockaded. We import Chinese solar panels and wind turbines for production of unreliable high-cost electricity that destroys food-producing land. We have destroyed cheap reliable coal-fired electricity, have no nuclear power and, as a result, have left Australia like a shag on a rock with no energy security. Defence has been weakened, there is no manufacturing base for producing defence assets, productivity is low, we suffer from welfare addiction and are living beyond our means. Far too many unproductive people with no skills and alien loyalties have been imported. The energy tragedy is exacerbated by career politicians who want to perpetuate their employment by oiling squeaky wheels, running up debt and not working for the national good.

(2025)

Minerals critical crisis

All minerals are critical minerals for the modern world. The most important critical 'mineral' is energy which must be cheap and reliable to enable low-cost mining, beneficiation, smelting, refining, manufacturing and food production. Australia has not had cheap reliable energy since the introduction of 'renewables' and cannot rely on the rest of the world for energy. Because of geological variability, no country can be completely self-sufficient although Australia has mines and unmined deposits of most basic commodities. Tier 1 mineral deposits are very large tonnage with a high metal content and operational in the bottom quartile of low-cost producers for at least 25 years of production and sustaining capital to survive changes in exchange rates, metal prices, smelter charges, subsidised mining by overseas competitors, labour costs, union hostility, age costs and anti-mining governments and activists.

Surface outcrops of Tier 1 deposits in Australia led to mines at Bendigo (1851-1954), Ballarat (1851-2014), Cobar (1870-present), Mt Lyell (1882-2014), Mt Morgan (1882-1990), Broken Hill (1883-present), Renison Bell (1890-present), Rosebery (1890-present), Kalgoorlie (1893-present), Mount Isa (1923-present), mineral sands (1930s-present), bauxite (1963-present), Pilbara iron (1966-present) and Cadia (1998-present). These Tier 1 deposits were not plain sailing as there were loss-making periods and even closures due to loss of manpower during wars, weather events, rail line closures, economic depressions, strikes, high exchange rates, low metal prices, fatalities, environmental lawfare and government edicts.

In good times, gouging governments put their snouts in the trough and extracted higher royalties, taxes and union-driven labour costs which were not reduced during the inevitable bad times. There was once a time when Australian mines had scores of copper, lead, zinc, nickel, gold, silver, tin and iron smelters on site or at ports to convert concentrate to metal. These added value and reduced transport costs. There are now only a few smelters in Australia. Most concentrates are shipped abroad because of the high energy, labour and regulatory costs and our remaining smelters are struggling.

All mineral deposits have a finite life. On current reserves and geological factors, the unexposed Olympic Dam deposit (1975-present), coastal and inland mineral sands deposits and the Pilbara iron ore deposits will be the only operating Tier 1 deposits in 25 years time. Most of our Tier 1 mines are old, reserves have been depleted and exploration for reserves replacement is hampered by land access, approvals delays and red, green and black tape. New Tier 1 mines have not been discovered in Australia.

With reduced Tier 1 minerals exports in a few decades time and no major manufacturing industries, Australia will be pushed into poverty. The problem can't be solved when the shortage occurs. If I have a geological idea for mineral exploration today, it will take 25 years and massive high-risk capital before successful exploration can lead to minerals production and payment of royalties. This is because regulatory processes including future nature-positive restrictions, environmental and Aboriginal lawfare, tenement acquisition, surface exploration, deep geophysics, deep drilling, metallurgical testing, financial due diligence, acquisition of capital and mine construction all take time. Approvals from three tiers of government and Aboriginal groups can take years. During this 25 years there are at least 8 terms of government when community attitudes will change and fickle markets can cripple project economics. Governments operate on short-term election cycles and do not consider the long-term stability and sustainability necessary for employment- and revenue-generating industries. Not many investors have an appetite for such long-term high-risk investments when there are more attractive investments elsewhere in the world.

Exploration for the McPhillamys gold deposit near Blayney started in 1980 and, after more than four decades of exploration, evaluation, mine planning, approvals, support from the local recognised native title-holders, support from the New South Wales government and vast expenditure, at the eleventh hour after massive sunk costs Minister Tanya Plibersek cancelled approvals after an indigenous artist's objection based on her own paintings of a mythical bee. This was concocted. In some countries, the fraudulent artist would be convicted as an economic terrorist. Why would an investor risk spending a penny on exploring to replace exhausted mineral deposits in Australia?

Australia is a very high-risk country for mineral exploration and mining, almost on par with many despotic Third World countries. Many Australian companies are now risking capital raised in Australia for exploration in Africa, the Middle East, Southeast Asia and South America where the ability to explore and bring a discovery to a productive mine puts Australia to shame. Minerals produced on the other side of the world by an Australian company doesn't mean Australia will have access to these commodities. Other countries want to add value by constructing smelters and refineries to treat their own concentrates and gain export earnings.

More than half of Australia has very old rocks that are prospective for exploration for Tier 1 deposits because, in the early history of the planet, metals were transported and concentrated at well-defined geological times while the planet settled down to its normal daily dynamic business. Gone are the days of a deposit poking out at the surface. Now explorationists use a diversity of scientific techniques and research knowledge to search for unexposed deposits at depth.

Measurements of magnetics, gravity and radioactivity from altitude with follow-up ground truthing are undertaken; satellite infra-red imagery and other spectra are evaluated; deep electrical conductivity and resistivity plus the seismic properties of the substrate are measured; surface rocks are mapped; and the chemistry of soils and rocks is measured. Even plants, soils and air are sniffed for volatile chemicals that may indicate ore at depth. Mathematical analysis of huge data sets indicates whether more work needs to be undertaken or drilling can commence to provide a 3-D picture.

For Tier 1 porphyry-copper deposits, such as those in central-western NSW, at least 150,000 metres of drill holes will have to be drilled at hundreds of dollars a metre before metallurgical, mining and financial evaluations can be undertaken. Time, deep pockets, persistence, patience and highly skilled professionals are needed. For every 10,000 tenements granted, only one will result in a producing mine. Even though discoveries are frequently made, only five out of a hundred discoveries result in a mine. Of these five mines, three will financially struggle. Many marginal discoveries are chestnuts, warmed up for the stock market if prices rise.

Exploration is not for the faint-hearted. If governments want Australia to be a critical minerals force and stay affluent from mining revenues, they must support exploration, stay on message for decades, support the resources industry from concept to concentrate by taking it off the election cycle political agenda and add value by encouraging smelting and refining in Australia.

We don't need a population Ponzi scheme to prop up the economy. We need an economy that turns rocks into metals, non-metallics and energy to support secondary industry; that turns soil into food, fibre and fermented fluids; and harvests our territorial waters. This requires knowledge, experience, vision and leadership by politicians to build the country rather than their own selfish political careers.

(2025)

Fertilise or fail

On a Tuesday 140 million years ago, the western part of the giant southern supercontinent of Gondwana comprising Africa and South America separated from the eastern part (Australia, Antarctica, and India). Later, the South Atlantic Ocean formed as South Africa and South America drifted apart. India separated from Australia and raced northwards until it hit Asia and pushed up the Tibetan plateau at the collision boundary. Australia drifted away from Antarctica 100 million years ago at up to 7 centimetres a year. The cargo on this drifting continental ark was tropical rainforest with its adapted fauna. Australia then was blessed with an inland sea, rivers, lakes and associated wildlife in areas that are now desert.

Once isolated and further north from Antarctica, Australia enjoyed a long period of tropical weathering and erosion. Rocks were decomposed to soils which were leached of nutrients over tens of millions of years. Most of Australia is now covered by the nutrient-poor residual soils and endemic flora which has adapted to survive on these soils.

The long weathering period left a flattened stable land surface with meandering watercourses and rivers. Remnants of this old flat land surface can even be seen in uplifted parts of the country such as the Darling Ranges, Great Divide, Barrier Ranges and Flinders Ranges. Aridity over the last few million years led to inland sand dunes, salt lakes and concrete-hard precipitates of soils rich in limestone, silica and iron.

Unlike Europe and North America, mainland Australia was not scoured by advancing and retreating glaciers that removed old soils and allowed fresh new fertile soils to form after glacier melting started 14,400 years ago. This gave little time for leaching of nutrients. Only six per cent of the Australian landmass has arable soils and a very small part of this six per cent has soils as fertile as those of the Northern Hemisphere. Our best soils have formed in higher rainfall areas by the weathering of geologically young basalts such as in Tasmania, western Victoria, New England, the Darling Downs and the Atherton Tableland and on alluvial flats where exposed rock has been decomposed to soil and transported downslope onto flood plains. These soils have only been slightly leached. We are not a fertile green land because of our old soils and low rainfall.

Even on our best fertile soils, crops still need added essential elements such as phosphorus, potassium, nitrogen and sulphur from fertilisers. Traces of magnesium, iron, zinc, copper, manganese, molybdenum, boron, chlorine, cobalt and sodium are also used by plants, and grazing animals require minute traces of chromium, iodine, selenium and fluorine.

Phosphate rock reacted with acid makes superphosphate. In former times bat guano phosphate rock was mined from caves. Surface bird guano was once mined on Christmas Island. Australia's only domestic source of phosphate is Phosphate Hill, 135 kilometres south of Mount Isa. The mine is struggling due to high costs. Australia imports phosphate rock from Morocco and superphosphate from the USA, India and Vietnam. Massive resources of phosphate rock have been found at Wonarah and Ammaroo in the Northern Territory but they are a long way from nowhere with no infrastructure.

All potassium fertilisers are imported. We have large tonnages of potassium in salt lakes in Western Australia and a couple of companies are attempting to build solution mining operations. Australia has no rock salt MOP (muriate of potash) or SOP (sulphate of potash) deposits. SOP is imported from China and MOP is imported from Canada, Russia and Belarus.

Nitrogen fertilisers were once produced from human urine and cow dung. European farmers house cattle over winter and mix the accumulated dung with water for spraying on fields in spring giving the typical rural pong ironically called *Landluft*. Farmers have been known to use the dung-water mixture to spray on anti-farming protestors, gypsy squatters and houses of parliament.

Nitrates such as saltpetre were mined from the Atacama Desert in Chile and Peru for explosives and fertiliser. These deposits are now exhausted. There are no nitrate deposits in Australia and nitrogen fertilisers such as urea, ammonium nitrate and ammonium sulphate need to be synthesised using air, ammonia, natural gas and energy. Australia produces 2.4 million tonnes per annum (Mt pa) of urea at Karratha and imports four Mt pa from the Middle East, SE Asia and China. More than one Mt pa of ammonium nitrate is made at Kwinana and Newcastle, mainly for the mining industry. There is a domestic supply shortage requiring imports of almost 150,000 tonnes per annum (tpa) of ammonium nitrate from Indonesia, Vietnam, Thailand, Lithuania and South Korea. Some five per cent of the world's ammonia production is made at Dampier, much of which is exported. About half of Australia's 250,000 tpa of ammonium sulphate is imported, the rest is made by reacting ammonia with sulphuric acid.

Australia does not have enough base metal smelters to produce by-product sulphuric acid and imports sulphuric acid from South Korea, Japan, Taiwan, China, USA, India and Malaysia. It is used for making superphosphate, SOP and sulphate of ammonia fertilisers.

In the 1980s, there was a flood of peer reviewed scientific papers from Chinese authors claiming that if rare earth elements are added to fertilisers, then crop yields increase. It was later shown that crop yields did not increase and in many cases crop yields decreased, rare earth elements were phytotoxic and entered the food chain, and rare earth elements in soils and waterways created environmental damage. This was a crude fraudulent attempt by the Chinese to sell rare earth elements mined at Bayan Obo (Inner Mongolia) which, at that time, had a very small market as there was no miniaturised electronics industry.

Australia is not self-sufficient in phosphate, potassium and nitrogen fertilisers which are essential for food production. We import fertilisers and acid so that we can eat. To become self-sufficient, it would take time, huge amounts of capital and a decade or so battling regulators for approvals with incessant lawfare about the mythical vadose songlines of the Krakatinnie tribe.

More than 70 per cent of food produced in Australia is exported with most production in areas of rainfall above 600 millimetres per annum. Fertiliser costs keep rising. Fertilisers require ship transport from abroad or around our coast followed by long-distance truck haulage.

The delusional Chris Bowen claims that expensive intermittent energy using components from countries hostile to Australia will drive an industrial revolution. Pull the other one. An industrial revolution to enable energy, mineral and food security is well overdue. Why is it that Sweden, a country of 10.5 million people with six nuclear reactors and a GDP of $US585 billion, can build cars, guns, military and commercial aircraft, naval vessels, submarines and intelligent ammunition yet Australia with a GDP of $US 1.73 trillion cannot? It was the crisis of the second world war that accelerated industrialisation in Australia driven by Essington Lewis.

Where is our Hercules to clean the Augean stables and industrialise Australia before the inevitable next crisis?

(2025)

Egyptians and leftie loonies

I'm too old and take too many pills to dream about normal things. I dream about the periodic table of elements, the only classification system in science that works. It was not devised by the dominant German, Swedish, English or French scientists in the 18th and 19th centuries who regarded themselves as intellectually superior to American and Russian scientists. The French happily disposed of their most famous chemist with the guillotine and, in the 19th century, Russian organic chemistry was so boring that chemistry professor Alexander Borodin took to writing music. Borodin was no slouch and actually has a chemical reaction named after him. Another Russian chemist Dmitri Mendeleev, born a year after Borodin, was not interested in the structure of music, counterpoint, transcription of folk dance music and hauntingly eerie music describing the steppes. He was interested in the orderly classification of the chemical elements known at that time. Mendeleev's classification was remarkable and he was able to predict the physical and chemical properties of the many elements that had not yet been discovered.

Some of the data used by Mendeleev came from the ancient Egyptians, Greeks and Romans who used all sorts of chemicals in high society. The upper classes used mascara (kohl) which was either the antimony sulphide stibnite or the lead sulphide galena. Kohl was painted on infants' eyelids to stop the 'evil eye'. Eye lashes and upper eyelids were painted black with kohl whereas the lower eyelids were painted green using the copper mineral malachite. Some green cosmetics also contained the green iron arsenate scorodite. Blue tints were from the copper mineral azurite. Stibnite and galena were roasted to give yellow, orange and brown oxides and, for those of pale complexion, the face was dusted with yellowish-brown antimony oxide or orange lead oxide whereas those with a somewhat darker complexion painted themselves with lead carbonate (cerussite) which gave a glowing lustrous complexion. The earthy reds in lipsticks and rouge derived from the iron oxide haematite but upper-class ladies used the far more lustrous pigment cinnabar, mercury sulphide. The foundation for powder was the inert clay mineral kaolinite. Up until 50 years ago, many talcum powders contained a small amount of chrysotile asbestos, a mineral commonly associated with talc and historically mined in parts of the old world.

I know many of you have tortured yourselves about why pharaohs and Greek and Roman emperors had a succession of wives who died young and had concluded that it was from misogynistic male behaviour. No. It was probably from females using fashionable heavy metal-based cosmetics. They slowly poisoned themselves with cumulative heavy metals partially soluble in water, gave themselves brain and central nervous system damage and shortened their lives.

Egyptian princesses glowed rather than perspired or sweated in the Nile heat, and their saline perspiration dissolved very small amounts of the gold from jewellery. As a cumulative poison, large doses of gold attack internal organs. The wearing of silver or copper jewellery resulted in metal oxidation from perspiration producing partially soluble metal compounds on the skin which are strong anti-bacterial agents.

One of the theories for Napoleon's death was that he was exposed to and poisoned by arsenic. Neutron activation analyses of a bit of one of Napoleon's hairs show it had a very high arsenic content suggesting he had died from internal organ failure from long-term arsenic poisoning. A nuclear reactor is required for high precision analysis on such a small sample. It was suggested that the arsenic derived from wallpaper. At that time, green lustrous insect-resistant wallpaper was stained with Scheele's green, a copper arsenite. However, the French have the paranoidal view that Napoleon was deliberated despatched by the English administering arsenic poisons. But they are French! Today, a highly poisonous green chrome copper arsenate is used to treat timber to prevent rot and insect damage. Unless you want a good dose of heavy metals, don't burn treated timbers or use them around your veggie garden.

Here is something confidential just for you. *Sotto voce.* Many *Speccie* readers probably have very good reasons to be poisoned by their spouse. If you suspect you'll be poisoned, take a bit of commonly available arsenic-based rat poison each day and slowly increase the dose. When your spouse comes in for the kill with that high dose of arsenic, you'll not die from the sudden overdose. You may die far later from long term cumulative arsenic poisoning but your spouse will not have the satisfaction of their dastardly deed.

I have my truths, and you are quite free to have your own truths. Both are unrelated to evidence. My first truth is that in my lifetime, we have changed from a diet with meat protein from free-range lamb (but mainly mutton) in the 1940s, 50s and 60s to one that, from the 1970s onwards, had oestrogen-fed caged chicken as a common source of meat protein. Could it be that this has slightly changed the hormones of young men, many of whom now appear more effeminate? If we can have an evidence-free anthropomorphic climate change theory that has swept the Western world despite no one showing that human emissions of carbon dioxide drive climate change, then I can have my chicken hormone theory. Try espousing my chicken hormone theory to an alphabet soup LBGTQ+ person and experience the peaceful world that many of them seek.

My second truth is about the appearance of those lefties who behave as if they are totally mentally unbalanced. In fact, they may be nursing damaged brains. You know the type, blue hair, tattoos and studs in visible and in unthinkable invisible places. I have often wondered about the effects of long-term exposure to traces of heavy metals and brain-altering complex organic molecule dye toxins. Tattoo dyes also contain traces of lead, cadmium, mercury or arsenic oxides; contain azo inks, which give vibrant colours, and are very complicated large organic molecules; contain polycyclic aromatic hydrocarbon compounds; and contain hydrocarbons, glycerol, alcohols and resins. Blue hair dyes are a cocktail of anthraquinones and all sorts of other complex large-molecule organic chemicals. Studs are normally a nickel-chromium alloy, others have inert titanium and niobium. The oxidised forms of both nickel and chromium are highly toxic and affect the brain.

We know that heavy metals and many organic compounds have an effect on the brain yet we know very little about the exposure to traces of these chemicals over a lifetime because the high-precision analytical techniques did not exist 50 years ago to give a baseline. The accumulation over time of slight traces of heavy metals and complex organic compounds may contribute to the modern leftie lunacy. That's my truth which, for reasons of emotion and not evidence, I stick to. If the Egyptians can poison themselves, so can the loopy lefties.

(2025)

Incurable disease

When a child, my parents sent me to a central western NSW farm to recover from glandular fever. In order to shake me off, every day the grazier sent me down to the creek with a gold pan. Recuperative days were spent in the sun panning, collecting gold, sapphires and zircon and having a watchful eye for snakes. I became fascinated with geology. I recovered from glandular fever, was infected with gold fever, an incurable disease and, when an adult, chased gold all over the world as a geologist.

Cosmic processes billions of years ago created element number 79 which can be drawn into wire, moulded, crafted, beaten into sheets only a few atoms thick and alloyed with other metals to make it harder. There is no colour or lustre like that of the evocative yellow metal.

Gold is the first mineral mentioned in the Bible. In Genesis 2:12 the riches of the land of Havilah were described *And the gold of that land is good;....* Here we have the commodity: gold. The market was created only ten verses later in Genesis 2:22 which states that *the rib, which the Lord God had taken from man, made he a woman, and brought her unto the man.* Commodities need a market and about half of all the gold produced now is used in women's jewellery, mainly in Middle Eastern and sub-continental cultures. The rest of the gold is used in electronics, central bank holdings and for investment.

Gold and mythology go hand-in-hand. Norse mythology underpinned Wagner's first Ring cycle opera, *Das Rheingold*, where maidens guard the immense alluvial gold treasures of the Rhine River. Like many myths, there is an element of truth. The Rhine River contains alluvial gold derived from the Alps of Switzerland and Austria where Celts mined surface gold and Roman slaves mined reef gold underground. I have been to a number of these mines. After Roman mining, they were covered by glaciers, exposed in Medieval times, covered again by glaciers in the Little Ice Age and exposed again in modern times. *Das Rheingold* is about the theft of gold which, when crafted into a ring, gave the wearer dominion over the world.

There is a Chinese myth that, in the long ago, a noble patrician suicide was to drink molten gold. The momentum of heavy liquid gold at a temperature greater than 1064 degrees Celsius was enough to do the job. Painfully. Maybe it's not a myth.

Philosopher's stone was a legendary substance with the power to convert base metals such as lead into gold and to create the elixir of life thereby granting immortality. Again, there is an element of truth. There are well-known chemical exchange reactions to convert aluminium to iron, a process used for the welding of railway tracks across the Nullarbor, and change iron into copper, used in some solution copper mines. Fundamental laws of chemistry however prevent conversion of base metals to gold.

Gold and theft also go hand-in-hand. Where there is visible gold in underground mines, normally it is one piece for the boss and one for the miner. Or is it two or three? The same occurs with alluvial mining where there may be a few nuggets amongst gold dust awaiting theft.

The gold-mining city of Kalgoorlie has the gold police, officially known as the Gold Stealing Detection Unit. Gold from every mine has a unique trace element fingerprint and isotopic signature which can be used to identify the source of the gold, even if it has been melted down, mixed with gold from other places and poured into ingots or fabricated. I shouldn't tell you this but you can outsmart the gold police. Peg a mining lease next door to the target mine for theft and mine a little bit of your own gold which could easily be "confused" with stolen gold from the adjacent operating mine. It should have exactly the same trace element and isotopic signature. If it doesn't, that's your bad luck. In gold treatment processing plants, every depression, bend or kink in pipes and drains is where gold accumulates ready for the picking.

Gold has fostered greed, war, killing, betrayal and invasions. There are far too many examples. The last Inca emperor, Atahualpa, was captured in what is now Peru in 1532 AD. In exchange for his release, the Incas agreed to fill a room with gold to the height of a raised arm and give it to the Spanish. The Spanish stole the gold and Atahualpa was executed in 1533 by the Spanish conquistador Francisco Pizarro. This double-crossing ended the Inca Empire.

Many times I have seen gold sticking out of surface rocks in outback Australia. Australian aboriginals also must have observed gold in rocks and rivers. It was, however, never prized or used by the Australian aboriginals for jewellery, trade or currency as it was in almost every other culture. Why not?

After a quarter of a century of travel over 24,000 km to the mysterious eastern cultures in Cathay, the Venetian Marco Polo co-published his book *Travels of Marco Polo* in about 1300 AD wherein he described the monetary system of the Yuan Dynasty. There is a chapter entitled *How the Great Khan Causeth the Bark of Trees, made into Something Like Paper, to Pass for Money over All His Country*. Marco Polo was incredulous that people exchanged real money such as precious metals, gems and pearls for mulberry bark banknotes cut into different sizes, dyed, stamped with official signatures and seals by the Kublai Khan and widely used for trade and commerce.

Traders refusing to accept mulberry money were executed. Paper money substituted gold coins. By this means real wealth was transferred to the rulers. The same occurs today when banknotes substitute for precious metals. Until 1971, the US dollar could be exchanged for a fixed quantity of gold. This gold standard maintained purchasing power and allegedly prevented excessive money printing, hyperinflation, trade deficits and spending. Loss of the gold standard has allowed governments to borrow to pay the interest on previous borrowings. If all the world's banknotes and paper gold were redeemed today for gold, there wouldn't be enough physical gold. Some countries such as China are accumulating gold. The price of gold has not risen but the value of paper money has fallen. Ever since the time of Jesus, a carpenter, the value of an ounce of gold has been roughly the same as a week of a carpenter's time.

I leave George Bernard Shaw with the last words:

> *You have to choose between trusting to the natural stability of gold and the natural stability of the honesty and intelligence of the members of the government. And with due respect to these gentlemen, I advise you, as long as the capitalist system lasts, to vote for gold.*

(2025)

Spanish lesson, Imbaburra, Ecuador, 2020

www.ingramcontent.com/pod-product-compliance
Lightning Source LLC
Chambersburg PA
CBHW051100030726
47504CB00006B/1720